The New American Eskimo

by
Nancy J. Hofman
&
Cathy J. Flamholtz

ON THE FRONT COVER: American Eskimo illustration by Chet Jezierski.

ON THE BACK COVER: National Grand Champion, Grand Champion Stevens' Toybear Apollo, owned by Rosemary Stevens. *Van Winkle & Associates photo°*

ON THE TITLE PAGE: Gr. Ch. 'PR' Hofman's Country Coolpas Luke, owned by Nancy J. Hofman & Julie D. Young.

DRAWINGS ON THE FIRST PAGE OF EACH CHAPTER: Our thanks to Linda Cummings, Rick Rivera, Rosemary Stevens and Paul Brown.

THE NEW AMERICAN ESKIMO

ISBN 0-940269-10-4

© 1995 by OTR Publications

All Rights Reserved. No part of this book may be reproduced or transmitted in any form or by any means, electronic or mechanical, including photocopying, recording or by any information storage or retrieval system—except by a review to be printed in a magazine or newspaper—without permission from the publisher.

Hofman, Nancy J., 1935-
    The new American Eskimo / by Nancy J. Hofman & Cathy J. Flamholtz.
       p. cm.
    ISBN 0-940269-10-4
    1. American Eskimo dog.   I. Flamholtz, Cathy J.   II. Title.
SF429.A69H645   1995
636.7'3--dc20
                                               95-38577
                                                 CIP

Printed in the United States of Ameria

10 9 8 7 6 5 4 3 2 1

Although the authors have extensively researched sources to ensure accuracy and completeness of the information contained in this book, we assume no responsibility for errors, inaccuracies, omissions or any inconsistency herein. Any slights of people, their dogs or organizations are unintentional.

OTR PUBLICATIONS
P.O. Box 481
Centreville, AL 35042

NANCY'S DEDICATION

To my late sister Marcia Kolar who never failed to encourage and support me.

To the memory of Thomas Maxwell (1924-1986), the most influential man in the history of the breed. His dedication to the American Eskimo gave us both a history and a future.

To my family and friends, who encouraged me to write this book.

To all those who appreciate and love the American Eskimo breed.

CATHY'S DEDICATION

To William Ledbetter, a great dog lover and fan of all Spitz breeds, for his generosity, curiosity, scholarship and total dedication to helping fanciers, throughout the world learn about dog breeds. The dog world needs more such people.

To Eÿke Schmidt-Rhode, the grand dame of the German Spitz, who through her writings, breedings and commitment has worked tirelessly to further the interests of her breed.

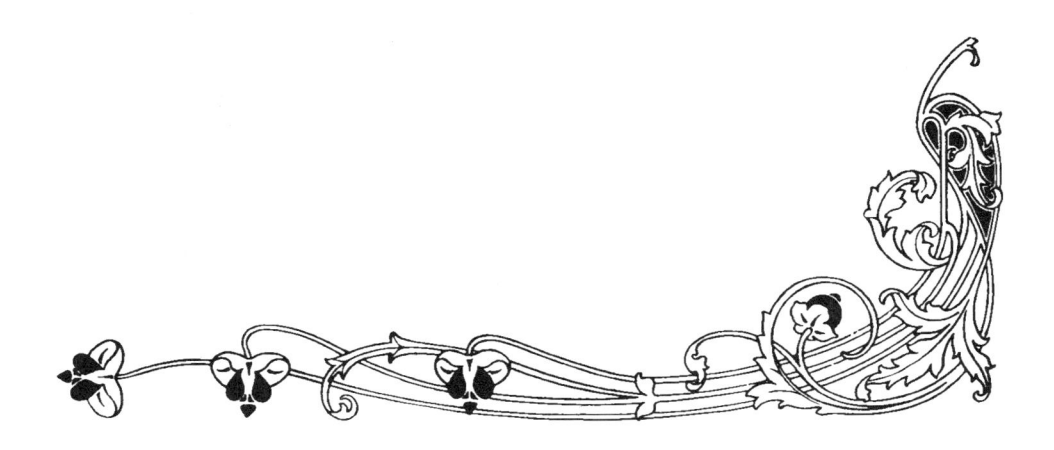

About the Authors

Nancy J. Hofman is well known to American Eskimo breeders throughout the nation. Her "Country" line has earned honors in the show ring and, more importantly, has had a lasting impact on the breed's bloodlines. A number of kennels have based their own lines on Country dogs and many fanciers will find the Country name in their pedigrees. A tireless promoter of the American Eskimo, Nancy Hofman's greatest contribution may well be her writings on the breed. Her unequaled research into the breed's background has revolutionized what we know about the history of the American Eskimo. *The New American Eskimo* is her third book on the breed.

Nancy Hofman purchased her first American Eskimo in 1971. It was a pivotal time in the breed's history. The National American Eskimo Association (forerunner of the American Eskimo Dog Association) had only been in existence for two years. *'PR' Hofman's Misty of Frost*, Nancy's foundation bitch, was bred by John L. Wilson, first President of the National club. It's difficult for today's fanciers to realize just how precarious the plight of the American Eskimo was 25 years ago. It was a dying breed, with few dedicated breeders. Most people didn't know what an Eskie was and breeders had to have people lined up to purchase their puppies, in advance, before attempting a breeding. Nancy found herself foursquare in the midst of the movement to save the breed.

The Country American Eskimos have shared the home and lives of Nancy, her husband, Darrel, and their three children (now grown with children of their own). "Our dogs are pets first, and show dogs second," Nancy says. "We'd love them no matter what they did in the show ring."

But, excel they have. *Gr. Ch. 'PR' Hofman's Country Diamond*, became the first Grand Champion on the Pacific Coast, a Dog World obedience award winner and a noted sire. Though used sparingly at stud, he produced a National Grand Champion, four grand champions (including the nation's top female in 1984) and three other champions. *Gr. Ch. 'PR' Hofman's Lil' Bit Country*, also sired champion and grand champion get. The bitch, *Ch. 'PR' Hofman's Solo Diamond* produced four champions and the prepotent *Gr. Ch. 'PR' Denali's Country U-Kay-C*, produced champions and/or grand champions in each of her litters. Current stars include *Gr. Ch. 'PR' Country's Ima-E-Z-Bud-E*, whose pedigree contains every one of Nancy's Eskies, and *Gr. Ch. 'PR' Hofman's Country Coolpas Luke*, who has an AKC major.

Cathy J. Flamholtz also entered the world of purebred dogs in 1971. She has owned dogs of several breeds, including champions and those with obedience and field titles. From the start, it is the amazing diversity of dog breeds which has captivated Cathy's interest. An avid student of the origin and history of the various breeds, Cathy has always taken delight in learning more about each breed.

Cathy's broad based knowledge, coupled with her unbounded enthusiasm, has proven invaluable in her writing. She has been in the forefront of the rare breed movement and is considered a top authority in the field. She has edited both local and national newsletters. Her many articles have appeared in magazines, both in this country and abroad. She earned an award from the prestigious Dog Writers' Association of America for a series of articles.

She is best known, however, for her many books, which have gained her a national following. Several have been nominated for top national awards. Her books include *A Celebration of Rare Breeds, Volumes I and II; The Toy Fox Terrier* (with Eliza L. Hopkins) and the award-winning *The Tibetan Mastiff* (with Ann Rohrer). She recently revised and edited *The Venerable Tibetan Mastiff* (originally written by Max Siber in 1897) and *The Goodger Guide to the Pug* (originally done by Wilhelmina Swainston-Goodger). In cooperation with Nancy J. Hofman, she has written *The American Eskimo* and *The New American Eskimo*. In addition, she has edited several other books which have been nominated for and/or won top awards.

An avid dog book collector, Cathy's personal collection numbers more than 2,000 volumes. She also collects paintings, prints, sculpture and other dog items. She lives in Alabama with her husband Harvey and son Matthew.

Contents

About the Authors 5
Foreword by John Miller, Jr. 6
Foreword to the First Edition by Rosemary Stevens 7

1. The American Eskimo—A Family Dog 9
2. American Eskimo History, An Introduction 11
3. What's in a Name? 13
4. In the Beginning 17
5. The Spitz in the Ancient World 21
6. The Spitz in Germany 33
7. The Spitz in England 41
8. The Spitz in America 55
9. Famous Owners 75
10. American Eskimo Relatives 87
11. Official United Kennel Club Standard 95
12. Official American Kennel Club Standard 97
13. Reflections on the Breed Standard 99
14. Understanding Correct Movement 121
15. Selecting an American Eskimo 125
16. Caring for Your American Eskimo 131
17. Grooming Your American Eskimo 135
18. The Stud Dog 141
19. The Brood Bitch 147
20. Having Puppies 153
21. From Birth to Maturity 161
22. Showing Your American Eskimo 167
23. Training Your American Eskimo 181
24. Obedience Competition 185
25. The Good Neighbor 191
26. American Eskimo Heroes 193
27. The Versatile American Eskimo 197
28. Those Lovable Clowns 205
29. A Tribute to the American Eskimo 209

Foreword to the Second Edition

I would suspect that if the members of the American Eskimo fraternity were to be polled as to their choice of a person to write a book on their breed, that person would be Nancy Hofman.

Nancy has spent most of her adult life in devoted service to the breed she loves. I remember coming to know Nancy about 12 years ago, mostly through phone conversations and her articles in *Bloodlines*. We would talk about the progress of the breed, changes in registration policy, the new (at that time) obedience program—whatever. Highly opinionated, she would always let you know what she thought of something. The thread that ran through all her opinions was the well being of small white dogs.

At that time she was the most prolific writer the magazine had. She wrote a regular column on behalf of the California American Eskimo Assn., and a feature column almost every issue. For several years she was also publicity director of the National American Eskimo Assn. For the past ten years Nancy has been CAEA's president. The California American Eskimo Assn. was the nation's third American Eskimo Association and Darrel and Nancy Hofman were instrumental even then. It is in large part a tribute to Nancy Hofman that CAEA has grown to be the nation's largest AE association.

To their credit authors Hofman and Flamholtz thoroughly researched the history of this breed, and have written the most thorough and accurate breed history yet recorded. Further to their credit, they did not opt out for histories of convenience or romance, a temptation to which so many other breed book authors have fallen...the authors' conclusions reflected my own; yet they went much further. The authors rightly point out the confusion created by giving the breed the name American Eskimo. Their conclusions as to the whys of this mirrored those I'd reached...

...There's a ton of useful "how to" knowledge, succinctly stated. Unlike many breed books containing generic information of this type, this is written specifically for the owner (or prospective owner) of an American Eskimo...

There is no question that this is the best book written on the American Eskimo yet....It was written to be read, understood, and completed—to not sit on a book shelf gathering dust. The major areas of the most important aspects of the breed are covered... For 95% of new or experienced American Eskimo owners, it's all they'll ever need....

American Eskimo clubs would do well to make a pledge, for each member of the club to donate a copy of this book to a library in their area. The dividends could almost not be measured.

John Miller
Former Editor
Bloodlines *magazine,*
official publication of the
United Kennel Club

Foreword From the First Edition

It is with great delight and true pleasure that I write this foreword to *The American Eskimo*. For many years, we have needed a comprehensive book on this breed. Often, Eskie owners have searched in vain for information about our breed. How wonderful it is that we now have a book of our very own.

Nancy Hofman is eminently qualified to author a book on the breed. Nancy acquired her first American Eskimo in 1971. Since that time, she has bred many Champions and Grand Champions. The first two Champion Eskies on the West Coast were owned by Nancy. In addition, she owned the first two Grand Champions in California. Nancy has served the breed well, both on the national and local levels. She was the Publicity Director for the National American Eskimo Dog Association and, for the past ten years, has served as President of the California American Eskimo Association. For the past fourteen years, she has written and edited the California American Eskimo Association's newsletter. Her articles, aimed at promoting the Eskie, have appeared in many dog magazines.

Nancy Hofman's dedication to the American Eskimo is unquestioned. Indeed, she has made this breed her life's work. She spends countless hours talking and corresponding with those interested in the breed. Those who know Nancy can attest to her honesty, integrity and dedication. It is Nancy who is always there to remind us to "keep the breed in mind first." In fact, I have never met anyone with a more thorough and extensive knowledge of the American Eskimo.

Nancy has an uncanny ability to get people involved in our breed. She has extended a hand to many new owners and they, in turn, have become dedicated American Eskimo enthusiasts. Whether it is helping to organize a dog show or talking a new owner, via telephone, through the whelping of that first litter, Nancy is always there when needed.

Those of us who know Nancy love her. We have great respect for her knowledge and expertise. The dog world needs more of her kind. This book is one more step in Nancy's tireless quest to promote the American Eskimo. I believe all Eskie owners will enjoy her book. *The American Eskimo* is truly a tribute to the breed we know as "The Dog Beautiful."

Rosemary Stevens
Past President
National American Eskimo Dog Association
1989

A Note About Titles

Dogs who have a "Ch." (Champion), "Gr. Ch." (Grand Champion) or "Nat. Gr. Ch." (National Grand Champion) before their names were awarded these titles from the United Kennel Club. UKC obedience titles are listed before the name and preceded by the designation "U-". American Kennel Club championships are identified as "AKC Ch.". AKC obedience titles are listed after the dog's name with no further elaboration. Titles from other organizations are identified. For example, "SKC Ch." or "SKC CD" refer to titles offered by the States Kennel Club.

The New American Eskimo

Chapter 1

The American Eskimo A Family Dog

The American Eskimo is a family dog *par excellence* as anyone who shares his home with one of the breed can attest. "The Dog Beautiful," as the Eskie has been christened, richly deserves praise for his devotion and loyalty. A proud, spirited and lovable animal, he lives to please and protect his family. And yet, despite his many laudable qualities, this is not the ideal breed for everyone. Those who want a yard dog, who will be happy left to his own devices, had best search for another breed. The Eskie is not for the weak willed owner, either. This breed is assertive and determined and, if you allow it, will manipulate and dominate you. For those up to the challenge of Eskie ownership, however, the rewards are many. They will find in the American Eskimo a whimsical clownish spirit. Eskies can be wonderfully mischeivous, bouncy, curious and always lively. They are also so very, very expressive. Coupled with a sensitive and affectionate nature, the Eskie has an uncanny ability to understand people.

We hope, in this chapter, to honestly discuss the American Eskimo character. It's true that the Eskie attracts attention wherever he goes. And why not? This natural breed is extremely beautiful. In fact, many owners obtain their first dog strictly because of the breed's looks. Time is best spent, however, getting to know the dog beneath that glorious white coat. The true beauty of the American Eskimo lies not in his flashy looks, but in his sterling character.

All those considering obtaining an Eskie, must fully understand the breed's long guardian tradition. For centuries, the breed we know as the American Eskimo has been bred specifically to guard his family and their property. By his very nature, the Eskie is an instinctive and territorial watchdog. He is incorruptible in his mission to protect his family and will not be tempted by tidbits proffered by a stranger. Nothing can convince him to abandon his duties. An American Eskimo bonds so closely with his family that he considers both them and their property as belonging to him. In his mind, they are "his" and must be defended at all costs.

These guardian qualities lend the Eskie a reserved, aloof attitude with strangers. Most Eskies simply won't approach, much less, lavish attention on outsiders. The breed is apt to be extremely mistrustful of newcomers. For this reason, socializing your Eskie is an absolute must. If you have frequent and regular visitors, take the time to introduce them to your American Eskimo. Once he understands that their visits are not cause for alarm, he will accept them as part of his routine. Eskie puppies should be taken out in public frequently, particularly during their young formative months. Take your dog for walks and encourage people to pet and speak to him. This is not usually hard to arrange for the American Eskimo is so beautiful that he naturally attracts attention wherever he goes.

As with all dogs in the Spitz family, the American Eskimo has a tendency to bark. Indeed, some dogs seem to enjoy the sound of their own voices. While this may not be a problem for the country living Eskie, it's apt to be seen as a nuisance in city and suburban situations. Barking is a natural extension of the Eskies' watchdog proclivities. When anything seems amiss, he will announce it to his owners with a sharp bark. With his keen sense of hearing, he rarely misses a thing. Young puppies should be reprimanded with a firm "No" for excessive barking. Soon your dog will learn to separate the real threats from the imaginary.

Above all, the American Eskimo demands to be a part of your family. For hundreds of years, he has lived in close proximity with his owners. He revels in their love and can become destructive when denied their attention. The Eskie is not happy being relegated to a kennel run in the backyard. His glorious personality and innate intelligence develop fully only when he is able to share his master's hearth. He accepts his part as a member of the family as his due. With his quick intelligence, he adapts readily to the lifestyle of the

American Eskimos can become very attached to children. Donna Hays' granddaughter, Ashley, curls up with Gr. Ch. 'PR' Winterset Sweetie Pie. Ashley fell asleep with her Eskie friend and the dog stayed in place for over half an hour for fear of upsetting the child.

Eskies are universally acknowledged for their intelligence. Nat. Gr. Ch. Gr. Ch. 'PR' McKee's King Jacob, owned by Gordon & Dottie Patterson, has even taken up reading.

family. While Eskies love all members of the family, it's not unusual for them to single out one person as their very favorite. He can often be seen following this person about the house. He will lie quietly while they are busy, but feels that it's his duty to be near them as their private guardian. I often suspect that he also wants to be close by in case you have a free moment for a little hugging and affection.

One should never underestimate the intelligence of an American Eskimo. These are "people dogs" and you will find yourself dealing with the dog as though he were another human. It's uncanny how the Eskie has the ability to understand not only your tone of voice, but what you say. You will marvel at how expressive your Eskie can be. His warm eyes and body language, once you come to know him, will tell you volumes. Be forewarned, however, if you let your American Eskimo get the upper hand, you're doomed. He can and will take over your house if you let him. He will demand to be hugged when it pleases him...and it always pleases him!

While you want to express your affection, you must be careful. Eskies can become spoiled very quickly. Always eager to please, your Eskie lives for your approval. He can look so dejected and crushed when you discipline him. The American Eskimo hates incurring the wrath of his owner. And yet, discipline him you must. As hard as it may be for him to accept, your Eskie must realize that you're the boss. You will love him and praise him when he acts correctly, but you won't reward poor behavior. The Eskie can be quite headstrong and you must begin, as early as possible, to curb such behavior.

Many American Eskimos share their homes with other pets. Don't be surprised, however, if your Eskie insists on being number one. Initially, he may resent the presence of another animal. You must, therefore, make certain that you give all your pets an equal amount of affection. Let your Eskie know, in no uncertain terms, that you will not tolerate spats with other animals.

American Eskimos are fun dogs to own. Their keen intelligence and extraordinary desire to please make them adept at learning tricks of all kinds. For years, Eskies were the star performers in both circus and rodeo acts. Today, the breed is more apt to demonstrate its prowess and trainability in obedience and agility trials. Spend some time with your Eskie. Play with him and, by all means, train him. Even if you do not wish to obedience train your dog, teach him a few tricks. Eskies delight in learning and are proud of their accomplishments. Whether it's playing ball, catching a frisbee or demonstrating a special trick, Eskies are born hams. There's nothing they love better than showing off. American Eskimos are tremendously agile and quick. Their ability to jump, with little effort, must be seen to be believed.

Don't hesitate to include your Eskie in family outings. He will love to go hiking or camping with you and the family. Take your Eskie along when you go for a swim. While not all dogs will take to the water, many Eskies love it. Mine love the water and even enjoy playing in the rain. No matter what you want to do, the Eskie is up to the challenge.

I must warn potential American Eskimo owners of one complication. *Eskies are habit forming!* It's difficult to stop with just one. Soon you'll want another of these beautiful white dogs sharing your home and your heart.

Chapter 2

American Eskimo History
An Introduction

The American Eskimo has been registered, in this country, for over 80 years. Despite this lengthy history, little was known about the breed's background. Fantastic and unbelievable tales, totally lacking any concrete foundation, were often repeated in the absence of factual research. It is only in recent years that a serious attempt has been made to document the background of these beautiful white dogs. It was not until the appearance of the first edition of this book, entitled simply *The American Eskimo,* published in 1989, that an effort was made to chronicle the history of the breed. The discoveries detailed in that book have now become an accepted part of the American Eskimo story. They have been repeated in official brochures and later books on the breed.

We could not have realized, when we wrote that first book, that we were opening a Pandora's box. The enormous enthusiasm with which Eskie owners embraced the story of the breed's background was a surprise, even to us. It became immediately apparent that there was a tremendous thirst for additional information. American Eskimo owners, captivated by the breed's past, wanted more...more...more.

That first book also provided access to a wealth of additional information. Sensing our enthusiasm, owners of Spitz breeds, from around the world, began to correspond with us. Their generosity in sharing information has been especially touching. We now have available many texts which had never before been translated into English. This inspired us to dig even deeper. We delved into the works of archaeologists, sought out translated texts of early Greek and Roman writers, culled through more than 2,000 English and American books for any information we could find on the breed. We reviewed paintings, prints, sculpture and drawings which would help in our quest. We were often aided by other owners who shared our interest. To be honest, we were sometimes surprised by what we found.

Gradually, a fuller and more complete picture of the American Eskimo's illustrious past began to emerge. Indeed, the Eskie has evolved from Stone Age dogs, which were surely among the first ever to be domesticated by man. Amazingly, the general breed type has changed remarkably little over the millennia. The dogs seen thousands of years ago are unmistakably the same dogs we see today. These white dogs seem to have always been esteemed, no matter where they resided. At times, they have been the companions of the common man—the helpmates of farmers and boatmen, the one spot of cheer in the otherwise drab existence of factory workers. They have also been status symbols—the pampered companions of the wealthy and the treasured pets of emperors, pharaohs and kings. But the road has not always been an easy or pleasant one. During their long existence, they have been, at times, a source of food, a victim of political persecution and borne the brunt of superstitious beliefs and rumors which led to their deaths.

In our last book, we said that it was our hope "to piece together the history of our white dogs. And, hopefully, by exploring the American Eskimo's background, we can come to understand the breed more fully and see how the many wonderful qualities we so admire developed." That is still our goal.

And so, in this book, we will expand our exploration into the American Eskimo's past. We have donned our detectives' caps in hopes of tracing the breed's evolution, from the earliest dogs to the show rings of today. We invite you to come along as we follow the track of the American Eskimo.

A study of the breed's history shows that the American Eskimo is a direct descendant of the white German Spitz. He has the happy smiling face of his German counterpart. This is Lisa Castellan's U-CD 'PR' Eskipades Little Jake CD. *Hislop photo*

While many Eskies love the snow, they are not descended from Arctic dogs. Here are three generations of the O'Sullivan's Shamroc bitches. In front is Gr. Ch. 'PR' Shamroc's Dybrk Shandale, followed by her daughter Gr. Ch. 'PR' Shamroc's Lethal Weapon and granddaughter Ch. 'PR' Shamroc's Candid Image.

Through the years, the American Eskimo has been known as an unusually hardy and healthy breed. This is Gr. Ch. 'PR' Snobirds S-Ka-Pade, a Standard male, owned by Judy Jones.

The Eskie is an Americanized version of the German Spitz. You will notice the resemblance when you compare this photo of Gr. Ch. 'PR' Apollo's Lucky Star, owned by Sandy Tocco, with pictures of the Great German white Spitz.

American Eskimos can also live successfully in hot, arid regions. U-CDX 'PR' Kaz Northern Bandit, owned by Doug and Esperanza Kaz, enjoys life in Phoenix, Arizona. *Doug Kaz photo*

Since earliest times, Spitz dogs have been exemplary companions. The Eskie follows in this grand tradition. This is Gr. Ch. 'PR' Kort-Mar Vegas Hit It Big, owned by Sally Bedow.

Chapter 3

What's in a Name?

Before we begin our journey, it's necessary for us to clear up some of the misconceptions surrounding the American Eskimo. The confusion about the breed's name, its relationship to other breeds and the purpose for which it was bred have stymied many researchers. We will attempt, in this chapter, to explain these discrepancies.

It's doubtful if any other breed, in all of canine history, has been known by such a wealth of different names. American Eskimo, Spitz, German Spitz, Fox Dog, Wolf-Dog, Pommer, Pomeranian, Pomeranian Spitz, Lou-Lou, Loup-Loup, Chien Loup, Mistabella, Spitzhund, Wolfspitz, Niederrheinischer Fix, Mannheimer Spitz, Löwenspitz, Friesländer Spitz, Volpino, Zwergspitz, Kleinspitz, Mittelspitz, Gross or Große Spitz, Keeshond, Dwerg Keeshond, Kleine Keeshond, Middenslag Keeshond, Grote Keeshond and Wolfsgrauwe Keeshond—this seemingly endless stream of names all apply, generally, to one and the same dog. Is it any wonder that writers and fanciers have had such difficulty tracking the breed?

DOG OF THE NORTH?

Much of the confusion surrounding the history of the Eskie lies in the adoption of the name "American Eskimo," by the United Kennel Club. This appellation suggests the breed was developed entirely in the United States and was, perhaps, descended from dogs kept by the Eskimos. Nothing could be further from the truth. And yet, the UKC should not be criticized for adopting this misnomer. Indeed, as we shall see, inaccurate names have always been applied to these dogs. As the record will reveal, there were sound, logical reasons for designating a new breed name, when the dogs were first registered in this country. These will be discussed in detail in the chapter on the breed in America.

A clear distinction should be drawn between the *American Eskimo*, and the *Eskimo*. The latter was a true sled dog, born and bred in the Arctic and once recognized by the American Kennel Club. "Originating, in all probability, in Eastern Siberia he has since been taken by his Eskimo owners to Alaska, Northern Canada, Baffin Island, Labrador and Greenland," old copies of *The Complete Dog Book* tell us. "In all these sections he is still fairly plentiful though at present there is considerable danger of his type being lost by indiscriminate cross breeding." Sadly, interest in the Eskimo was to wane. As the Siberian Husky and Alaskan Malamute became more popular, fewer people were interested in the Eskimo. In 1959, the American Kennel Club dropped the Eskimo dog from its rolls.

Nor should the *American Eskimo* be confused with the *Canadian Eskimo Dog*. This sled dog breed, known as the Kingmik, by his Inuit Eskimo owners, is said to have been brought to the Canadian polar region some 1,100-2,000 years ago. The breed was on the verge of extinction when, in 1974, William Carpenter and John McGrath, of the Northwest Territories, began a program to save the dog. They searched for and purchased some 40 dogs to help revive the breed. The Canadian Kennel Club now registers this native breed.

There has also been much confusion over the American Eskimo's purpose. Again, the name American Eskimo conjures up images of sled dogs, hauling loads through arctic snows. This was never the case. The American Kennel Club has placed the breed in the "Non-Sporting" group, while the United Kennel Club lists the American Eskimo in the "Northern Group" and the breed standard refers to it as a "working" breed. In this chapter, we hope that we will be able to explain these seeming inconsistencies.

THE SAMOYED

Many writers have declared that the American Eskimo is a direct descendant of the Samoyed. Again, nothing could be further from the truth. It's true that both breeds have white coats and black pigmentation and are members of the Spitz family. Both share the appealing "smiling" appearance. There are, however, many type differences as well. Furthermore, the temperament and character of the two breeds are dramatically different. As we shall see, the Eskie's true ancestors have, from the earliest times, served as valued watchdogs. With this, has come an extreme alertness and a tendency to bark. The Samoyed, by contrast, is not a barker and is often classed as an "indifferent" watchdog.

Some early American Eskimo breeders subscribed to the Samoyed descent theory. The first official breed standard even declared that the Eskie was "a miniature Samoyed...identical except for size. The small size of the American Eskimo is due to years of breeding down in size from the larger type of dog." It was an unfortunate characterization, but an understandable one. Most early Eskie breeders had little knowledge of the German Spitz, the breed's true ancestor, which was not recognized in this country. There is absolutely no evidence to demonstrate that there was a concerted effort to breed down Samoyeds in size to produce the Eskie. In actuality, American Eskimos, though they were then known as Spitz, were imported to this country long before the Samoyed first made an appearance.

THE "SPITZ"

The generic name "Spitz" (pronounced 'shpits,' in German) refers to a very large group of dogs which are characterized by pointed noses, upright ears and tails which curl over the back. This group includes such breeds as the Siberian Husky, Alaskan Malamute, Samoyed, Chow Chow, Finnish Spitz, Keeshond and Pomeranian.

If we trace the history of the word "Spitz," we will find that it is of Germanic derivation. It means "sharp point" or "tip," and may refer to the dog's pointed muzzle or, possibly, the pointed ears. In Germany, the term is not generic in nature. It refers to a specific breed of dogs which has been known on German soil since pre-Biblical times. These dogs were known in all parts of the country and, as the breed developed, they would be found in many sizes and colors. As we trace the

The "Eskimo," a breed once recognized by the American Kennel Club. Interest in these dogs waned and, in 1959, it was dropped from the list of recognized breeds.

background of the American Eskimo, we will find that he is the direct descendant of these German dogs.

During the Middle Ages, the Spitz was known as the "Mistabella," a term we will explain in the chapter on the breed in Germany. Today, we tend to think of Germany as one united country. If we focus on divisions, we are likely to think of East and West Germany. This, however, was not always the case. Before the mid-1800s, Germany was a collection of, more or less, independent provinces. At times, the Spitz dogs were often identified with the provinces where they were most common. Thus, small black German Spitz were often called "Mannheim" or "Mannheimer Spitz." In her fine book, *Unsere Spitz (Our Spitz Varieties)*, published in 1985, Gerda Umlauff tells us that the large gray Spitz, recognized in this country as the Keeshond, was known as the "Niederrheinischer Fix," or "Watch-Dog of the northern Rhine."

SPITZ OR POMERANIAN?

Large white Spitz, approximately equal in size to our Standard American Eskimos, were often seen in the province of Pomerania. "This does *not* necessarily mean, however, that *Pomerania* was where our German Spitz *originated*," wrote the renowned German dog writer, Richard Strebel, in 1904-05. "Perhaps this name was adopted due to the fact that the northeastern German province of Pomerania was, in the period around the year 1700, particularly well-known for developing and promoting the superb White German Spitz varieties of a very superior quality."

Naturally, the use of the name Pomeranian has confounded many writers who have not traced the entire history of the breed. When we think of a Pomeranian today, we immediately picture small toy dogs, available in a variety of hues. These little dogs, however, did not become fully established until the late 1800s. Before that date, the word Pomeranian, or at times, Pommer, was applied in Germany to *all* Spitz dogs. "Up until the beginning of the 19th century, the name Pommer was the name most commonly used for the German Spitz here," wrote the authority Ludwig Beckmann, in his 1894-1895 book *Geschichte und Beschreibung der Rassen des Hundes (History and Description of the Breeds of Dogs).*

The name Pomeranian was first adopted in Great Britain, in the 1700s. During this period, the German-born Queen Charlotte imported "Pomeranian" dogs for both herself and her friends at court. These new white beauties were also occasionally known as "Fox Dogs." In future years, British fanciers would shun the "Spitz" label, but it's clear that the dogs shared a definite link with the German dogs.

"Although some persons hold the idea that the dogs which have long been kept in Germany, and there called by the generic term of Spitz, are distinct from what in this country we know as Pomeranians, this is not the writer's opinion," wrote B. D. Drury, in 1903, "which is strengthened by the fact of his having had before him (as a judge) on many occasions specimens imported from Germany—in fact, in the early days of shows most of the best animals of this variety were imported."

"The Pomeranian was and remains the Spitz dog," Milo Denlinger wrote in his 1950 book *The Complete Pomeranian*. "This statement may be hard for some of the breeders and fanciers of Pomeranians to swallow, since the Spitz tribe is about the most plebian *(sic)* of the races of dogs. All aristocratic strains of dogs and men have derived from obscure and commonplace beginnings, and the proud Pomeranian is unable to deny his lineage."

WHAT JOB?

If the breed's name caused confusion, so did it's purpose. In Germany, the Spitz has always been considered a utility or watchdog. This description was to confound British dog writers. The British preferred highly specialized breeds, rather than the all-round dogs favored in other European countries. Thus, the English had special breeds for finding birds on land, other breeds for water work and still other breeds for hunting game other than birds. The Germans were likely to combine all these uses in a single dog, such as the German Shorthaired Pointer or the Weimaraner, which could be used for all these purposes. If a Brit wanted a guard dog, he could choose a Mastiff or Bullmastiff. If he wanted a sheep herding breed, there was the Collie. If he wanted a dog for vermin, there were terriers. And, so, when the Spitz made his way to England, writers struggled to fit him in one of these categories.

The white Spitz, or Pomeranian, was approximately the same size as a terrier and, therefore, he was tried as a ratter. Vero Shaw writes, in *The Illustrated Book of the Dog,* published in 1879, that "isolated specimens may on occasion do a little in the way of destroying rats, but we have seen many tried at all sorts of vermin, big and little, with the same result— an apparently irresistible inclination to get out of the pit as soon as possible, and leave their enemies to something which liked to kill them better. This experience is corroborated by almost every one who has seen the breed tried..."

Many writers considered the breed a sheepdog. "In his native country he is the ordinary sheep-dog...." writes Stonehenge, in *The Dog in Health and Disease*. "These dogs are common everywhere in the North of Germany, where they were sometimes used for herding sheep," wrote A. Croxton Smith, in *About Our Dogs*.

Since the two breeds share so many characteristics, historians have mistakenly believed that the American Eskimo was descended from the Samoyed. Yet, you can see that Am., Mex., Can. Ch. Alta of Deep Powders Am. CDX, Can. CD, Mex. PC, owned by Ann Hamlin, has many differences when compared with the Eskie.

While mistaken, there was a kernel of truth in these and the many other statements about the breed as a sheep herder. In *The German Shepherd Dog,* by von Stephanitz, there are two interesting photos. One depicts a "long coated Pomerian Old German Shepherd Dog," and the other a shepherd dog from northern Germany. White shaggy-haired dogs were found "throughout Pomerania, Posen, Brandenburg, Brunswick and Hanover as far west as Westphalia. They are met with only here and there and more often as watchdogs on the farms (where they are held in great favour as non-poachers and very reliable watchers) than with the cattle. Their other names 'yard-dog,' 'peasant's dog'....indicate that these shaggy-haired creatures also performed yard service, apart from the work with the flocks and herds...."

Von Stephanitz also refers to a variety of early German Shepherd as the "shepherd spitz." He tells us that, in northern Germany, early shepherd dogs were seen which had a "tendency to curl the tail....(and) the fully developed head of the dog shows some of the hallmarks of the spitz..."

During the late 1800s and early 1900s, a now extinct breed known as the "Pomerian" Shepherd could be found in northern Germany. It resulted from breedings of German Shepherds and Spitz dogs. British historians learned of this breed and, when the German Spitz was imported to England, they assumed that it had been used as a sheepdog.

Ludwig Beckmann, in his 1894-95 book, tells us that this "rugged, older variety of the German Spitz had coarser muzzles than present-day German Spitz varieties have; and they were often born without tails, or their tails were docked. Later this older variety disappeared completely. These dogs probably were assimilated into the production of our German Shepherd."

It appears, therefore, that early-on there may actually have been a variety of Spitz which was used for sheep herding. However, both Beckmann and von Stephanitz agree that this type of dog disappeared at an early date.

Clearly, the American Eskimo is one of the most misunderstood breeds in all of American dogdom. It is our hope that by explaining the confusing wealth of names applied to the breed and its ancestors, dispelling the Samoyed link and clarifying the inaccurate assumptions about the use of these dogs, it will clear the way for us to begin a detailed discovery of the Eskie's true history.

Chapter 4

In the Beginning

"The Spitz-like dogs...represent undoubtedly the *oldest* form of our domesticated dog." So wrote German authority Ludwig Beckmann in his 1894-95 book *Geschichte und Beschreinung der Rassen des Hundes (History and Description of the Breeds of Dogs)*.

Indeed, archaeologists trace the Spitz back to the Late Stone Age (4,000-1900 BC). Prior to this time, humans were largely hunter-gatherers. They lived a nomadic existence, following the migrations of wild animal herds while culling what plants and herbs they could find along the way. During the Late Stone Age, though, a variety of changes took place. Our early ancestors made the monumental discovery that they could raise their own food. The general warming of the climate, no doubt, made a major contribution to the adoption of agriculture, which had a dramatic impact on their lifestyle. Suddenly, Stone Age man could rely on a stable existence, allowing him to build permanent settlements. According to University of Frankfurt Professor Jens Luning, this transition was "the revolutionary event in human history."

With the increase in available food, supplemented by hunting, the population expanded. Historians tell us that by 4,000 B.C. there were over 86 million people in the world, eight times as many as only 2,000 years earlier. With food easier to acquire, Stone Age man began to store food, domesticate animals, make extensive use of copper and fashion tools and pottery.

We know that these early humans chose the land around lakes as their dwelling places. These sites provided a ready source of water for drinking, washing and agriculture. The lakes teemed with fish, a ready source of food. It is also likely that they attracted the animals that man routinely hunted. Settlements of 50-200 people sprang up in such sites. Homes, constructed of wood, were built on stilts over the lakes or on pilings at the marshy edge. While all this provided a more permanent existence, it was not without danger. There were competing tribes, or clans, which would mount raids on the settlements. It was easier, after all, to raid stores of food than to go to the trouble of raising your own. Plunder and death often followed in the wake of these raids. It's possible that prisoners were sometimes taken to be used as slaves.

THE TORFSPITZ OR PEAT MOSS DOG

It's obvious, under these living conditions, that a keen-eared watchdog would be valuable. And we know conclusively that these early humans did, in fact, have dogs. Numerous complete and partial skeletons, as well as bone fragments, have been and continue to be unearthed in both Germany and Switzerland. They are visible testaments to the dogs owned by Stone Age man. Scientifically, these dogs are designated as *Canis familiaris palustris* or *Canis familiaris palustris Ruetimeyer*. Commonly, they are referred to by a variety of names: Torfhund, Torfspitz, Moorland Dog or Peat-Moss Dog. This is because the remains were found buried in layers of peat moss on the lake shores. This proved to be a boon for archaeologists. Peat is rich in tannic acid, which is an excellent preservative. Therefore, we can tell much from these wonderfully conserved specimens.

"The lake-dwellers' settlements had these dogs in large numbers. The skulls of these dogs are extremely uniform in size, as compared to the wide range of variability in the skull sizes between the various modern breeds," write Thomas Althaus and Marc Nussbaumer, in *Vom Torfhund zum Heutigen Rassehund (From the Peat-Moss Dog to the Modern Dog Breeds)*, a booklet published, in 1979, by the Museum of Natural History, in Bern, Switzerland.

The first scientist to undertake a critical examination of these skeletons was Karl Ludwig Ruetimeyer. He discovered that the size and shape of the skeletons corresponded very closely with the German Spitz, standing approximately 11 to 14 inches at the shoulder. The well known German Spitz breeder, judge, writer and authority Eÿke Schmidt-Rohde tells us that a "medium sized dog of Spitz type was reconstructed from these remains. It had a head similar to a fox, ears were upright, fangs not too long, neck was medium to long, short back, and tail was rolled up above the stocky looking body..."

Dr. Conrad Keller did much research on these early Spitz dogs. He detailed his findings in *Die Abstammung Alteste Haustiere (The Origin of Ancient Domestic Animals)*. Keller divided *Canis familiaris palustris* into three categories: the Wolfspitz, the House-Spitz and the dwarf Spitz.

Researchers tell us that the Peat-Moss dogs performed a variety of functions. "The Torfhund (Peat-Moss Dog) was...probably used as a watch-dog and companion-dog in the dwellings of the lake-dwellers during the Late Stone Age," Althaus and Nussbaumer tell us.

"The...moorland dog, the lake-pile dwellers spitz who no doubt was the same old yelper as his present-day descendants, may also have taken his share of guard duty in the settlements," writes von Stephanitz, while discussing German breeds in his classic book *The German Shepherd*.

From what we know about life in the settlements, it's easy to see how valuable a good watchdog would be. He would warn of possible attacks and signal the appearance of wolves and other wild animals. Such a dog could make a priceless contribution. We can also see that the Spitz tendency to bark has been an ingrained characteristic since the earliest of times.

While we say that the Torfspitz was a "companion," it's not likely that that word had the same context as we use it today. We do not know how affectionate the adult members of the clans were with their canine companions. Despite the adults' attitude, though, it seems certain that the village children would not have been able to resist the charm of young puppies. And, as we shall see, at a later date both adults and children forged a tender relationship with their canine companions.

Most primitive peoples did not put out food for their dogs. Instead, the dogs scavenged for what they could find in the village. They subsisted on leftovers. These Lake Dwellers simply tossed their waste onto trash piles, which often mounded up to a considerable height. The remains of meat, left on bones, the grains (primarily barley) which fell from the primitive mortars, gleanings from the waste pile, any scrap of food he could find...these were, most likely, the daily fare of the Torfspitz. This served another very valuable purpose. This scavenging kept the rodent population under control and helped to deter wild animals who might otherwise be attracted to the settlement.

The Battak Spitz's lifestyle has helped to provide cynologists (those who study the history and origin of dog breeds) with clues to the early history of the German Spitz.

While we may not like to think about it, it is entirely possible that the Torfspitz also served as a source of food. After all, times were hard. Dogs breed quickly and there are only so many that a small village can accomodate. "Since open dog skulls, from which no doubt the brains had been removed, have often been found heaped up in piles in the settlements of prehistoric man, it is thought that these dogs were probably eaten," Althaus and Nussbaumer state.

German writers on the breed tell us that these early Torfspitz were most likely white or light in color. It is believed that white colored dogs were easier to spot at night, thus helping the early owners to distinguish their own dogs from marauding wild animals, such as wolves. The village dogs, therefore, would be less likely to be killed. The color of many of our present white livestock guardian breeds evolved in a similar manner.

It's also possible that these white, or light colored dogs, may have played a religious role in the life of the village. Many prehistoric peoples have revered white animals. "A king of snakes was supposed to be white; white elephants were sacred; white cassowaries in Patagonia were not to be killed, or the species would die out," writes Edward Ash, in *Dogs, Their History and Development*. "White animals were preferred as victims for sacrifices. A white dog was sacrificed by the Iroquois; this dog was killed in January, and the ashes sprinkled at the door of every house...So in some places white was bred for, with great care; every dog had to be white..." So, although we don't know conclusively, it is possible that white Torfspitz may have been sacrificed on special occasions.

THE BATTAS

To get a feel for the role the Torfspitz may have played in the lives of the Lake Dwellers, we can look to the dog known as the "Battak-Spitz" or "Batta-Spitz." This breed was first mentioned by Strebel in 1904-05. Shortly before his book was written, German authorities had discovered a primitive tribe of people, the Battas, living in the interior of Sumatra. These scientists said that the Battas lived "under the same conditions as the lake-dwellers of the later stone age of Europe." Therefore, a look at the environment of the Batta spitz may offer an invaluable glimpse into that of our German Spitz's ancestors.

Like the Lake-Dwellers, the Battas lived in huts built on piles. While the humans were not overly kind to their dogs, the animals were allowed to share their homes and the dogs seemed quite devoted to their human masters. "He is an excellent watch-dog," observed Mr. Siber in his report on the expedition, "and invaluable to his owner on account of the many attacks provoked by feuds which the Battas have among themselves. Slavery or imprisonment is the penalty for those who allow themselves to be surprised by attackers...."

Men used the Batta Spitz as a hunting dog, driving the quarry into prepared traps. "Otherwise," Siber writes, "the dog belongs entirely to the woman, accompanying her as guardian and protector when she is at work outside the house, or when bathing. On the latter occasion each dog watches the clothes of his mistress which are placed in a row on the river bank. He is very useful in the poultry yard, for he keeps away the vermin from the chicken runs which are situated some distance from the huts. His resources are very scanty: refuse and leftovers from the meals (near the rice mortars one might see the dog fighting with the chickens for the occasional grains which are thrown out), bones thrown to him, and even excrements..." The dogs also supplemented their diets with the mice they caught.

As with the Torfspitz, the Batta Spitz was also occasionally consumed for food. "If he grows large and fat on this luxurious diet, he will eventually grace his master's table as a much appreciated dish." Dog meat seems to have been the preferred menu at Batta wedding celebrations. The researchers anticipated that dog lovers would cringe at this observation. "The gruesomeness of this state of affairs is not weakened by the fact that, as late as thirty years ago, the Battas preferred human flesh to all other meat and that their laws provided the penalty of a criminal being eaten alive, piece by piece."

We do not know if the Batta Spitz still exists today. As late as the early 1900s, the breed was reported to be exceedingly rare.

EARLY SPITZ DOGS

The Torfspitz must have carved a valuable niche for himself for these dogs continued to proliferate in succeeding centuries. Indeed, they seem to have spread far beyond the German and Swiss lake settlements. By the Bronze Age (1900-800 BC), we find that the Spitz dog now comes in two different varieties. The larger dog is still found, but now there is a smaller version, measuring 9-11 inches in height.

We also know that, by this time, the Spitz was regarded as a loved and treasured companion. Early man has always buried his most cherished possessions with him when he departed this world. And so, we begin to see carved depictions of Spitz dogs found in human graves. These charming relics are hands-on testaments to the love of early man for his dog. They may also signal a belief in the afterlife, where prized possessions would still be needed.

In an article entitled, "Carved Prehistoric Figurine of the German Spitz Progenitor," William Ledbetter reports on a carved figurine found during a renovation in Darmstadt, West Germany. There, deep beneath the cellar of an old house lay a little figurine which was "found along with three pieces of pottery and a black amber ring jewel..." According to Ledbetter, these artifacts most likely "belonged to a female member of a Germanic tribe; after cremation, as was the burial custom...her ashes along with treasured personal belongings had been collected and buried in an urn, which resembled a bucket-shaped earthenware pot."

Deftly carved from black amber, a petrified hardwood, the two inch high by two-and-two-thirds inch long dog has been damaged in the intervening centuries. The ear tips have broken off and the legs are only half their original length. Yet, the tiny model still strikingly

This carved black amber Spitz-type figurine dates to 200 B.C. The ears have been broken off and the legs are only half their original length. It is one of many artifacts that have been discovered in Germany.

Long before the birth of Christ, German children played with these little figurines. We know they were prized possessions for they were often buried with their young owners.

Detail of a Spitz-type dog found on the famed German "Silver Kettle of Gundestrup," which dates to 100 B.C.

displays German Spitz characteristics. Mr. Ledbetter draws our attention to "the neat, wedge-shaped little head with a fine muzzle and ears mounted high on the head....The tail, so characteristic of our modern Spitz turns over the figurine's back and unmistakably proves this ancient dog's identity as a representative of the Spitz family, to which our modern Great German Spitz, of course, belongs."

The carving has been dated to approximately 200 BC and closely resembles some of the Greek figurines we will discuss in the next chapter. Bill Ledbetter reminds us that this is not an isolated find. "Up until now, eleven similar figurines....have been discovered at nine different locations within a 50-mile radius of Frankfurt, West Germany."

"Such ancient figurines of the German Spitz progenitor were commonly made and treasured by female members of the Germanic tribes originally inhabiting the Elbe River regions of North Germany,"

says Dr. Werner Jorns, a prominent archaeologist. "Numerous works of art which have been discovered here in Germany since the turn of the century...show that this ancient progenitor of the present-day German Spitz varieties was always *the* most treasured household possession and companion."

Dr. Conrad Keller tells us that the Lake Dwellers' settlements ceased to be inhabited around the first century A.D. Our knowledge of the Spitz in Germany during this time period is quite sketchy. "It is very strange that the Spitz was almost completely forgotten or disregarded during the period from around 400-1800 A.D.," says Richard Strebel in *Die Deutschen Hunde und ihre Abstammung (The German Dogs and Their Ancestry)*, published in 1904-05. "It is my opinion that the Spitz was so common and well-known everywhere during this entire period of time that nobody considered it important or worthwhile to document his existence."

Chapter 5

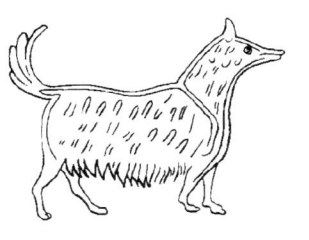

The Spitz in the Ancient World

We do not know exactly when or how the Torfspitz spread to the world's oldest major civilizations. We do know, however, that early humans were avid traders. Evidence tells us that there was contact, across the Alps, between the early peoples of the Mediterranean and those residing in Germany and Switzerland. We know that the Lake Dwellers had parsley and peppermint, plants indigenous to the Mediterranean area. And the earliest Mediterranean peoples kept delicately fashioned white "pearls," made of limestone found in Switzerland.

In our quest for the American Eskimo's predecessors, we will travel to many of the world's first great civilizations. In both ancient artwork and literature we find ample evidence that the Spitz dog was indeed present as the companion of early man. In the various types of artwork, we see the indelible breed characteristics—upright ears, typical coat, tail curled over the back—all are there. Both artwork and literature firmly establish that these dogs were, even before the birth of Christ, treasured family companions.

ARTWORK

There is a great body of artwork which depicts the Spitz in the ancient world. In this chapter, we shall try to examine these artifacts in approximately chronological order. In this way, we can hope to gain an appreciation of the presence of the Spitz through history.

In Persia

In the days before the emergence of the great Persian Empire, the southwestern region of what is now Iran was ruled by a people known as the Elamites. Still a mystery to historians, the precise derivation of the Elamite people is unknown. Even to this date, their language has never been successfully deciphered. In the early days, Elam was an independent kingdom with its own cultural heritage. Later, it became an important trading crossroads and its culture was greatly influenced by Sumeria and Mesopotamia.

It is the early independent period, around 3200 BC, with which we are concerned. In this era, Elam's capital was Susa, or Shush. In 1850, French archaeologists began to excavate this ancient capital. Their finds date back to 4,000 BC, in Neolithic times. The French unearthed a storehouse of treasures. There were cuneiform inscriptions and outstanding statuettes of the Elamite kings and gods, formed from gold and silver. Thankfully, for our purposes there were also small models of guardian animals, which were probably used as amulets. These small charms, or talismans, were said to protect against evil spirits. The treasures from Susa can now be seen in museums around the world.

One of the oldest known depictions of a Spitz dog, dating to 3200 BC, may be seen in the Musee des Antiquities Nationales, at Saint Germain-en-Laye. We thank German Spitz authority Eÿke Schmidt-Rohde for bringing it to the dog world's attention. While attending a dog show in Paris, she made a visit to the museum. "In the display cases in the foyer,...I immediately found what I was looking for," Mrs. Schmidt-Rohde writes in the German club's magazine, *Der Deutsche Spitz*. "I spotted a small Spitz of pure gold!" Though tiny, a collar can clearly be seen on the small statuette, proving that dogs such as these were kept as pets. Similar statuettes, in both gold and silver, can be found in other museums.

In Egypt

Probably the most famous of the early civilizations, Egypt has long captivated the imagination of laymen and archaeologists alike. The colossal pyramids, concealing the gold laden tombs of the Pharaohs, still leave us awestruck. The annual flooding of the Nile River, provided the ancient Egyptians with

This little statuette, dating from 3200 B.C., is one of the oldest known depictions of a Spitz dog. Made of pure gold, it comes from Elam. If you look closely, you can see that the dog sports a collar, a clear sign that the Spitz was a valued pet.

not only a stable food supply, but a surplus. A government, complete with the first bureaucrats, was established to keep track of the abundance. To aid in this task, the Egyptians developed a system of writing. The kingdom also housed a whole group of specialized people, from priests to scribes to craftsmen of all sorts. So well established did the Egyptian Empire become that it's strong monarchic government lasted for more than 3,000 years.

We know that, throughout their long history, the Egyptians loved and even revered dogs. One of their gods, Anubis, is pictured with the head of a dog and other gods took the form of dogs.

Pet dogs were held in high esteem. There were large cemeteries, specifically for dogs. Funerals were held for dogs and the entire family went into mourning when a beloved pet died. Indeed, some members of the family even shaved their heads as a sign of grief.

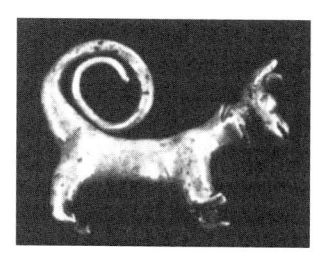

Like the statuette above, this Spitz dog also traces to Elam, during the same time period. This model is made of pure silver. Like his golden counterpart, he too sports a collar.

Several of these pet cemeteries have been excavated and were found to contain a high percentage of small pet dogs. What they tell us about these canines is quite interesting. Many of the dogs had intricate collars of twisted leather. One, clearly owned by a wealthy family, even had tiny ivory bracelets on his legs. Researchers say that many of these animal companions had very bad teeth and were suffering from pyorrhea. This condition could only have arisen if the dogs were given soft food, a sure sign that they were house pets.

We know that the Egyptians had a variety of dog breeds. Mastiffs and several types of Greyhounds can be seen in the spectacular paintings found in ancient

A figure showing the typical Spitz characteristics—erect ears and a tail which curls over the back. This was found in excavations at Fayyum, Egypt and dates to 300-600 B.C.

tombs. In the IVth Dynasty, according to British writer Bryan Vesey-Fitzgerald, a dog of Spitz type appears in tomb paintings. A statue of a Spitz dog, dated 3,000 BC, has been located. It shows what appears to be a larger dog, with the typical erect ears and curled tail, but lacking the fine foxy finish of muzzle that we associate with the German Spitz and its relatives. Some

This tombstone, which dates to the third century B.C., was discovered in Alexandria, Egypt. Gravestones from this time period often depicted the departed with their favorite possession. This Spitz dog was clearly special to this young child. Some historians have classified this as a Miniature Spitz, or Pomeranian, but it may also be a puppy.

authorities contend that the dog is more reminiscent of the Chow Chow. All we can say for sure, though, is that the dog is a member of the Spitz family.

A very important find was made at Fayyum, an oval basin located in the plateau of the Libyan desert, about 50 miles from Cairo. It dates from 600-300 BC. In the excavations there, two little statuettes of small dogs were found. One is clearly a small Spitz (modern historians have dubbed it a "Pomeranian"), while the other is probably a Maltese. We do not know specifically the use of these small items. They may have been amulets, charms or toys.

While we know conclusively that the Spitz was present in ancient Egypt, we still do not yet have a full picture of the dogs which were kept there. Excavations in Egypt continue and may add to our knowledge. As this is being written, a new catacomb of more than 50 tombs has been discovered.

In Greece

In southern Europe, on the Aegean, lay the golden civilization of Greece. Borrowing the very best of the Egyptian and Mesopotamian cultures, the Greeks formulated a shining kingdom where arts and thought were elevated to a high level. It was a culture which revered intellectual development, social spirit, sports, arts and humanities. Indeed, the Greek influence persists to this day. Much of our present day culture can be traced directly to the ancient Greeks. The first history and geography books were written by them. The first texts on philosophy and science were Greek innovations. Plays, epic novels, poetry —all these were perfected by the Greeks. The *Iliad* and the *Odyssey,* Homer's brilliant epic sagas, are still studied today. The works of Aeschylus, Euripides, Sophocles, Socrates, Xenophon, Plato and Aristotle still provide food for thought. Every four years, we gather to commemorate the Olympic games, which began in Greece. Many of our sports—bowling, wrestling, gymnastics, marathon running—all had their genesis there.

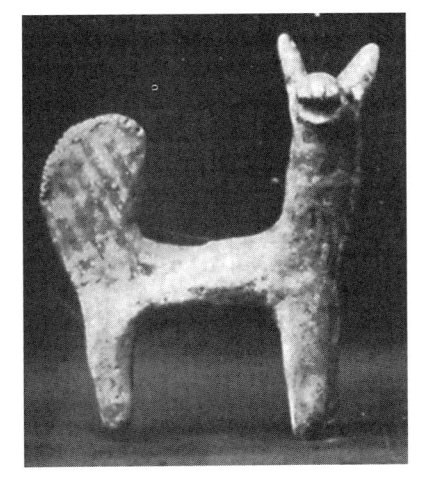

An early Greek artifact, dating to what is known as the "Archaic period," which covers anything before 800 B.C. It demonstrates a more primitive style than is seen in later Greek art. Such small objects were often kept as good luck charms.

During the period between 750 and 500 BC, the Greek influence spread far and wide. From the Aegean, Greek colonists fanned out to all the countries of the Mediterranean and into Europe. They ventured all the way to the Ukraine. It was through these colonies that Greek thought and products spread.

The influence of the ancient Greeks persisted even after the golden empire had vanished. During the grim years of the Middle Ages (500-1500 AD), much of European culture was devastated. Historians tell us that it was the study of Greek literature and art that led to the rebirth known as the Renaissance.

Ah, Greece. For the American Eskimo historian, searching for the breed's ancestors, Greece is the mother lode. We have many lovely vases, wine pitchers and jars from Greece which show dogs that appear almost identical to today's modern American Eskimo. These Spitz dogs are all solid white in color. Many fanciers have jokingly observed that some of these dogs could walk off these ancient vases and into today's show rings.

There are several aspects of these magnificent artifacts which are helpful to us. We know that the Greeks kept other breeds, besides the white Spitz, and they, too, are shown on pottery and other items. Thankfully, these breed depic-tions all exhibit a wonderful realism and are anatomically accurate. In all cases, they present us with not generic pictures of dogs—instead, these are true to life portraits of individual breeds.

We are also fortunate that the Greeks show us the relationship between the humans and their Spitz dogs. The

A young Greek boy plays an ancient instrument known as a "chelys." His white Spitz dog keeps him company, no doubt chiming in on a note or two. (c. 400 B.C.)

A selection of Greek vases from 400 B.C. All feature white Spitz dogs, which will seem very familiar to American Eskimo owners. What is interesting to note is that the dogs are usually depicted interacting with people, clearly indicating that these Spitz were pets. We see the dogs cavorting with their owners, standing on hind legs begging, jumping up to play and walking with them.

The Spitz in the Ancient World

Another Greek vase, c. 400 B.C. It's clear that the dog in the foreground is a white Spitz.

dogs are often seen in charming, playful poses. At times, they gaze at their masters with the devotion we see in our own dogs today. The dogs appear with both adult men and women, as well as children of all ages. There can be absolutely no doubt that these are treasured and cherished pets.

In addition to the paintings of Spitz dogs which appear on vases, etc., we also have sculpted depictions of these dogs. They appear primarily on reliefs and tombstones. The Greeks paid great respect to their dead and fashioned impressive tombstones to honor departed loved ones. Trips to these elaborate resting places were often a great consolation to the family. Furthermore, on the anniversary of the loved one's death, the ancient Greeks would often host parties to celebrate the departed's memory.

Writers have reported seeing such a monument on the "Street of Graves," in Athens. There can be seen a white Spitz puppy with a young child and three adults. James Watson, in his 1906 *The Dog Book,* says that at "the Metropolitan Museum in Central Park will be found a replica of the mural tablet at the tomb of Karallion,

Single portraits of a dog on a vase, such as this one from 400 B.C., are rare.

wife of Agatha, at the Dipylon gate, Athens. This lady is represented facing left and sitting, while facing her in a low relief is the figure of a man whose costume extends to the ground, and showing against the bottom of this flowing garment is a small dog looking anxiously up at his mistress. The head is a good representative of the Pomeranian type, while the body is covered with a tufty coat." Watson also viewed a book, published in London, *Die Attischen Grab-reliefs,* which pictured more than 20 tombstone dogs, "the great majority of them being the same small Pomeranian type..."

A detail engraved on a bronze jar which dates to the second century, B.C.

This little toy dog, with erect ears and a tail curling over the back, is made of lead and dates to 200 B.C.

This sculpture, which hails from the ancient Greek city of Tanagra, dates to 100-300 B.C.

The Etruscans

The area between the Arno and Tiber Rivers, in central Italy, was the home of the Etruscans. The first people to settle Rome, they were greatly influenced by Greek culture. For centuries, scholars have tried to solve the riddle of these people for they had a distinct language, totally unrelated to any found in the Mediterranean or Europe. We know that the Etruscans had a vibrant literature, written in Greek. Sadly, none of it has survived.

During their existence (800-100 BC), the Etruscans flourished. They built bridges, canals, temples and roads. They are said to have had magnificent cities, but these are located beneath the sites of many present day cities and, therefore, have never been excavated. Outside of their cities, however, the Etruscans established "cities of the dead." Here, wealthy families built elaborate tombs, which housed generations of the departed. In these burial vaults, they recreated their houses, complete with furnishings. Life-sized statues of deceased relatives, jewelry, etc., were found in these final resting places. It is from such tombs that we have learned something of Etruscan life.

Etruscan bronze work and delicate gold jewelry rivals the best that man has ever produced, even in modern times. Sadly, we see few depictions of dogs in Etruscan work. It's a great loss considering their extraordinary skill.

It seems logical that, with their close association with the Greeks, the Etruscans must have known the Spitz. The only picture presented in old dog books, however, shows a leashed dog with his wealthy owner. From a vase, discovered in the Etruscan city of Vulci, the illustration is less than pleasing to those searching for true Spitz type. The dog shown has the upright ears, but the tail does not curl tightly over the back and we are uncertain about the coat's texture and length. Clearly, this does not establish definitely the Spitz type we see in Greek art.

More convincing is the copper coin, weighing 2.5 grams, which hails from the city of Arezzo. Hercules, his head symbolically surrounded by a lion's mane, can be seen on one side. On the other side a Spitz is pictured.

In the course of researching this book, we searched for other concrete proof that the Etruscans did, indeed, possess dogs identical to those found in Greece. The photo of a part of a horse harness depicts graphically and undeniably a Spitz dog of excellent type. The upright ears and tail curled over the back, sculpted magnificently in bronze, clearly show that the Spitz was familiar to these little known peoples.

In the 1800s, the German historian Keller made a study of Greek art. During the research for this book, we obtained access to his rare works and present this drawing of a Spitz dog accompanying a chariot.

In Rome

The Romans overtook and replaced the Greeks and the Etruscans. They would establish the great and mighty Roman Empire, which would serve as a model for future types of government. A succession of Roman Emperors spread their influence throughout Italy, most of the Mediterranean and then turned their eyes northward. The Empire would eventually rule most of France, all of Belgium and Luxembourg, much of Britain and part of Germany.

The Romans' approach to their conquered peoples was markedly different from that of earlier warrior nations. They did not merely subjugate defeated nations, demanding tribute and treating them as vassals. No, the real genius of Rome was that they incorporated these new territories into their own nation. Roman citizenship was extended to almost all conquered peoples. Representatives were invited to join the Senate and take part in governing the Empire. Foreigners were even elected to the position of Emperor. However, lest we begin to think that the Romans were egalitarian, we must remember that slaves

Another Keller drawing from Greece, late 300 B.C.

were a part of every wealthy family's household. Some were, later, granted the status of freed men. The Romans made other contributions to the areas they conquered. These ancient builders constructed canals, roads, fortifications and impressive buildings throughout their kingdom. A network of roads, some surviving to this day, linked all parts of the Empire.

The Spitz was known to the Romans, as he appears in their artwork and literature. Sadly, Roman art lacks the wonderful realism and high polish that we see in Greek art and, unfortunately, it is not as plentiful. The British Museum houses an Apulian vase featuring a Spitz. It is dated to the third century BC.

On her trip to Paris, Eÿke Schmidt-Rohde discovered a gravestone, from the Roman era, commemorating Aspinosus Iclus, a small boy from Entrains. "His Spitz and his rooster accompanied him to the death chamber when he died," she writes in *Der Deutsche Spitz*. "On his gravestone he carries a hatchet and little pot to help make his way. His face looks sadly in the distance." Like the Greeks, Romans also gathered at the graveside to pay tribute to their departed loved ones. This is the purpose, Schmidt-Rohde says, for the "loving, lifelike decoration of gravestones."

We know that the Spitz already existed in Europe before Roman times. However, the continual interchange of people and goods on the newly constructed

Another of Keller's drawings, depicting Spitz dogs with their fashionable Greek owners.

A Spitz dog jumps up on a child on this bas-relief, from the fourth century B.C., which was discovered in Athens, Greece.

Roman roads, must certainly have served to disperse the breed throughout the Empire.

Other Civilizations

Was the Spitz known in other ancient civilizations? Probably so, though without concrete evidence, we are left only to wonder and speculate. As we have seen, the breed appears to have spread far and wide. It seems likely, therefore, that the Spitz was known by other early peoples.

Among the most likely candidates were the Phoenicians. Situated along a coastal strip of land in present day Israel, Lebanon and Syria, the Phoenicians were incredibly avid traders. Alone, they turned the ancient world into a colossal maritime trading nexus. These sea-faring specialists plied the waters of the Mediterranean, of course, but even ventured as far as the Atlantic Ocean and the Red Sea. They established regular trading posts at their port stops to barter or buy goods to carry to other countries. We know that dogs were among their wares. Many canine authorities have credited the Phoenicians with dispersing different breeds, throughout the world, via their trading ships. Since we know that the Spitz was a highly valued dog, often owned by the wealthy, wouldn't he likely have been a valued trading commodity, as well? Wouldn't wealthy people, eager for those tempting goods from faraway countries, have offered Spitz puppies as barter? It certainly seems probable.

No history of dogs, in the ancient world, is ever complete without considering the Assyrians. The name will be instantly recognizable to those familiar with the Old Testament. These were the legendary warriors who, at one time or another, conquered most of the Middle East. They were famed for their ruthlessness and cruelty in battle.

The Assyrians occupied part of Mesopotamia. They settled in the fertile valley between the Tigres and Euphrates Rivers, in present day Iraq. One of their most famous kings was Ashurnasirpal II. He mounted ambitious military campaigns, conquering many small kingdoms, plundering their treasures and demanding tribute to be paid annually. This tribute took the form of valuables offered to Ashurnasirpal as an acknowledgment of his power and status as ruler, and also as a means of buying protection.

Naturally, a king of such stature deserved a great capital and Ashurnasirpal II certainly had one. The impressive city of Nimrud (the Biblical Calah) included the King's richly elaborate palace and a huge terraced pyramid, known as a ziggurat.

Starting in the 1840s, the British began to excavate Nimrud, as well as three other Assyrian capitals. The world thrilled to the massive stone architectural wonders, the carved detailing of the bas-reliefs, the intricate mosaics and other treasures. Now stored primarily in the British Museum, these relics have greatly influenced all modern canine historians. They have led to conclusions which may not, in fact, be accurate. Found on bas-reliefs, particularly those at Nineveh, are compelling depictions of large, fierce Mastiffs, shown in the guise of war dogs and big game hunters. The greyhounds and pet dogs seen in the art of other contemporary civilizations are absent. This has led writers to conclude that Mastiffs were the only dogs owned by the Assyrians.

Recent discoveries in Iraq, however, may change all that. In 1989, archaeologists with the Iraqi Department of Antiquities announced that they had made a major find at the Nimrud site. They discovered a complex of royal tombs, filled with huge caches of exquisite gold jewelry, crystal and semi-precious stones, as well as other artifacts. Reports say that there were over 125 pounds of gold jewelry alone. This includes necklaces and charms, some in the shape of guardian animals. British Museum archaeologist John Curtis, has been quoted as saying that this discovery rivals that of King Tut's tomb, in Egypt. The similarity doesn't stop there. While excavating the grave of Princess Yabahya, the researchers translated a marble tablet inscribed with the curse, "If anyone lays hands on my tomb...let the ghost of insomnia take hold of him for ever and ever."

Will these treasures add to our knowledge of the Spitz? Perhaps. We know that this dog was considered a guardian animal in many nearby countries. Iran, home of the Elamites and, later, the Persians, was close at hand and, at one time, under the Assyrian yoke. Under Ashurnasirpal's leadership, the Assyrian army ventured all the way to the Mediterranean. And, for a period of time, part of Egypt was under Assyrian rule. It seems entirely likely, therefore, that they were acquainted with the Spitz dog.

Before now, no evidence has been presented in dog books to show that the Etruscans owned Spitz dogs. Indeed, depictions of dogs in Etruscan artwork are rare. In researching this book, however, we came across this ornamentation on a harness. The ears and tails of some of the figures have been broken, but the typical Spitz characteristics are easily seen.

Sadly, it may be some time before we have any answers. The recent conflicts in Iraq have made them reluctant to welcome foreign scientists. *Time* magazine was allowed to photograph part of the treasures, but other outsiders have been forbidden to see these ancient marvels. Therefore, it may be years before we have answers to this tantalizing question.

LITERATURE

In addition to the artwork which offers us a pictorial view of the Spitz dog in the ancient world, we also have some literature available which mentions the breed. This appears in Greek and Roman texts, translated largely in the 1400-1600s. These sources are invaluable because they offer a glimpse of the attitudes and thoughts with regard to the dogs. Unfortunately, we do not have surviving texts from the other ancient cultures. In order to appreciate these translations, however, we will have to clear up the names applied to the Spitz.

What's in a Name, Again

As has always been the lot of the Spitz, the names applied to this breed have confused translators. As we have seen, breed names have a habit of changing through the ages, particularly with older breeds of dogs. To make matters worse, Greek and Roman writers give only the sketchiest of physical descriptions. Not much help there.

Greek and Roman writers frequently mention a small white pet dog, which they identify as "Melitaie" or "Melitæus." This has led modern writers to assume that these ancient wordsmiths were speaking of the Maltese. This, therefore, is the breed name they used when translating Greek and Roman texts. Even though we know full well, due to our study of the artwork of the period, that the Spitz was a widely kept pet dog, white in color, we find mention only of the Melitaie. We have to ask ourselves *why*.

Fortunately, there is one pivotal instance where art and literature fuse together and provide our answer. A Greek vase, dated 500 BC, shows a young man with what is undeniably a Spitz dog. Printed in Greek, above the dog, are the words "O Melitae." Here is visible testimony that the ancient Greeks referred to the Spitz dog as "Melitae."

"...I must here point out a great source of confusion which lies in the fact that there were two Melitas and more than one breed of Melitæus toy dog," writes Judith (Lady Wentworth) Lytton, in the rare 1911 work *Toy Dogs and Their Ancestors*. "...the original Melitæus universally kept by the Greeks from 800 BC was the now so-called Pomeranian. The Pomeranian was the true Maltese pet dog....

"We do not come across the Maltese as we now know it till 200 BC, when it is found represented in Egypt, together with the Melitæus, though there is no evidence to show whether it originated there or was brought over with the other Melitæus. The latter supposition, however, seems the most probable, owing to the model of the Pomeranian Melitæus which we know from Greek vases and literature to have originated in one of the two Melitas."

Mrs. Lytton believed much of the confusion stemmed from the fact that there were two islands named Melitæ. One, which was described by the famous historian Pliny, was located in the Adriatic, between Corcyra and Illyricum. The other ancient Melitæ, described by Strabo, is now known by the name of Malta. Pet dogs were bred on both of these crossroads islands, as well as on Sicily.

When we examine the selected literature, therefore, we will see the dogs called Maltese dogs, Maltese terriers and, sometimes, Sicilian dogs. The Honorable Judith Lytton believed that these were merely translation errors and that the ancient texts really referred to the Spitz dog. It's difficult to tell for sure, but we include these stories for the perusal of American Eskimo fanciers.

Prized Pets

Asterius, the Bishop of Amasia, wrote in about 375-405 AD, about conditions in Læonia. He tells us that there were many stray dogs, roaming the city, which were "left to shift for themselves in the street." Country dogs were used, occasionally, for hunting. Among the Turks, occupying the area, it was not the custom to keep pets, except for the Maltese *(Spitz)* dogs, "which the women of good family rear for pleasure."

Epaminondas, who died in 362 BC, was a famous Greek general. He led armies to a victory which, in 371 BC, established Thebes as the supreme power in mainland Greece. Years later, Aelian would record a number of incidents from his life.

After a victory over Lacedæmon, Epaminondas was dragged before a court of law, charged with continuing to command the Theban army four months longer than he was authorized to do so. The penalty, should he be found guilty, was death. After the charges had been read, Epaminondas rose. He, and he alone, should be held responsible for the event, he declared. His men should be absolved of any blame.

Esteemed German Spitz breeder and author Eÿke Schmidt-Rohde discovered this tombstone, from the Roman era, in a Paris museum. We thank her for allowing us to include it here. The young boy was buried with his pet rooster and Spitz.

Slowly he walked to the witness stand, every bit the victorious general. "My actions are my best apology," he stated, defiantly. "If in your eyes they count for naught I am ready to suffer the punishment of death." Then, taking the offensive, he demanded that a monument be erected, praising his military victory. The engraving should read: "Epaminondas forced the Thebans, although they resisted him desperately, to carry fire and sword into Lacedæmon, which, for five hundred years, no enemy had dared to penetrate, to rebuild Messene, which had been razed to the ground two hundred and thirty years before, to bring the Arcadians together again into a common territory and last, but not least, to restore to the Greeks freedom to live according to their own laws."

By the time Epaminondas was finished, the judges, quite ashamed of themselves, unanimously acquitted him. As he stalked from the courtroom a Maltese *(Spitz)* dog approached, wagging and jumping upon him. "This animal is grateful for the good I have wrought," he announced to the gathering, "but the Thebans, to whom I have rendered the greatest services, would have me put to death."

Saint Clement of Alexandria (c. 150-215 AD) is considered one of the fathers of the Roman Catholic church. This Greek was an early convert to Christianity and sought, through his many writings, to fuse Greek philosophy with Christian teachings. In his "Treatise on Education," he observes that the women "make pets of Indian birds and Median peacocks....And they would look down upon a modest widow and think her inferior to a little Maltese *(Spitz)* dog. They would scorn a good old man, who is worthy of more honor, if I mistake not, than any fantastic creature purchased with gold, and they would offer no shelter to an orphan child; but they take no end of trouble over rearing parrots. The children born within their walls they abandon and expose by the wayside, but they harbor any number of cocks and hens. In a word, they give senseless animals the preference over creatures endowed with reason." This clearly demonstrates that "Maltese dogs," or more rightly small Spitz dogs, were favorites of wealthy Greek women.

Claudius Aelianus (170-235 AD) was a history teacher in

This Roman plate dates from 200 B.C.

Rome. Two of his works, both written in Greek, have survived. One, *De natura animalium,* or *On the Nature of Animals,* is a curious collection of stories which all include moral lessons. "I am now going to relate some wonderful examples of the extraordinary affection of dogs," he writes. "...When his relatives placed Theodorus the harper in his tomb, his little Maltese *(Spitz)* dog, flinging itself into the coffin in which the corpse lay, was buried with its master."

Several passages in a work called *Symposium,* dated 190 AD, tell us about a people known as the Sybarities. Evidently, they were very fond of dogs. "It is customary among them, even for the children, until they are grown up, to wear purple robes and curls plaited with gold. It is also customary for them to bring up in their houses...dwarfs, and also little Maltese *(Spitz)* dogs, which follow them even to the gymnasia..." Another passage says that the Sybarities "cared for nothing but Maltese *(Spitz)* puppy dogs..."

We may never know the entire story of the Spitz in the ancient world. After all, we are left to piece together the clues that are available to us. Literature, which is promising but not entirely clear, and artwork, clearly depicting the breed, are our only sources. However, as more archaeological wonders are revealed and more Greek and Roman works are translated, hopefully, the picture will become clearer. Future writers may be able to offer us a more comprehensive portrait of the American Eskimo's ancestors in the world's first great civilizations.

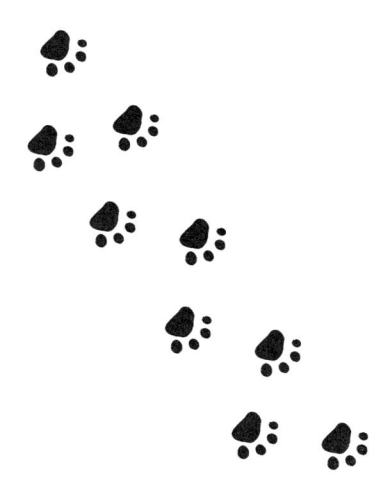

The German Spitz was exported to countries all over the world and was often immortalized by artists. (Top left) *Portrait of Mme. Adelaide*, 1750, Nattier; (Top right) *The Morning Walk*, c. 1785, by Gainsborough; (Bottom) *Two Fox Dogs*, 1777, by Gainsborough.

Chapter 6

The Spitz in Germany

As we follow the Spitz breed's course, through time, we encounter a giant gap. We find mention of dogs in the texts of the ancient world, but there is nothing else until we reach the 1450s. This, however, is not as unusual as it would first appear. During this "missing period," books were handwritten by scribes, chiefly monks. Naturally, their works were primarily on religious topics. In 1440, the German goldsmith Johann Gutenberg began to experiment with printing via movable type. By 1450, he had perfected his press and it was available for commercial work. Perhaps it is sheer coincidence, but this is the point where we, once again, pick up the Spitz story.

THE 1400 AND 1500s

"...it is extremely difficult to trace the history of this breed any further back than the middle of the 15th century," Ludwig Beckmann writes in the 1894-95 book *Geschichte und Beschreibung der Rassen des Hundes (History and Description of the Breeds of Dogs)*. During the Middle Ages, Beckmann tells us, watchdogs were routinely kept in German yards. The "larger watch-dogs...were called the Hovawarth (Yard Watchers)..." These should not be confused with the resurrected breed known by that name today in Germany.

"...the smaller, yapping watch-dogs of the farms out in the country were called Mistabella (Manure-Pile Yappers)...These smaller dogs were mainly Spitz-like," Beckmann says. Sounds pretty awful, doesn't it? What is most likely meant, though, is that the Spitz's dog-house was placed atop what we know today as a compost heap. On farms, such piles are often left for more than a year to ferment fully into wonderfully rich black earth. There would have been a further benefit: The rotting material gives off heat, thus providing the dog with a warm resting spot. It's important to see, once again, that barking is one of the oldest breed characteristics.

Count zu Sayn

The first actual mention of the word "Spitz," can be found in 1450, in the *House Rules and Regulations*, of Count Eberhardt zu Sayn. The Count was a feudal nobleman, who made his home in Germany's Rhine Valley. His holdings consisted of thousands of acres of land, very rich in game. Here, Count zu Sayn indulged in splendid hunts, often entertaining fellow nobles. There is evidence to suggest that feudal lords like Count zu Sayn may have presented Spitz dogs to their tenants.

In the 1951 German book, *Dogs and Dog Care,* Ulrich Klever writes: "Straying and chasing game are things he does not know, because in comparison with his master's house and property, nothing is of any importance to him. When the hunting lords gave their tenants a Spitz, this was calculated generosity. They knew full well that a Spitz never chased game, no matter how rich a preserve he might have lived in."

Many authorities believe that the Spitz had, indeed, been bred through the preceding centuries to obviate his hunting instincts. To noblemen, of Count zu Sayn's era, it was absolutely imperative to prevent all hunting and poaching on their lands. Hunts were major sources of entertainment and hosting impressive hunt parties was the sign of a truly rich lord. Reports of such events tell us that, often, hundreds of wild animals were killed during such extravaganzas.

In England, a series of "Forest Laws" was enacted to preserve all possible game. People living on the gentry's land could only own dogs small enough to fit through a precisely measured wire loop. Unless you had a special waver, you could not own a Greyhound, Mastiff or other medium-sized or large dog. Should you wish to have a dog of that size, his feet had to be mutilated to prevent hunting. Future generations would pay for these hunting excesses as all the large game was gradually eradicated from many European forests.

Apparently, it was the habit of Count zu Sayn's servants to condemn those they did not like by calling them *Spitzhunds*. Perhaps the Count admired Spitz dogs, or he may just have wanted to ensure harmony. At any rate, he issued an edict prohibiting the derogatory use of the word.

Other Books

We also first find the term "Spitz" in German dictionaries from the 1500s. The name appears in the children's book, *Reineke Fuchs,* the German version of *Reynard the Fox.* The context of the word differs depending on which authority you believe. One writer says that one of the characters is a Spitz, who acts as the defender of the homestead. Beckmann, however, says that the book includes "the expression *spitzhut* (in this story meaning *accuser* or *plaintiff*) is found; this term is probably based on the derogatory word *Spitzhundt."*

Curiously, we find no mention of the breed in the work of the world famous naturalist Gessner. His *Natural History of the Four-Legged Animals,* published in 1552, describes other breeds, but neglects the home-grown Spitz. Beckmann says that there is, additionally, no mention "in the publication of Crescentius or any other agricultural publications of the period..."

THE 1600s AND 1700s

The popularity of the Spitz continued to grow. During the 1600s and 1700s, the German Spitz was one of the most commonly seen dogs in the country. Germany had not yet become an industrial power. Instead, most citizens relied on agriculture for their living. In most sections of the country, nobility continued to rule over vast estates, with labor provided by peasants, who were responsible to the feudal lord. In other areas, people owned their own small plots of land.

The German Spitz became the cherished dog of the common man. On the farm, he was esteemed as a multifaceted, all-around watchdog *par excellence.* When the peasant was at work, a Spitz would stay by the door, protecting the home. The owners could go about their daily tasks, secure in the knowledge that no stranger would be permitted on their property.

The German Spitz was esteemed as a guardian of home and property. When the family went to town, it was the dog's duty to protect the wagon and cargo. This rare engraving, by an unknown German artist, shows both a black and white Spitz at work.

The Spitz was especially appreciated by the woman of the house. It was she who usually tended the vegetable garden, which provided food for the family. Yet, it was also her responsibility to watch over the children who were not yet old enough to work. Very often, it was one of the family's Spitz dogs who came to her aid. The baby would be placed on a blanket, at the edge of the garden plot, while mom attended to the planting, weeding and harvesting. Beside the child, lay the faithful Spitz dog. He served as the youngster's playmate, ever ready to bark should the child cry, crawl off or should a stranger approach. From the earliest days of a German child's life, therefore, the Spitz would become his best friend and loyal playmate.

The dog was equally valuable, however, to the man of the house. When the goods produced on the farm were taken to town for sale, one of the Spitz dogs always accompanied the cargo. Riding beside his master, in the wagon, the dog assured that no one would steal any of the produce.

In the province of Swabia, in southwest Germany, the Great German Black Spitz (equal in size to our Standard-sized American Eskimos) would become the esteemed companion of wine growers. The "Vineyard Spitz," as he was dubbed, protected the valuable grapes from predation by both four-legged thieves and birds. Flitting here and there, ever on the go, his sharp bark chased the birds from the crop. So esteemed was he in his work that, in later years, a monument would be erected to him.

William Ledbetter, an avid Spitz fancier and historian, in an article entitled, "Notes on the Origin and Development of the German Spitz," recalls the days when vintners brought their wine to town.

> "Under the coach seat or behind the wine keg always lay the family's Spitz, watchfully observing the unfamiliar surroundings. After business had been transacted and the wine had been brought down into the cellars of the restaurants, the wine producer celebrated with his patrons. In the evening, after the wine producer had left the city and was approaching his home area, it usually occurred that he fell asleep on the seat of his coach. The horse, of course, knew the way back to his stall—and the Spitz? He had control over *everything:* the farmer, the horse, the wagon, and, above all, the farmer's wallet!!! No one dared to approach his master!"

The Spitz was equally popular in the coastal regions of Germany. Boats, engaged in fishing and trade, plied the Baltic Sea, as well as all the major rivers. Most took Spitz dogs with them, to protect their goods. When the boats docked, the men went ashore. Remaining behind were the Spitz dogs, who prevented any strangers from boarding. These Germans traded with the Scandinavians to the north, and the rest of Europe to the south and west. The dogs were admired in many ports where German ships docked, and it seems likely that there developed a lively trade in Spitz dogs.

"The character of our Spitz is markedly stamped by his having been bred for thousands of years as a watchdog," Richard Strebel wrote in his 1904-05 book, *Die Deutschen Hunde und ihre Abstammung (The German Dogs and Their Ancestry)*. "Before trains began to traverse our fatherland, the Spitz was the constant companion of freight coach drivers, stage coach drivers and river boatsmen...Thus, the characteristic of vigilant watchfulness has been preserved, intensified and is now a striking, bred-in characteristic. We should have had the opportunity to watch the Spitz on the coaches and riverboats of former years: now up to the front, then back to the rear, up on top again, now back down below—nothing escaped his keen hearing capability, his sharp eye-sight—and he reported every irregularity with a light, cheerful voice."

While we know that the Spitz was, indeed, the companion of the common man, this does not mean that he was overlooked by German nobility. Indeed, he seems to have been a great favorite with a number of royal houses, include the Hanovers. The Great White Spitz (identical to our standard-sized American Eskimos) was often known as the most beautiful of all the German Spitz varieties. Particularly popular in the provinces of Pomerania and Mecklenberg, he would journey with the young Queen Charlotte, when she made her way to England with the soon to be crowned King George III, who ascended to the throne in 1761. When wealthy British patrons expressed an interest in the breed, Queen Charlotte procured specimens from Pomerania for them.

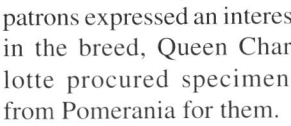

THE 1800s

In the early and mid-1800s, we once again find the Spitz performing his traditional watchdog duties. He remains the coachman's companion, the protector of boats and barges and the all-around farm dog.

"The German Spitz surpasses all other domestic dog breeds with regard to watchful vigilance," wrote Ludwig Beckmann in his great opus on dogs. "Constantly distrustful,

The essence of loyalty as depicted in a painting from the 1700s.

The Spitz dog, or Loup-Loup, as drawn by Buffon in his *Histoire Naturelle*, in 1835.

A sketch by Swiss writer and artist Richard Strebel showing how the German Spitz appeared at the turn of the century. Note how little the breed has changed.

skeptically observing all that is happening in his surroundings, the slightest suspicious noise or movement sets the Spitz into a state of alarm. I know of many examples, whereby the German Spitz showed extreme devotion and loyalty, not only to his home, but also to his master. I remember particularly a Great German Black Spitz kept on a small, remotely isolated farm out in the country. Every Saturday evening, as soon as he was released from his kennel, he raced at top speed over the fields and through the forest, over an hour's distance away, to the forest's exit, where he patiently awaited the return of his master, who customarily went to town every Saturday on his horse-drawn buggy."

It is during the 1800s that people first began to take an interest in the physical characteristics of the breed. Beckmann tells us that, during that century, the "German Spitz varieties were limited to (a) wolf-gray or wolf-sable with grayish yellow, regular markings, (b) uniform pure-white or (c) uniform jet black. German Spitz in other colors (such as red-orange, reddish-brown, spotted or checked) have never been popular here in Germany and are, at the present time, almost always a definite indication...that the dog is *not* a pure-bred German Spitz....there is no essential difference (except for color) between the three different sub-breeds or varieties: (1) Wolfsspitz," known in this country as the Keeshond, "(2) Great German White Spitz and (3) Great German Black Spitz."

The Dog Show Era

By the mid-1800s, Germans had begun to hold dog shows. The first International Dog Show was held in Hamburg, in 1863. This seven day extravaganza had a total entry of 450 dogs—quite impressive for its day. The show was truly "international" in scope, for there were many exhibitors from European countries, including England. Indeed, a British judge presided over the Spitz classes. We do not know about the total Spitz entry, but we do know that the appearance of three Miniature Black German Spitz quite surprised the judge. "In England this *smaller* variety is unknown..." Beckmann tells us. We must remember that only the Great German White Spitz had been exported to England prior to that time.

Obviously, dog shows caught on. The German nobility embraced this new interest in purebred dogs. Arthur Seyfarth built a huge, palatial kennel in Köstriz/Thüringen, in 1874. From

An old German woodcut, from Beckmann's 1894 book, showing the three varieties found in the Great German Spitz at that time. On the left is the Wolfspitz, or Keeshond, the largest and most ruggedly built of the trio, together with the Black and the White color varieties.

This print, from the 1800s, depicts breeds traditionally associated with Germany—the Spitz and the Dachshund.

A Spitz waits patiently, perhaps guarding the luggage, as people alight from a coach.

A lovely white Spitz

that date to the early 1900s, he would issue an elaborate catalog, complete with wonderfully commissioned drawings, to list the more than 50 breeds he offered for sale. The catalog tells us that Seyfarth sold "several thousand" dogs, often exporting them "to all parts of the world." Canny businessman that he was, this name-dropper included mention of his illustrious purchasers. Saint Bernards, Great Danes, Dachshunds, Poodles, German Pinschers, Pugs, Maltese, Seidenspitz and, of course, German Spitz were among the breeds offered for sale. Mr. Seyfarth proudly proclaimed that he could provide any type of dog you wished, whether you wanted one to guard your house or go hunting with you. In the days before modern vaccinations, distemper was the bane of both breeders and owners. Seyfarth confidently declared that every dog, leaving his kennel, carried with it a can of distemper pills, which were sure to get him through the illness.

In Hannover, in 1882, a five-day International Canine show was held. This time we do know something of the Spitz entries. In the "large" classes, only Great German Black Spitz were entered. The "middle" classes consisted entirely of German Black Middle Spitz. The judge must have been pleased for his report says: "A truly wonderful class, in which almost each entry could receive a top rating." For the "small" and "dwarf"

It would be easy to assume that this exquisite painting was of American Eskimos. Yet these are German Spitz, circa early 1900s. Can there really be any doubt that the Eskie is the transplanted German Spitz?

This painting, entitled "The Grandfather's Visit," is from 1910 and clearly shows the Spitz as a member of the family, living inside the house.

classes, there was a single entry, according to Beckmann "a very tiny little fellow in pure snow white."

The Birth of the German Spitz Club

Interest in purebred dogs and dog shows continued to grow. Charles Kammerer, an elderly breeder from Vienna, must go down as one of the pivotal figures in German Spitz history. He bred Great German Spitz and may also have bred the smaller varieties. In April 1899, Herr Kammerer wrote to *Hundesport und Jacht,* a popular canine paper. He urged all Spitz owners to rally together to form a club for the breed. Breed fanciers took his appeal to heart. In October, they met to form the Verein für Deutsche Spitze (Association for German Spitz Varieties), which is one of the oldest dog clubs in the country.

An avid Spitz fan, Kammerer told Richard Strebel a story, demonstrating the breed's intelligence, which is related in *Die Deutschen Hunde und ihre Abstammung (The German Dogs and Their Ancestry).* "He (Kammerer) has a little water pool in his backyard, in which he sometimes lets his Spitz take a cooling bath, particularly during the hot summer weeks. Some of his dogs will independently jump into the pool immediately, others only upon command—only one Spitz of his chooses to shy away from the water pool completely, just as a tom-cat would. After the bath, his dogs are permitted to run out into a meadow, where they romp and fool about, rolling and wallowing, in order to dry off their coats. What does his water-shunning Spitz do? He runs straight to the meadow, where he immediately goes through all the *motions* as if he were drying off after having taken a bath! His master laughs about this sly trick of his, and thus he gets away without bathing very often! The same breeder wrote to me that he has observed that the larger Spitz varieties bark less and are more of the good-natured type than the smaller varieties are." Kammerer also noted that "envy or jealousy is a very pronounced character trait of the

The canine chorus, in this humorous 1902 print, inludes a German Spitz.

The Spitz in Germany

A White Spitz—a glamorous accompaniment to an elegant lady in 1914.

As we know Spitz dogs have a special affinity for children and believe they should be included in everything—including dinner.

German Spitz varieties—that 90% of the fights his dogs have with each other can be traced back to this jealous streak."

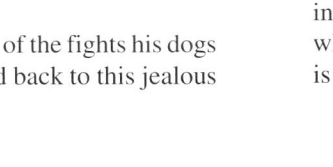

THE 1900s

As the new century dawned, Germans continued to take an interest in purebred dogs and shows. Arthur Seyfarth's kennel continued to provide a multitude of breeds to an eager public, both in Germany and abroad. We know that the German Spitz, under the name Pomeranian, had already become thoroughly established in England. He was also known in France, Belgium, Holland and other countries, including the United States. Obviously, he was known in Czechoslovakia, too, for we are told that, in 1901, there was an entry of 19 white Spitz in a show there.

The German Spitz continued to be a popular breed. Theo Marples, one of the founders of England's Pomeranian Club, says in his rare book *Show Dogs, Their Points and Characteristics, How to Breed for Prizes and Profit* (c. 1919), "It is a fact that dogs of this description, and even larger, mostly white" are found in "Pomerania and the whole of Northern Germany, where they may be seen in the streets everywhere. He is the common house-dog, carrier's dog, and, indeed,

A 1924 painting of a Spitz, which was used on a postcard.

39

A stylish woman, in 1906, poses with her Spitz.

general canine factotum..." A factotum is an employee or assistant.

Richard Strebel certainly confirms this fact, in his 1904-05 book. "We need only step out into the street and before long at all, we can catch glimpse either of a genuine, pure German Spitz or a Spitz blend. This is true wherever you are nowadays in Germany and also in all the other European countries, from Petersburg (Russia) down to Milan (Italy). There is nowadays no other dog breed that has such a wide range of distribution, yet on the other hand, for whom there are so few large-scale breeders. If we were to make a list of the recognized breeders here in Germany, in Switzerland and in Austria, we would be extremely surprised to see just how short this list would be. I have given this puzzling question considerable thought, but I have not been able to find a satisfactory answer or explanation, It cannot be due to the character of the Spitz, since otherwise the Spitz blends would not be so popular and found on every street throughout northern Europe. This proves that the Spitz is treasured everywhere that he is known. It may be due to the fact that our standard books on dog breeds here in Europe have treated the Spitz almost as a second-rate breed since the introduction of so many new fad-breeds in recent years."

1913 saw the publication of the very first stud book for the breed. There were a total of 1,050 entries. Of these, 699 dogs were of the larger varieties, while 351 were small or dwarf Spitz. Of the large Spitz registered, 247 were pure white, 222 were black and 221 were wolf-gray.

Thus, the Spitz became fully established as a registered breed in Germany. He has weathered many storms. World Wars I and II decimated the breed and it took time and dedication to gather dogs together and once again build breeding programs. From the perspective of the American Eskimo, we need not delve further into the German history of the breed, in the 1900s. The foundation stock which would form the Eskie breed, had already been transported to America.

Chapter 7

The Spitz in England

Undoubtedly, the vast majority of American Eskimo foundation stock, in the United States, arrived from Germany. It is also likely that some early white Spitz dogs came here from England. More importantly, though, many of the Americans' attitudes about Spitz dogs came directly from Great Britain. Due to the language barrier, most dog writers and knowledgeable dog show folk relied on British, rather than German, texts. As we shall see, this led to great misunderstandings and, often, virulent prejudices which would endure for years. By examining the genesis of these attitudes, we will be better able to understand the early years of the Spitz in America.

THE EARLIEST DOGS

Janet Edmonds, a pioneer in the recent re-establishment of the German Spitz in England, provides us with tantalizing clues about the earliest dogs in her country. In her booklet, on the German Spitz in England, she says that a Spitz skeleton, dating to Roman times, has been unearthed at Chedworth. It is now on display at this former Roman villa. It would seem likely, therefore, that the Spitz traveled with the Roman legions when they conquered England.

Ms. Edmonds has also located a medieval depiction of the Spitz. Found in the church of St. Mary the Virgin, in Higham Ferrars, in Northants, it dates to 1337. This brass rendering "shows a priest standing on two dogs fighting over a bone. One is a spaniel," Janet Edmonds writes, "the other a spitz. Unfortunately, memorial brasses were symbolic, not representational, so there is no way of knowing whether the small size of the two dogs represents their actual size or their importance. Either way, it is a charming piece, well worth going to see."

THE 1700s

A curious situation occurred in England, in the early 1700s. Religion was still a touchy point in the country, with great friction between Protestants and Roman Catholics. During the Protestant reign of Queen Anne, a document called the "Act of Settlement" was passed by Parliament. It rewrote the laws of succession, specifically barring the Stuart line, which was Catholic, from taking the throne. The crown would instead pass to the German Hanover dynasty, through Sophia (granddaughter of King James I) and her Protestant heirs. Henceforth, all British monarchs must be members of the Protestant Anglican church.

George I

Sophia died before Queen Anne, but her son George I, took the throne in 1714, to become the first of the Hanoverian kings. This brought quite a switch in attitude at the royal court. George spoke only German and, during his reign, as improbable as it sounds, never bothered to learn English. The new monarch embraced all things German. He brought George Frederic Handel, the great composer, to London, where the King bestowed special favors on him, gave him a home and granted him citizenship. Critics charge that George I's allegiance was really to Hanover and he even used the British navy to gain more territory for the German dynasty.

We have no documentary proof that the white Spitz was first brought to England during George I's reign. As we have seen, however, the breed was popular throughout Germany and known to the Hanoverians.

George II

When his father died, in 1727, George II took the throne. Born in Germany, before his father became King, George II maintained close ties with his birthplace, frequently making trips to Hanover. He did learn fluent English, but he continued to further the influence of the Hanover dynasty. Naturally, he also continued to embrace German culture.

A detail from the 1767 painting *Gamekeeper with Three Dogs,* by the famous artist Stubbs. This clearly demonstrates that the "Pomeranians" kept in England of this day were really German White Spitz.

Again, we have no evidence that the white Spitz made a debut, in England, during George II's reign. Still, with such close ties, it certainly remains a possibility.

George III and Charlotte

George II's son predeceased him and so, when he died, title to the crown passed to his grandson, George III. Crowned in 1760, he was to become the longest ruling British male monarch. A controversial character, George III was an idealist, who wanted to banish corruption from political life. Unfortunately, the way in which he went about it, led to much turmoil. Still, he did succeed in imbuing the court with a sense of morality and public spiritedness. Strong willed, he took an aggressive stand against the American Revolution and was so upset, following the Declaration of Independence, that he seriously considered abdicating the throne.

Much has been written about the marriage of King George and Queen Charlotte. Together, they would produce 15 children. Their relationship is portrayed in the recent film, *The Madness of King George.* The movie focuses on the period when George developed a disease which resulted in senility, bouts of insanity and blindness.

Unlike his predecessors, George took more of an interest in English matters and did not use the throne to further Hanoverian interests. This does not mean, however, that he eschewed German culture. When it was time to marry, he took as his wife, Charlotte Sophia, from the German province of Mecklenberg-Strelitz. German culture was still welcomed at court. We know, for instance, that Wolfgang Amadeus Mozart and his sister, Maria Theresa, performed for the King and Queen in the 1760s. It was here that Wolfgang wrote his first symphonies.

We know for a fact that the German Spitz was a popular breed during King George and Queen Charlotte's time. Clearly, Mozart, as we shall see in a later chapter, was an unabashed enthusiast of the breed. Again, we don't know if white Spitz dogs were already at court, brought with the first Hanoverian kings, or if Queen Charlotte brought them with her when she first journeyed to England. However, we have both written and pictorial evidence which leaves no doubt, whatsoever, that the white German Spitz was ***the*** breed of choice at court. He was the darling of British society and everyone wanted one. So popular did the breed become, that owners had to guard carefully lest they be stolen.

Certainly, Queen Charlotte took pride in her Spitz. She even helped to locate dogs for those who attended court. A letter survives, from the Queen, addressed to a Lord Harcourt. Dated 1767, it was sent with two young "Pommeranian" (as the Queen spelled it) dogs. The letter below was printed in Sari Brewster Tietjin's lovely book, *The New Pomeranian.*

My Lord,

When last I saw you at Windsor you expressed a fondness for the Pommeranian Dogs. I wrote to Germany and have received this morning from Pomerania through the means of G. Z. Freyborg two Pair, of which I now offer two in Truth very beautifull for that Species their Names, Mercury and Phebe. May I also give you a hint, that they ought not to be sent in the Square, for being the true breed they may become a temptation for Dog Stealers. I shall be glad to hear that they afford you some pleasure which may perhaps be the case,

The family of Sir William Young, including the white Spitz, are immortalized in Johann Zoffany's painting *The Young Family,* done in 1770.

The 1790 print, *The Return from School*, by W. R. Bigg.

for the messenger says, that they are young and clever at learning tricks.

Charlotte

We do not know, of course, how many other dogs Charlotte procured for her subjects. Fortunately, we do know what the "Pommeranians" looked like. Historians tell us that King George III was an avid collector of paintings. Master painters like Gainsborough and Stubbs included dogs when painting portraits of their illustrious masters. These snow white dogs were about the size of our Standard-sized American Eskimos.

We know, therefore, that as the 1700s came to a close, the white Spitz, known in England as the Pomeranian, was a popular breed, the companion of nobility.

THE 1800s

As the new century dawned, it was to open a new and puzzling chapter in the breed's history in England. The publishing of dog books, meant for the masses, had begun in the late 1700s and would increase dramatically in the 1800s. For some reason, which we can only partially explain, the Spitz became the victim of bad press. This is odd considering the fact that King George III still sat on the throne and still liked the white Spitz. Whatever the reason, the views of early writers would, pardon the pun, dog the breed for years and may have hampered its success in England. It certainly had an effect on the breed in America.

Bad Press

In 1800, *Cynographia Britannica*, written by Sydenham Edwards, was published in London. Edwards gives us the first detailed description of the "Pomeranian or Fox-dog." The head, he tells us, is broad at the back, narrowing to the muzzle. The ears are short, pointed and erect. "The tail is large and bushy, curled in a ring on the rump." He singles out the coat for special comment. "There is a peculiarity in his coat; his hair, particularly the ruff around his neck, is not formed of hairs that describe the line of beauty, or serpentine line, but is simply a semicircle, which by inclining the same way in large masses gives him a very beautiful appearance." Edwards says that the dogs may be of a pale fallow shade and also "some are white, some black, but few spotted." Lest we have any doubt about the size of the "Pomeranians" of this era, Edwards says that they should stand about 18 inches at the shoulder.

It's a remarkably good description for such an early book. The problem comes, however, when Edwards describes the breed's temperament. "He is of

The "Pomeranian," as the white Spitz came to be known in England, was the fashionable pet of royalty and the gentry.

The illustration of a Pomeranian which appeared in Rees' Encyclopedia, 1802.

little value, being noisy, artful, and quarrelsome, cowardly, petulant, and deceitful, snappish and dangerous to children, and in other respects without useful properties." Whew! He then includes an extremely contradictory statement. "Although his attachment is very weak, yet he is difficult to be stolen."

His statements had a lasting impact on other writers. Those less familiar with the breed, would parrot his opinions. The more widely read *Sportsman's Cabinet*, by Taplin, came out in 1803. Taplin's description is a paraphrased version of Edwards, adding only that the "nose and eyes" are "mostly black" and that the dogs should be 18-20 inches tall. He also adopts Edwards description of temperament, concluding that the breed lacks "one prominent property of perfection to recommend him." A closer reading of Taplin's entire book provides us with some clues to his prejudices. He seems to abhor *all* foreign breeds and derides any that are not used for sporting purposes.

Pomeranians as they appear on an English print dated 1803.

Meyrick added to the derision in his 1841 book *House Dogs and Sporting Dogs*. The breed, he says, is "certainly a pretty and graceful dog, but has the disadvantage of being neither clever nor affectionate, and is, in addition, possessed of a yapping restlessness that makes him quite insupportable to most people."

The *Illustrated Book of the Dog,* by Vero Shaw, is one of the most important dog books of all time. Written in 1879-81, shortly after the formation of England's Kennel Club, it included some of the earliest standards for breeds and became an immediate hit and much used reference work. A respected judge, Shaw's words were widely read, even outside of England. Together with the English writer Stonehenge, Americans would pay particular attention to them. For that reason, we print the bulk of Mr. Shaw's opinions here:

The Pomeranian is admittedly one of the least interesting dogs in existence, and consequently his supporters are few and far between. He has not that delicate beauty of outline which belongs to the Toy class generally, and his unsuitability for field sports renders him perfectly useless as a sporting dog. The Pomeranian is certainly a foreign importation, but to what country the credit of his production is due is a matter of conjecture. Good specimens of the breed have appeared from time to time amongst us, which have been picked up in Germany, Belgium, France, and other parts of the Continent, but the dog appears to be claimed by no one nation in particular...

As before observed, the virtues of the Pomeranian, whatever they may be, have failed to gain him many friends, and this is hardly to be wondered at when his good and bad qualities come to be weighed in the balance. Against a pretty coat, sharp and rather intelligent face, must be reckoned the snappish temper and lack of affection with which the Pomeranian is so generally credited. In fact, this breed looks far more intelligent that it really is, for it seems incapable of developing even an ordinary amount of instinct. As a guard to a house, however, if kept indoors, the Pomeranian is of some service, for his ears are keen, and an inclination to bark seems deeply rooted in the variety. On the other hand, though uncertain and treacherous in disposition, his courage is very much below the average, and a Pomeranian

A print from the mid-1800s.

would sooner run than stand his ground any day. From this it may be surmised that as a vermin dog, which from his size and shape of head he might reasonably be expected to be, in some shape or other, a dog of this breed is worse than useless....

Supporters Fire Back

One can only imagine the response these books engendered from those who had come to know and love the Spitz, or Pomeranian. Despite the language barrier, word of Shaw's description eventually reached Germany. We must assume that, in the fatherland, Spitz fanciers were livid. As we have said, the words of Shaw and the other early authors would continue to have an impact for years and years. When Richard Strebel wrote his famous *Die Deutschen Hunde und ihre Abstammung (The German Dogs and Their Ancestry),* in 1904-05, he was still fuming. In a peculiar way, perhaps we should be grateful, for Strebel's outrage inspired him to pen the most passionate and accurate description of the breed's temperament ever put down on paper.

>...In England the chapter on the Spitz in Vero Shaw's standard dog breed book completely misrepresents the Spitz...nothing could be further from the truth than this unbelievably shameless misrepresentation of the Spitz. But such devastating misrepresentations have been repeated, especially in England, more than once in the last few years. Therefore, I shall attempt to depict the character of the Spitz, just as I myself have had the opportunity to experience it first-hand; and my own experiences have been confirmed over and again by *all* of the ethical breeders and fanciers of this breed here in Germany. I ask my readers to particularly study the history of the Spitz and the characteristics of related breeds. Careful observers will comprehend the unique breed traits from the history and development of the German Spitz. It will then be clearly understood and obvious that a breed which was bred for a particular purpose over thousands of years will not suddenly, all at once and overnight, give up or lose all its good, valuable bred-in hereditary qualities....

>...His hearing capability is extremely well-developed, his ears are constantly in motion and his small, bright little eyes radiate watchfulness. This means that our Spitz is very suspicious; and curiosity is a very significant, pronounced breed characteristic. Our Spitz is never vicious: he barks and simultaneously retreats cautiously to a safe

This illustration of the "Pomeranian or Spitz" appeared in later editions of Stonehenge's *The Dog in Health and Disease,* which was first published in 1859.

position, so that he has sometimes been accused of cowardice. This is a misconception, since he only avoids, in this sly manner, coming in contact with an intruder's injurious hand; but he immediately will bite this intruder the very second he finds the appropriate opportunity to do so! This has led to the misconception that our German Spitz is deceitful. There is no breed that is more loyal, devoted and affectionate to his master than our German Spitz. He is, and this has never been emphasized enough, **UN-BRIBABLY** loyal to his master. Very numerous are the examples, indeed, in which our Spitz has risked or sacrificed his own life to guard his master's life or property. Our German Spitz is extremely intelligent, even though I cannot maintain that he is particularly suitable for the types of protection training (other than watch-dog duties), in which breeds like our German Shepherd excel...

Since our German Spitz is quite lively and a bundle of energy, he needs to be trained in a patient, yet consequent manner. It is not easy to regulate his character trait of being strongly self-willed, but once he has learned to obey his master, there is no dog on earth that could be more devoted, loyal and affectionate. With regard to watching over his master's house and homestead, the German Spitz is peerless....

The chapter, on the breed, in *Hutchinson's Dog Encyclopedia* also helps us to put this early criticism in perspective.

Large white "Pomeranians," often imported from Germany, were common sights at English dog shows in the mid-1800s. This drawing dates to 1863.

...The arrival of this dog in England,...was not hailed by dog-lovers and dog authorities in any friendly spirit. Indeed, they had no time for it, and looked askance at a type that did not seem to them to have any sporting value, and which, consequently, in their opinion compared most unfavorably with the British sporting breeds, such as the Mastiff, Bulldog, Greyhound, Pointer, Setter, Spaniel and the various breeds of hounds.

Much of their prejudice was distinctly insular; the Pomeranian was "a foreigner," and so the more said against it the better. It was not wanted here amongst British breeds, they opined. Although much of what they said was mere prejudice, there was something to be said in their support, and their reason of dislike is capable of explanation. If the reader has ever seen a Spitz dog in bad coat, he will know exactly why the olden-day authorities and dog-lovers had not a good word to say for the Pomeranian breed. With but few exceptions, all the dogs that were seen were in deplorable condition, for nobody in those days would go to the trouble of brushing a dog; the coat was allowed to grow anyhow, and consequently became unpleasantly matted; when such a coat became intolerable it had to be shorn off.

The Pomeranian was not largely kept. Leading authorities were so prejudiced against the breed that it is a wonder the breed did not die out altogether here. It speaks well for the owners of those dogs that, with so many enemies and so much said against the breed, they should have continued with it. However, not only did they continue, but, what was more important for the breed, they learnt how to improve the coat, how to look after it, and how to make the dog a smart and attractive member of the canine race. They showed the dog more ably. Prejudice, always absurd, gradually became less virulent, and many dog-lovers who had said much against the breed eventually discovered that it was very much like any other dog, just as friendly and nice, and they had to admit that with proper treatment it was indeed a handsome breed, with a coat that deserved admiration.

Those White Dogs (The 1870s)

While the press went about slandering the breed, the Spitz was busy converting dog lovers. It may be easy to hate a breed you don't know intimately. However, it's a different story when you come face to face with them. And, as we all know, the Spitz is not without his charms.

Henry Webb edited an 1872 book, *Dogs: Their Points, Whims, Instincts, etc.* "The Pomeranian" he tells us, "is a pretty and graceful dog. Always well known in Germany, it is of comparatively recent importation into our country. It's little sharp nose and prick ears give it a peculiarly knowing look; and although some writers affirm it is not of an affectionate disposition, we know several instances of its devotion to its mistress, which go far to upset such assertion. A lady, residing in a garrison town not a hundred miles from London, possesses two very beautiful specimens. They know all the shops she frequents and the families she visits, and if they miss her from home for any length of time, and they have an opportunity of escaping, they are off together, and go into all the shops, or bark at the doors of various houses, until they find her, when their delight is unbounded. One, the favorite, generally accompanied his mistress on her visits to distant friends. He was once left behind, and fretted to such a degree that he refused all food, and to save his life he was obliged to be sent off to her..."

In 1870, England's Kennel Club recognized the Spitz, giving it the name "Pomeranian." The next year, the breed was invited to compete at the Kennel Club Show, in June. There were three entries, "being composed of a trio of large white dogs," early

"Frisk," was Best of Breed at the Birmingham, England show in 1877. The somewhat exaggerated style is typical of artist Harrison Weir.

"Charley" was a big winner in English show rings of the 1880s. He stood 16 inches tall and weighed 18 pounds.

PICCO: A MEMBER OF THE TEMPERANCE SOCIETY

PICCOLO, or "Picco," the beautiful dog belonging to the Rev. Henry de Bunsen, of Dorrington Rectory (formerly of Lilleshall, Shropshire), is of the Pomeranian breed, commonly known in England by the name of "Spitz." He was born in the year 1865, in the village of Edgmond, near Newport. His parents, both fine dogs with silky white hair, are still alive, and greatly valued by their owner, Miss Alcock. When "Picco" came to Lilleshall, he was a small, fluffy, white puppy of six weeks—snowy white, and very much like the toy lambs you can see in the shops. His first development of character showed itself in his being constantly on the alert, and always ready to bark his little shrill bark if he heard any footstep outside the door. His education during the first six months of his life proceeded very rapidly. He learned to beg in a few lessons, and with little difficulty waited until *ten* was counted before he would eat the biscuit put before him! There was usually a pet cat or two in the room with him, so "Picco" easily got over the canine aversion to cats. Miss Pussy, indeed, became very fond of rubbing her nose against him, and frequently followed him about the garden. From being constantly in attendance at the family meals, "Picco" soon got to know the sound of his favorite biscuit, and he has also learned never to come and *beg* for it till his own dinner, which is given him after the family have dined. The only exception he makes to this rule is on his "tub-day," when he fancies that he has an additional appetite after his bath; and so on *that* day he comes regularly to be fed at luncheon.

When his own dinner of rice and scraps is prepared, and some one calls out "Picco, go and fetch your table-cloth," he gets up and walks to the sideboard

Ch. Koenig of Rozelle, a top winner in the 1870s and 1880s, was owned by Miss Hamilton, the first President of the Pomeranian Club. She had one of the country's top kennels of large white dogs.

cupboard, which he opens with his nose, and brings out a copy of *The Times* newspaper in his mouth, which is laid on the carpet. On this *paper* table-cloth his plate is placed. He then begs, looking slyly out of the corners of his eyes to see when the finger goes down as the word *ten* is pronounced. He then daintily smells all round the plate to see if his dinner pleases him; very often this is *not* the case, and only by dint of coaxing, or calling "Puss, puss," can he be induced to eat his dinner. When that is accomplished he is told to fetch his biscuits, when he trots to the kitchen and picks up a covered basket, which he brings to Mrs. de Bunsen, and throws it down with a bang by her side. He will stand up by her side while she puts a piece of biscuit in front of him, saying "Trust," and, till he hears the words "Eat it," he will not even dare to look at the tempting morsel. Then he will dance on his hind legs and walk round the room for a piece of biscuit or bread, and hold it on his nose till his mistress counts ten, when he lifts it off with his two fore paws. But the most remarkable trait in "Picco's" character is his great dislike of any kind of wine or beer. He knows the look of a wine-glass, and nothing will induce him even to smell it! In the kitchen he refuses to drink out of any tumbler offered him there, with but one exception; for, strange to say, he will walk straight up to and drink out of the glass of the teetotal house-maid, for he knows that *she* only drinks water! Peter, the butler, always has him to sleep in his room at night, where he sleeps very soundly till awakened by the alarum *(sic)* at six o'clock. When Peter gets up, then "Picco" stirs himself, and goes into the next room, where the groom sleeps, on whose bed he jumps, and *pulls* off the clothes till the inmate rises. "Picco" knows Sunday quite well, and never offers to go to church with the family, though he flies after them if he sees any of them putting on their out-door things on any *other* day. He also never barks at the Sunday-school children who come into the house to their classes, though one footstep on a week-day makes him furious. When the family are away, "Picco" will never take a walk with strangers; he keeps company only with those who live in the house.

At the annual meeting of the Lilleshall Temperance Society in June last, we had the pleasure of seeing "Picco." The dog was on the platform, much to the amusement of all present. One of the speakers, in referring to "Picco's" firmness in his water-drinking habits, asked, "Is not 'Picco' worthy of being enrolled as a member of the Lilleshall Temperance Society?" Amidst loud and hearty cheers, "Yes, yes," resounded from all parts of the large assembly. The next morning we had the pleasure of visiting the clean and tidy cottages of several of the Lilleshall miners in company of their devoted friend, Miss Battersby, when one of the miners met us on the road, and, politely touching his hat, said, *"I hope, sir, that I shall keep from the drink as true as that dog Picco!"*

Ah! what a change would come over thousands of homes that are now scenes of sorrow and desolation if men and women were all as wise as "Picco!"

Band of Hope

The dog who sounded the death knell for the large white "Pomeranian." This is Marco, purchased by Queen Victoria while on a trip to Florence, Italy. The red 12-pound dog started a craze for small, colored Poms.

breeder Miss Lilla Ives reports. A bitch named Floss topped the class. Early entries, even at the most prominent shows, generally consisted of only one or two dogs. Six is the largest turnout mentioned by early writers, during that decade.

We do know something of the dogs which existed during that period. As in King George and Queen Charlotte's day, white was the preferred color. Theo Marples, who would later help form the Pomeranian Club, tells us that "only the big white dogs were exhibited. A Pomeranian of any other color at that time was a *rare avis*...."

And what was the size of those dogs? Marples, in *Show Dogs, Their Points and Characteristics, How to Breed for Prizes and Profit,* tells us that the dogs of the 1870s weighed between 18 and 24 pounds. "Some of the greatest of the whites exhibited were as large as 28 pounds," writes Milo Denlinger, in *The Complete Pomeranian.* Other authorities put the weight as high as 30 pounds. In fact, a dog named Patrick won at the Colchester show, in a class for "any other variety over 30 pounds."

It would, of course, be more useful if we had shoulder heights, rather than weights, to go by. The only such measurement we have been able to locate is found in Vero Shaw's book. In *The Illustrated Book of the Dog,* he includes a drawing of Charley, born in 1877, owned by Mr. J. Fawdry. It was the habit, at the time in England, to take copious measurements of dogs and Shaw includes Charley's particulars: Nose to stop, 1 and 3/4 inches; stop to top of skull, 3 and 1/2 inches; girth of forearm, 5 inches; girth of pastern, 3 and 1/4 inches; height at shoulders, 16 inches; height at elbows, 10 inches; height at loins, 15 and 1/2 inches; height at hock, 3 and 1/2 inches.

Miss Hamilton, who would later become the first President of the Pomeranian Club, had one of the most important kennels of large whites. Rozelle Kennels was the home of such illustrious winners as Ch. Rob of Rozelle and Ch. Koening of Rozelle. Whites were tops at Belper Kennels, owned by Miss Chell, too. Her Ch. Belper Flossie became the very first female Pomeranian champion and her Ch. Belper Snow and Ch. Belper Fritz were consistent top winners.

1880-1887

The white Spitz continued to be kept as a pet during the early 1880s. But, let's face it, this was not a popular breed. Fortunately, he had gained a few supporters in the press, although those nagging old assertions "snappish" "bad-tempered" "untrustworthy with children" etc., continued to rear their ugly heads.

One of the Spitz converts, Gordon Stables, did speak out, though. In the chapter on the "Pomeranian, or Spitz Dog," in *Our Friend the Dog,* he writes:

This is a breed of dog to which I must also confess a partiality. The Pomeranian has a great many good qualities to recommend him. He is very obedient, very tractable, and teachable. He can be taught nearly as many tricks as a Poodle, and to retrieve and carry into the bargain. Moreover he is an excellent guard to property, for he is very watchful, and, if he cannot fight, he can at all events give warning, and if forewarned be forearmed, that is half the battle.

The Pomeranian is extremely affectionate towards those he really loves, and will remain faithful to the very death. His good qualities ought to make him a greater favourite...he is but little known.

Some people will tell you that the dog is apt to be uncertain in temper. To strangers he *may* be at times, although even of this I have my doubts. Some people say the very same thing about our national favourite the Collie. It is so easy to take away a dog's character.

White was still the favorite color. Dogs had to be "all white....entirely free from any tinge of lemon. Lemon ears would disqualify an otherwise excellent dog." Dalziel described the color as "pure flake white." He also gives what must be the earliest description of snow nose in the breed. He says that "perfectly black noses often change to brown or flesh-color, when the dogs are allowed to frequent the hearth and be exposed to the heat."

"On the whole the history of the breed was not a happy one," says *Hutchinson's Dog Encyclopedia,* "on account of the prejudice against it,...." Rawdon Lee suggests, however, that there were other reasons. In *Modern Dogs,* he writes, "white specimens of excellence were most difficult to produce, especially when accompanied by dark...eyes and a perfectly black nose. Fawn or fallow marks on the ears are continually appearing, and red noses are far more common than black ones. Then there was the difficulty in washing and in getting them up for show, in which latter respect white dogs are always more troublesome than coloured ones."

Indeed, by the mid-1880s, some predicted that the breed would soon become extinct altogether in the British Isles.

Floss: The Canine Innkeeper

This letter about George Nash, owner of the Alexandria Hotel, and his dog Floss, was recounted in *The Stockkeeper,* in 1883.

> This hotel is provided…with bells to each room for the purpose of calling the attention of the waiters, each bell having a different sound. There is also an ordinary door-bell, which is rung by a handle at the front entrance of the hotel, this bell similar in all respects to the others, saving a slight difference in tone, and is fixed on the same board as the others. Now, persons calling at the hotel for refreshments may ring as often as they please at any of the inside bells, and Floss will not take the slightest notice of them, but let anyone ring the door-bell, and though she be to all appearances asleep before the kitchen fire, which is at the opposite side of the house to the front door, Floss will jump up and rush to this door, barking all the while, as if she would clear the house in a minute; and until she is perfectly satisfied that there is nothing wrong she will not return to her warm quarters.
>
> What is still more remarkable is, that she can distinguish the sound of the door-bell even when one of the other bells is ringing at the same time. Floss is about six years old, but has only been at this hotel for twelve months, and her peculiar qualification was only noticed by her owner a few weeks ago, since which time the poor Floss has been repeatedly roused from her quiet slumbers by persons desiring to test the accuracy of the…statements.

1888-1900

In 1888, fate stepped in. Once again, a Queen would have an extraordinary effect on the breed in Britain and many other countries. It would signal the rise of the "toy" Pomeranian, which would soar to the heights of popularity. Unfortunately, it almost sounded the death knell for the white Spitz, in England.

The well-loved Queen Victoria was an avid dog lover. There were special kennels, at Windsor, to house the 15 different breeds that she would fall in love with. Though she was the granddaughter of Queen Charlotte, she was unaware of the white Spitz dogs who had been court favorites. In 1888, she went on a tour of the Mediterranean. On a stop in Florence, Italy, she fell in love with a Spitz, or Pomeranian, named Marco. Weighing 12 pounds, he was, according to Drury, "red, somewhat of the shade usually associated with Chows." He quickly became Her Majesty's devoted companion and soon there were other Pomeranians in the royal kennels.

In one of the master publicity moves of the era, Charles Crufts, founder of the famed Crufts dog show, persuaded the Queen to exhibit some of her dogs at his show. Soon, the entire country would read, in the newspapers, of the wins of "Windsor's Marco" and his kennelmates.

The extraordinary rise in Pomeranian popularity had begun and would forever change the fate of the white Spitz in England. G. M. Hicks, writing in Leighton's *New Book of the Dog,* gives us a feel for the swift increase in popularity. Hicks tells us that the largest single entry in the breed, at the Kennel Club Show, prior to the Queen's sponsorship, came in 1881, when 15 dogs were exhibited. Several years later, there was not one dog. In 1891, there were 14 dogs, in 1901 there were 60 entries and by 1905 this had jumped to 125 entries.

"Pomeranians are seemingly popular with all classes, from Royalty downward," wrote Charles Lane,

On the left is Park Swell and on the right is Ch. Belper Snow. These turn of the century show winners were among the last of the "Overweight Pomeranians" seen in British show rings. They were quickly replaced by the toy dogs we now know as Pomeranians.

in his 1900 book, *All About Dogs*. "Her Majesty the Queen has a large kennel of them at Windsor, which I had the honour of an invitation to inspect, and can testify to the great interest taken in the breed, and the number of specimens kept, with every care and consideration shown for their happiness and comfort. Her Majesty's collection, when I saw them, some time since, consisted almost entirely of what I should call 'off colours' that is, not white, black, brown or blue, but shades and mixtures of those and other colours, some exceedingly pretty, and although somewhat larger in size, being mostly 'small medium,' and not so fine in head as many of the dogs now shown, are so good in other respects, that they have often successfully competed with well-known specimens, when Her Majesty has entered any at the Royal Agricultural Hall and Crystal Palace Shows. A great many are also kept by persons in the higher, middle and lower ranks of life, both in this country and the continent of Europe (where, no doubt, the breed originated), and it is a common occurrence, when a popular judge is officiating at one of the larger shows, to see over fifty entries of Pomeranians in the various classes. I have frequently had one hundred, and sometimes even more entries to judge, at the larger shows, and a puzzling job to undertake, on a dull day, in a failing light, is to tackle a class of from twenty to twenty-five black specimens, and try to find out the respective merits of each when there are probably ten or a dozen really good ones amongst the lot, though, to an outsider, they all look much alike. Small, good specimens fetch very long prices, and the breed is exceedingly popular." As Herbert Compton put it, "today you find the breed 'fancied' in the drawing-rooms of dukes and the parlours of the proletariat."

English fanciers went color mad. The race was on to raise Pomeranians in ever more exotic hues. The Pom breeder Theo Marples tells us that "fanciers now journeyed to Germany to procure the best specimens of the breed that could be obtained." This put the white Spitz at a distinct disadvantage. As we have seen, breeders had already experienced difficulty getting pristine white coats with black points. With the rage for smaller size, many breeders had an added difficulty in trying to produce the white color in the newly fashionable tiny dogs.

Size continued to decrease. By the late 1800s, specimens as small as four pounds were regularly seen in British show rings. Indeed, it must have been a confusing sight with these four and five pounders in the same ring as 25 pound dogs. The Pomeranian Club, established in 1891, sought to clear up the problem. While some of the members, including the President, still bred the larger Spitz type dogs, most members had jumped on the toy Pom bandwagon. In 1894, a resolution was passed, dividing the breed, for show purposes, into two classes. Separate classes were offered for dogs over 16 pounds, those 7-16 pounds and for those under 7 pounds. Dogs under 7 pounds would be referred to as "Toy Pomeranians." In 1899, this weight division was again changed. The divisions were for dogs over 12 pounds, those between 8-12 pounds and those under 8 pounds. The larger dogs were now known as "Overweight Pomeranians."

As the century grew to a close, interest in the larger white Spitz, or Pomeranians, had definitely cooled. Still, the dogs were eligible to compete at shows. Under the above weight separations, dogs in each of these classes could earn Challenge Certificates (similar to our classes which award points) and, thus, it was still possible to breed larger champions. All that was to change, however.

THE EARLY 1900s

By the early 1900s, the Pom had become the most popular toy breed, bar none. He had edged out the Pug and Italian Greyhound, the previous favorites. Fantastic prices were paid for specimens, quickly surpassing previous levels for sales of toy dogs. At the Ladies' Kennel Association show, in 1903, there were 322 entries.

In 1916, however, an action by England's Kennel Club was to sound the death knell for the larger Pomeranian or, as Edward Ash writes, "the heavy-weight Pomeranian met its Waterloo." In that year, the Kennel Club decreed that there would no longer be any weight divisions. All dogs would be registered together and only two challenge certificates, one for each sex, would be given. Naturally, this put the large dogs at a tremendous disadvantage. With the huge number of toy entries, they had virtually no change of achieving championships.

Breeders of large Pomeranians complained bitterly to the Kennel Club. The K.C. suggested that the larger dogs should be considered a separate breed and registered completely apart from the small Pomeranians. Breeders took their advice to heart. They formed the Spitz Club and the KC agreed to register their dogs as "Spitz." All told, 247 dogs were entered in the stud books under this new/old appellation. However, it never really caught fire. Sadly, the effort to establish a new breed, known as the Spitz, died.

By the 1920s, speaking of these dogs, Barton would declare in his *Kennel Encyclopædia,* "White Pomeranians are almost extinct in this country..."

Hutchinson's Dog Encyclopedia tells us that, by the mid-1920s, "the large Pomeranian had virtually disappeared and was seldom, if ever seen...; it was looked upon as an absurdity, an overgrown specimen of the true Pomeranian! The public had learnt to expect a Pomeranian to be a dog round about 4 or 5 lb. in weight, and dogs weighing 16 lb. or more appeared to them grotesque. Attempts to re-arouse interest in the larger breed failed. These dogs were no longer wanted, and the owners of the larger breed had to realize that the public and fashion had not responded to them. The cult of the smaller dog continued..."

A white Pomeranian from the early 1900s.

IN ENGLAND TODAY

Thankfully, we do not have to leave the history of the Spitz dogs in England on such a plaintive note. In the 1970s, Averil Cawthera, Rosemary Bridgeman, Janet Edmonds and Julie Smith joined forces to once again establish the Spitz in England. Ms. Bridgeman suggested the romantic name "Victorian Pomeranians."

Several dogs were imported from Holland (where the small dogs were registered as "Klein Keeshond," the Dutch name for the Small German Spitz). These were later joined by an outstanding Austrian import. Breeding these dogs, the dedicated fanciers worked to reestablish the old breed and gain Kennel Club recognition.

A club was formed, but the Spitz breeders ran into opposition from Pomeranian fanciers. This resulted, primarily, from the choice of "Victorian Pomeranian" as the breed name. It soon became obvious that selecting a new name would expedite acceptance. This caused a great deal of friction for the quaint "Victorian" name was very near and dear to the hearts of some members. Ultimately, however, they elected to call the breed the "German Spitz."

Today, the German Spitz is a recognized breed in England. The dogs are divided into two size classifications: "klein" (small) and "mittel" (middle). Britain still, of course, recognizes the Keeshond and Pomeranian. Now, finally, the large Spitz of old, made popular by English royalty, can be seen in the show ring and can, once again, earn championships.

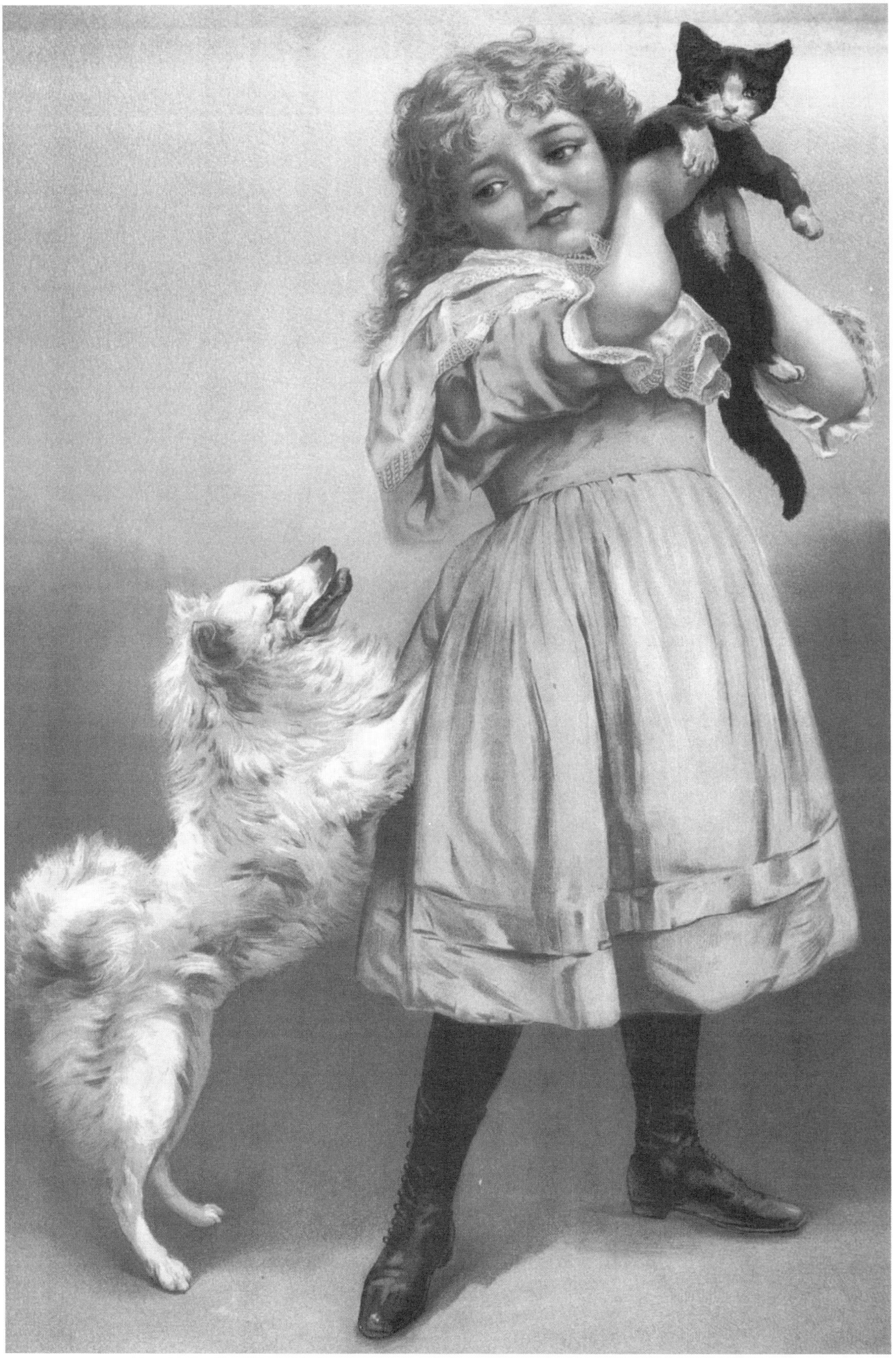

Chapter 8

The Spitz in America

The early history of the American Eskimo, in this country, has always been somewhat of a mystery. This is particularly true with regard to the 1800s and the first part of the 1900s. Our research, however, has uncovered a few facts which shed some light on those early years.

Undoubtedly, the main stock for the breed, which would become known as the American Eskimo, came from Germany, as we shall demonstrate. It appears likely, based on several sources, that some large white Spitz also arrived from England, during the 1800s.

Several recent articles have reported that Japanese Spitz may have arrived on the West Coast and been incorporated into the breed. *We can find no evidence to support this theory.* In fact, as we shall see in a later chapter, it was actually the other way around. The Japanese tell us that our American Eskimo is a likely *ancestor* of their breed! While some reports say that there was limited breeding of Japanese Spitz during the 1930s, the breed was not recognized, in that country, until the 1950s. It was only after that date that widespread breeding took place and the breed became well known. By this time, of course, the American Eskimo was a well-established breed, long registered with the United Kennel Club. Therefore, it seems highly improbable that the Japanese Spitz would have been introduced into U.S. bloodlines at this late date. Furthermore, a survey of the bloodlines, of California Eskies, shows quite clearly that their foundation stock hails from the Midwest.

FROM GERMANY TO AMERICA

America has always been a powerful lure for those seeking a better life. From the earliest days of this nation, German immigrants have journeyed to our shores. The first Germans arrived here in the 1600s. There were sizable German populations in our original 13 colonies. They could be found in Pennsylvania, New Jersey, New York, Virginia and the Carolinas. Some, like the Mennonites, came seeking religious freedom. Others were searching for land and prosperity. William Penn, founder of Pennsylvania, actively encouraged German immigration. He authored pamphlets which were distributed in Germany's Rhineland, describing well heeled newcomers who now wore fine flashy clothes and whose pockets were filled with jingling coins.

Many Germans came to this country during the 1700s. Most were peasant farmers who would settle in the East. All told, between 1700 and 1800, more than 200,000 Germans immigrated to the New World. We do not know, for certain, if any of them brought their Spitz dogs with them.

We do know, however, that Spitz dogs came to this country in the huge tide of immigration that swept our shores during the 1800s. Indeed, between 1815 and 1914, more than 30 million Europeans made the journey to settle in America. Historians describe it as the greatest mass migration in human history.

Several factors encouraged this mass exodus. Around 1820, the first of what were called "America letters" was published in Europe, including Germany. These glowing reports, penned by recent émigrés, on life in the United States, promised low prices, high wages and freedom from government repression.

Shipping firms handed out flyers boasting of the benefits of moving to America. In the Midwest, land speculators opened special offices to appeal to immigrants, including those from Germany. Midwestern states even opened their own immigration offices, which offered inducements, such as the right to vote after only six months.

Germans, in search of freedom and economic opportunity, poured into the Midwest. From Ohio to Wisconsin to Texas, they established communities. They brought their traditions, culture and know-how to the heartland and their influence can still be seen throughout

The New American Eskimo

This drawing appeared in the famed early natural history book *Animate Creation,* **published in 1885.**

the region. During this period, 38,000 Germans settled in Wisconsin and, by 1900, one out of every three Texans was of German descent. Their influence can still be seen in towns such as Hermann, Missouri, which was established in 1837. Here they still produce Rhineland wines and the streets proudly bear the names of Mozart, Guttenberg, Schiller and Goethe.

These Midwesterners, so proud of their German heritage, would play an integral part in the story of the American Eskimo. We know that they brought their dogs with them and, on the farms in the region, they would continue to breed their German Spitz dogs. This explains fully why the Midwest has always played such an important role in the history of the American Eskimo. It should come as no surprise that the first National Club for the breed was founded in the Midwest and that the majority of early breeders came from the heartland.

THE "MAD DOG" SCARE

While the Spitz dog prospered in the Midwest, the same could not be said of his cousin in the cities of the Northeast, particularly in New York. Indeed, a very sad fate was to befall these city relatives.

In the late 1800s, Americans, particularly those in the Northeast, began to take an interest in purebred dogs. With the Civil War over, life had settled down to normal and there was increased time for leisure. Soon the first dog magazines would appear and the first dog shows would begin. As always, Americans were greatly influenced by the English. We know that books by British authors were widely read. Some British judges even crossed the Atlantic to judge at early shows.

There was a great rush, particularly among the wealthy, to import dogs of all breeds to this country, from England. There was a status to owning an imported dog. At least one dog, however, seems to have crossed the Atlantic in the opposite direction. Vero Shaw, in his 1879-81 work, *The Illustrated Book of the Dog,* reports that, "This breed is fairly popular in America where it is known under the title of Spitz dog, and we have seen a very good specimen imported into this country by a lady who had visited the United States."

Authors, such as the well respected Stonehenge, sought to appeal to the new American market. His book, *The Dogs of Great Britain and America,* included information on dog shows and topics relevant to both British and American readers. It was widely distributed in the United States and some of the standards included in his book were used by judges. Of the "Pomeranian or Spitz-Dog" he says, "This variety of dog has become very popular as a house dog in America, but of late has fallen into disrepute on account of his snappish disposition."

It was from these early books that many Americans would first learn about the Spitz. Their first impression was not favorable. The character assassination, which took place in the British press, appears to have been primarily a result of not wanting to promote any "foreign" breed. The Spitz's general use as a watchdog for the house, too, was misunderstood in Britain. It was the age of specialization and the Spitz did not easily fit into English breed categorization. Whatever the reason, the rampant denigration of the breed was to have tragic results in this country.

The famed dog expert Stonehenge featured this woodcut of a "Spitz Dog" in his 1879 book *The Dogs of Great Britain and America.*

Around the 1870s, rabies was reported in New York City. Soon, panic swept to other cities in the Northeast. Superstition was rampant as many people did not understand the disease or its mode of transmission.

"Among the stupid popular ideas prevailing at the present time with regard to a mad dog is the belief that persons who may have been bitten by the animal a long time previously, and when it was healthy, are in danger of developing hydrophobia upon its subsequent appearance in the dog," reported *Popular Science Monthly*. "This notion would seem almost too ridiculous to mention were it not so common that a dog who bites a person maliciously is almost invariably killed, with the sole intention of rendering the human being secure from hydrophobia. A little reflection should convince those who entertain this foolish superstition that by killing the animal they are depriving themselves of the only means of certainty as to its actual condition, for if in the first vague stages of rabies it must exhibit pronounced symptoms within a very few days, whereas if it remains healthy by no possibility can the person bitten suffer other consequences than those ensuing from an ordinary wound."

"It is the duty of every person to endeavor to lessen the present panic on the subject of rabies..." wrote the director of one animal shelter, "and...to supply information which may tend to allay general excitement, and to remove the fears of nervous people....It is true that many hundreds of mad dogs, so called, have been brought to the home, where they have been isolated, kindly treated, and fed with appropriate food. In not one instance has rabies been discovered in such animals. Some of the cases at the time of their arrival were designated as raving madness, and stories were told of

An advertising card, probably dating to the late 1800s, from the Dellac store, in New York City.

hydrophobia, yet without the slightest foundation in reason."

Any dog which experienced a convulsion, for whatever reason, was immediately identified as rabid. The shelter owner reported the case of a part Pug who had gone into a convulsion on a street corner. A police officer was called. "The officer was alarmed, a crowd collected, and a cry was sent up, 'Kill him, he is mad!' 'Knock his brains out!' 'If he bites you, you are a dead man!', etc. The dog was taken up by one of the keepers, brought into the home, and soon recovered, and at this moment is romping with two kittens before my office fire."

Somehow, in the midst of this panic, a rumor started: It was the Spitz dog that was responsible for the start of the rabies epidemic (although it is debatable whether there was really any epidemic at all). The oldest book we have found which mentions this dark period is the very rare *The Practical Dog Book,* published in 1880. "The excitement that ran high several years ago, concerning the rabid characteristics of the Spitz, caused so many of the breed to be ruthlessly slaughtered, that good specimens are scarce."

The esteemed writer Rawdon Lee also refers to this period. In his 1899 classic *Modern Dogs,* he reports:

This may well be the first *photograph* of a Spitz published in an American book. The 1901 work *Our Devoted Friend, The Dog*, contained this photograph of "Madam Spitz and her second family of puppies." Her owner was identified as Mrs. F. W. Toedt, of Hamburg, Iowa. Note that this was a town founded by Germans. The bitch has flop ears and a look that is not wholly typical, but the puppies look more promising.

"Some few years ago there was a mad dog scare in New York, and in official quarters the origin was said to be traced to the Spitz dogs, a great many of which were destroyed without any proof being forthcoming either one way or the other."

"They always had the general reputation of being snappish and as very unsuitable for children to play with on that account. This reputation followed them to this country," writes James Watson, in *The Dog Book*. As we have seen the "reputation" which Mr. Watson points to came not from the Spitz's homeland, Germany, but from England. "...there was so much talk about them as being prone to 'develop' rabies that no entries of Pomeranians would be accepted at the New York show. It is so seldom that we see any of these large Pomeranians at the present time that it is unnecessary to say more about them..." Those who wished to know what the breed looked like, Watson advised, could refer to the paintings of Gainsborough.

Since white Spitz are so beautiful, they were often used by early advertisers to appeal to their customers. This image appeared on a Prudential Insurance Company calendar from 1910.

We will never know how many Spitz were slaughtered in an attempt to save the cities from rabies. States and cities passed dog licensing laws, with annual fees that were prohibitive for many people. The Massachusetts law was typical. Each city was to appoint policemen to "kill or caused to be killed all such dogs whenever or wherever found" which were unlicensed. "Such officers...shall receive one dollar for each dog destroyed...." In some states, anyone could kill an unlicensed dog and receive a bounty.

Those who loved their Spitz dogs must have gone to great lengths to protect them. After telling us about all the Spitz dogs who were killed, *The Practical Dog Book* concludes: "It is the German element of this country who principally keep them; for they are not popular among people of other nationalities." This book says the weight of the dogs, in 1880, was 12-25 pounds. "The prices of a good specimen are: Males $15-25. Females $10-20. Puppies: males $10-15; females $5-10." This price was lower than many of the other breeds featured in the book.

In the book, *Our Devoted Friend the Dog*, there is the tale of a funeral held for a "Hamburg Spitz," named Trixy. Mrs. S. W. Whitney, of Tarrytown, New York, purchased the dog from "a German nobleman." The family's devotion to the dog is clear. In February 1899, he was buried in a special casket, under a willow tree, overlooking the Hudson River. Trixy was laid to rest on a floral pillow and was sprinkled with rose and violet petals.

While Spitz ownership was certainly highest among Germans, we do know of at least one non-German owner during this period. He was only two years old, but future President Franklin D. Roosevelt, at home in Hyde Park, New York, considered the white Spitz "Budgy" to be his best friend.

THE SPITZ AND THE AMERICAN KENNEL CLUB

At the turn of the century, the larger white Spitz dogs were to be found in this country. "Spitz" was, by far, the most common name, but the breed was also known as the Pomeranian. In 1888, a dog named "Dick" was entered into the American Kennel Club studbook, as a Pomeranian. The first Pomeranian to make an appearance in American show rings is believed to be "Sheffield Lad," who was entered in the Westminster Kennel Club show, in 1892.

A few dogs made sporadic show ring appearances for the next few years, primarily in the Eastern U.S, where they competed in the Miscellaneous Class. Charles Mason provides a critique of one of these dogs, a bitch named "Blanche," who appeared at the Boston show, in 1897. Mason considered Blanche "an indifferent specimen," and compared her unfavorably to Charley, a dog he had seen in London, owned by Mr.

Fawdry. You will recall that this is the dog who is pictured in Vero Shaw's *The Illustrated Book of the Dog*. Clearly, then, Blanche was the large type of white Spitz.

Many dog show fanciers, though, would follow Britain's lead. During 1899, a number of imports arrived from England. These were the toy dogs, in a rainbow of hues, which had changed the breed in Britain. They quickly became the fashion in this country, too. In 1900, the Pomeranian was officially recognized as a distinct breed and the toy dog was on its way. Larger Spitz dogs were no longer welcome in American show rings.

THE SPITZ AND THE UNITED KENNEL CLUB

In 1898, a mathematician, Chauncy Z. Bennett, founded the United Kennel Club. Unlike the American Kennel Club, which is a non-profit organization, the UKC is a private company. We can trace AKC records, through their published studbooks, to the earliest days of the organization. Unfortunately, the UKC never published its records or studbooks. We have been told, furthermore, that some of the original records were destroyed in either a fire or a flood. Sadly, since these were never published and otherwise distributed, they are lost to us forever. This makes the job of the American Eskimo historian a difficult one. We are left to piece together information from old issues of *Bloodlines*, the UKC's magazine, and stories which have been handed down.

The United Kennel Club first registered the breed in 1913. It appears that the breed was first recognized as either the "Spitz" or the "American Spitz." According to information provided to the authors by Fuhrman and Miller (the second and third owners of the UKC), the oldest pedigree dates to 1913. It was for a dog, whelped in 1910, and owned by Joseph Erland, of Pittsburgh, Pennsylvania. They did not tell us the name given to the dog. Also in 1913, Erland and Edward McBride, also of Pittsburgh, registered four litters. The first pedigree which included three full generations of UKC registered dogs, was issued in 1917. The recipient was a dog owned by John and Elizabeth Ireland, from Clay Center, Nebraska.

There were several prominent early breeders, including the Ottens Kennel, in Stoutsville, Missouri and the Bobands Kennel located in Youngsville, New York. By all accounts, the Bobands Kennel had a very extensive breeding program and claimed to have sold thousands of dogs throughout the New York City area alone.

The most influential of the early breeders, however, was Mr. and Mrs. F. M. Hall. This couple deserves the gratitude of all Eskie owners, for their love and dedication to the breed. These pioneers had been breeding the white Spitz for many years, prior to UKC recognition. Some reports say that it was the Halls who first approached Mr. Bennett, owner of the UKC, asking for the breed to be recognized. They presented Mr. Bennett with carefully detailed pedigrees which they had been keeping. This, however, does not explain why the first registrations were not of Hall dogs. We do know that the couple sought out dogs to supplement their breeding program, taking special care to obtain dogs from non-related stock. Reportedly, the dogs in their kennels ranged between 20 and 40 pounds in weight.

Reportedly, the Halls were very displeased with the name "Spitz." They did not know what the word meant and, when they turned to the dictionary, were unable to discover its meaning. Further, some people had told them that the term was synonymous with the word "runt."

There may also have been several other reasons for deviating from the common "Spitz" label. In truth, this general and rather generic term was sometimes applied, haphazardly, to many dogs who bore little resemblance to the white German Spitz. Many Finnish settlers had settled in the Midwest and brought with them their own "Spitz" dogs, which had a decidedly dif-

This lovely portrait of a Spitz, by well-known artist Louis Agassiz Fuertes, appeared in the 1919 National Geographic *Book of Dogs*.

In a scene from one of his movies, silent film actor Charlie Chaplin and a Spitz argue over a bone.

ferent appearance. These animals were red in color and are now recognized as "Finnish Spitz." In addition, it seems that many mongrel dogs were sold under the label "Spitz." This was apt to cause confusion and undermine the efforts of breeders producing dogs from a purebred bloodline. To this day, this attitude sometimes prevails. Therefore, American Eskimo owners have been very firm in their demand that the breed be called something other than simply a Spitz.

It is also entirely possible that the characterization of the breed, by dog writers, which would continue for many years, had an impact on the Halls. Clearly, it must have pained them, as it would any conscientious breeder, to have their dogs thought of as untrustworthy.

We must also remember that, in 1917, there was a compelling political reason for the name change. World War I had begun in 1914 and America was decidedly pro-British in its leanings. Britain had declared a naval blockade of Germany and the Germans retaliated by sinking a number of passenger ships, including those containing a few Americans. Then, in 1915, the British passenger ship the Lusitania was sunk by a German torpedo. More than 1,000 people were killed, including 124 Americans. A wave of anti-German sentiment swept the country. At first, the Germans announced that they would no longer sink vessels containing civilians. But, in January 1917, they did an abrupt about face. A month later the "Zimmerman telegram" was intercepted and decoded by British intelligence. Addressed to the German ambassador in Mexico, it instructed him to seek an alliance with that country should the United States enter the war. In return for fighting against the Americans, the Germans promised to give Texas, Arizona and New Mexico to the Mexicans. The entire country was outraged. Two months later, we declared war on Germany.

Sentiment against all things German, including dog breeds, was rampant. Dachshunds, which had previously enjoyed great popularity, went into a steady decline during the war years. When introduced to Great Britain, the German Shepherd would be given a new name, the Alsatian, to distance the breed from its German heritage. Some Americans, eager to avoid discrimination, denied their German lineage.

This attitude resurfaced again during World War II. During the Second World War, dogs were occasionally auctioned off to raise money for the war bond drive. A story is told of such an auction, held in California. The breeds offered on the auction block had each been commanding several thousand dollars for the war effort. However, the mood changed dramatically when a Dachshund was brought to the podium. There was not one bid and soon the crowd was yelling in anger, "Get that Nazi dog off the stage."

Thus, the political climate may well have played a part in the name change of the white Spitz. At that time, it may have been in the breed's best interest not to have it marked by an association with its German homeland.

We were the first to discuss this anti-German sentiment in *The American Eskimo*. John Miller, former editor of *Bloodlines,* said that it was "a time when anti-German sentiment was at an all time high. During the war it was common for Americans of German descent to be publicly beaten, and German owned stores were routinely burned. The loyalty of German-Americans was always in question. To give so German a name as 'White German Spitz' to a newly recognized breed would certainly have doomed it to failure in this country...."

How, then, did the name "American Eskimo" come to be associated with the breed? Once again, we must look to those breed pioneers, the Halls. They had named their kennel of white Spitz, the American Eskimo Kennel. It seemed an appropriate name for the breed which did, in some ways, resemble the dogs of the

Eskimos that were, during that period, being introduced to this country. The name was not immediately accepted by other breeders. As late as the mid-1920s, some breeders continued to advertise their dogs, in *Bloodlines,* as "Eskimo Spitz" or "American Spitz." Gradually, however, the name did achieve universal acceptance. The white German Spitz became known, once and for all, as the American Eskimo.

BREED PROGRESS

In the years immediately following recognition and registration by the United Kennel Club, breed progress was slow. The UKC is now the second largest registering body, but in those early years, many people did not yet know of its existence. Around the country, dogs continued to be bred and sold under the name "Spitz." In books and articles from this period, most refer to the breed by this simple name.

In 1919, the National Geographic Society issued *The Book of Dogs,* the first of its volumes on canines. The Spitz was featured in the chapter "Our Common Dogs," and a stunning portrait, by famed artist Louis Agassiz Fuertes, was included.

"...The true Spitz weighs about 25 to 30 pounds. The best dogs are white or cream-colored...They are bright, fascinating, pretty dogs; but it must be said they are very 'choicy' in making friends and very ready to repel with sharp teeth any unwelcome advances by dogs or humans they don't know. They are apt to be a real responsibility on this account."

Wood's Natural History, written by Rev. J. G. Wood, and published in 1923, gives a most positive description of the breed:

> It is a great favorite with those who like a dog for a companion and not for mere use, as it is very intelligent in its character, and very handsome in aspect. Its long white fur and bushy tail give it quite a distinguished appearance, of which the animal seems to be thoroughly aware. Sometimes the coat of this animal is a cream color, and very rarely is deep black. The pure white, however, seems to be the favorite. It is a lively little creature, and makes an excellent companion in a country walk.

The breed is occasionally mentioned in other books from the 1920s and '30s, such as John Leonard's 1928 work, *The Care and Handling of Dogs.*

The relationship between Spitz dogs and children is immortalized on this 1921 *American Magazine* cover, painted by the famous artist Norman Rockwell.

The California Fruit Exchange once sold their products under the "Spitz" label. Sadly, the head study used seems more reminiscent of a Samoyed than a true Spitz.

The breed was to garner one influential friend. Will Judy, the founder of *Dog World* magazine, and a prolific writer, was fond of the breed and did much to promote it. Apparently, he was not familiar with the UKC or aware that the Spitz had been recognized as the American Eskimo. He did know, however, that the breed was popular as a family dog. In his *The Dog Encyclopedia,* published in 1936, he wrote:

> This breed has not yet broken into high dog society although it is a popular breed and is a profitable pet shop article. Clearly it is to be distinguished from the much larger samoyede *(sic)*, a dog of a different type, and is a member, through the German...spitz, of the general lupine or pomeranian family, which embraces practically all Arctic dogs.

In 1936, Will Judy, influential writer and founder of *Dog World* magazine, made an appeal for dog lovers to take up the Spitz. This photo accompanied his pleas. Sadly, the dogs were not identified.

FIRST STANDARD OF THE SPITZ OR ESKIMO SPITZ (1936)

In "an effort to obtain uniform type" and encourage interest in the breed, Will Judy, founder of Dog World *magazine, crafted this first sketchy standard for the breed. While extremely brief and deficient in many areas, it does highlight many of the breed's essential qualities. It is historically interesting because it predates any official American standard by more than 20 years.*

The spitz should be pure white in color; cream and biscuit colors are not desirable but not disqualifying. There should be no markings of any kind on the dog.

WEIGHT—Should be from 18 to 25 pounds. Overweight is heavily penalized.

HEAD—Should be fox-like, muzzle pointed and the skull not coarse, not extra wide, and be slightly domed.

EYES—Should be black and preferably with black rim; slightly oblique rather than entirely round.

NOSE—Black.

EARS—Should be slightly tipped rather than rounded at the ends and close set rather than far apart. Carried erect when alert.

COAT—Should be outstanding, straight, and not curled or wavy; has a dense undercoat.

FRONT LEGS—Should be entirely straight. Rear hocks should be straight rather than bent.

FOOT PADS—Should be somewhat large but compact.

CHEST—Should be generously wide but not too deep.

On the whole the spitz should present a picture of liveliness, not too low to the ground, a dog able to move quickly and travel fast.

Junior: Loyalty Personified

Six-and-one-half years is a long time in a dog's life. But exactly what happened to Junior, a little white Spitz, in the six-and-one-half years he was absent from his Brooklyn home probably will never be known. One thing is certain: Nothing was able to erase from his canine soul the memory of that home.

It is a one-family house at 1475 Carroll St., where live Mr. and Mrs. Albert A. Weinstein, and their two daughters, Jean and Phoebe.

Junior came to this household nine years ago when he was a puppy. Phoebe was eleven then and Junior would follow her to school. One afternoon in 1937, Phoebe and Junior were playing on the sidewalk when an automobile came by. The driver opened the door and whistled. Junior, whose fluffy while tail became a semaphore of happiness at any kind of attention, bounded into the car and was gone.

For a long time the Weinsteins ran advertisements in newspapers, promising rewards for the return of Junior or even for information about him. Many Spitzes were brought to their door but none was Junior.

One day recently Mrs. Weinstein was sitting on the front steps. She saw a dog limping up the street. His coat was dirty and full of burrs. He paused, sniffed a moment and resolutely came up the walk. He whined once and fell at her feet, revealing bloody paws worn almost to the bone from the rough pavements. The dog perked up somewhat after she fed him, and he responded to "Junior." Mrs. Weinstein then picked the burrs from his long hair and put him in the bathtub. Soap and water revealed the silken sheen of his coat, and Mrs. Weinstein noted the two tiny patches of black hair near his left eye and on his nose. The Junior of six-and-one-half years ago was similarly marked.

As soon as he was dry Junior made a dash for an open door, then trotted up and down the block, sniffing at each child he passed, evidently hunting for Phoebe, the little girl he used to follow to school.

When Phoebe finally did come home a ball of white shot around a corner of the house into her arms. A red tongue laved her face with kisses.

The New York Tribune, 1944

The spitz at times has been termed the white pomeranian. Also wrongly it is called the chow spitz and the eskimo spitz. Likely the spitz is an effort to retain the popular white pomeranian or pomeranian spitz so common in Germany not many years ago—a large sized dog from which the present pomeranian has been bred down in size....

...It can be hoped that this breed in time will be recognized officially in every way not only for registration but also for show exhibitions. It is a dog of beauty, an excellent house dog and unusually popular. The spitz is a lively, hardy, intelligent dog of convenient size, beautiful in furry coat, a keen watchdog, and properly trained as a puppy, without viciousness.

Judy went so far as to draw up the first standard for the breed. It is quite sketchy, certainly when compared to the standards of today. It must be remembered, however, that this was the very first standard that had been written for the breed in the United States.

There are occasional mentions of the American Eskimo in books published in the 1940s and '50s. Most still refer to the breed, however, as the Spitz. Harry Miller, in his 1950 work, *Gallery of American Dogs,* includes a lovely drawing by famed artist Paul Brown. He also includes a photo which, unfortunately, is not at all typical of the breed. "Although he is one of the most popular companion dogs and has been well-known as a

Love of the American Eskimo often lasts a lifetime. This is two-year-old Ray Vernimme, in 1934, with his friend Beauty. He is now a licensed Eskie judge.

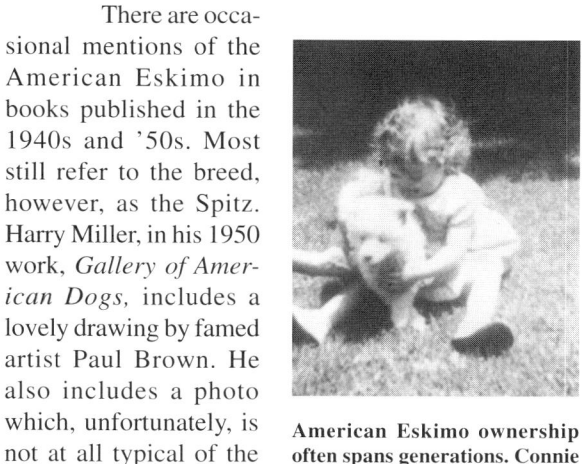

American Eskimo ownership often spans generations. Connie Jankowski can recall stories that her father and grandfather told of their dogs. This photo, from 1940, shows "Lindy" with Connie's cousin, Diane.

Professional entertainers Dean McCroskie, with McCroskie's Mike, and Jean McCroskie, with Spike the Houdini.

These born hams are McCroskie's Mike, Spike the Houdini and Spike's son, 'PR' Twin's White Chieftain.

house pet for many years, the Spitz is never seen at a regulation dog show....However, there are countless people who will immediately recognize a Spitz, whereas they could not name many of the purebred dogs." The breed, Miller tells us, is "sometimes called the Eskimo Spitz....he is greatly recognized by many people to whom pedigree and blue ribbons have no significance. He is essentially a good companion and a good watchdog, with a natural reserve and reluctance to make friends with anyone who comes along..."

Jeannette Cross and Blanche Saunders included the Eskie in their best-selling *The Standard Book of Dog Care,* published in 1952. A section on the "Spitz (or American Eskimo)" is included in the chapter "And These are Purebreds Too."

"...(The) Spitz is...the most frequently used name for one of the best known house pet breeds in America....The breed was, at one time, known as the German Spitz because of the fact that the first specimens brought to this country were from Germany. The United Kennel Club registers this breed as the American Eskimo, a name which seems a happy choice, as it connotes both the breed's arctic ancestry and its status as a popular breed in the United States." Cross and Saunders believed, as so many other ill-informed writers have, that the Eskie was descended from the Samoyed.

"The Spitz is bright, quick to learn, eager, and affectionate in temperament," they continue. "While not unfriendly, he does not take readily to strangers, which makes him a dependable watch dog....he is an ideal size for a house dog—large enough to make a hardy, active playmate for children but not too big for the average home nor expensive to maintain. With these assets, in addition to his snowy gleaming coat and dark expressive eyes, it is no wonder that the Spitz is one of America's favorite pets."

STAR PERFORMERS

While the breed continued to rank high as a watchdog and companion, it also gained a reputation for being super-intelligent. Many were seen in traveling circuses and rodeos. The Barnum and Bailey Circus maintained a troupe of traveling Eskie performers. Crowds cheered as the white dogs leaped onto the backs of horses and balanced precariously on tightropes. But the dogs also performed in less prominent, regional groups.

Current American Eskimo fanciers, Dean and Jean McCroskie, tell of their introduction to the breed. "In 1956, our Mother went with us to the White Horse Ranch, near Naper, Nebraska. This was a summer camp for young people interested in learning circus type acts. While there, our Mother bought us two white horses and our first two snow white American Eskimo puppies.

"These miniature male puppies were littermates. We named one McCroskie's Mike. The other...was Spike the Houdini. Their sire was Clipper...and their dam was Cindy..."

White Horse Ranch was founded in the 1930's by Mr. Caleb R. Thompson. On his 2,700 acre spread, Mr. Thompson trained animals for circus acts. The white animals were his trademark. He developed a breed of white horses, noted for their trainability. These were sold to circus folk, show people and movie producers. Accompanying the white horses, were white Spitz dogs. Personally trained by Mr. Thompson, these dogs learned an amazing repertoire of tricks.

Mr. Thompson trained many youngsters in the art of performing. "He and a group of his students toured the U.S. and Canada during the 1940's and 1950's with trick horses and trick Spitz dogs, plus a few other trained white animals," the McCroskies tell us.

Caleb Thompson was not aware that the white Spitz could be registered with the United Kennel Club. To ensure the preservation of his superlative performers, he registered the dogs himself. He used the White Horse Ranch designation and the first dogs purchased by the McCroskies bore the W.H.R. prefix, followed by a registration number. It was only when Dean and Jean McCroskie told him, that he became aware of the UKC. "He was glad we had registered Mike and Spike with the UKC," Dean and Jean recall.

The story of Mr. Thompson's success with the white dogs may have inspired others to use the breed in their acts. "In 1957 and 1958, we studied under...Mr. Bernard R. Baranoski." Nicknamed "Pinky Barns," for the pink chaps he wore, Mr. Baranoski conducted the Famous 101 Ranch Shows. He was the 1924 all-round champion cowboy and an accomplished trick roper and bullwhip artist. He was also a sought after pony, horse and dog trainer. Photos of his can be seen, today, in the Circus Hall of Fame. "In 1965, he wrote us," the McCroskies say, "and said he was using four standard and one miniature American Eskimos in his act. This was Pinky's breed of dog."

Today, twin sisters Dean and Jean McCroskie, carry on this performing tradition. And their dog of choice? The American Eskimo, of course. Currently, their act includes "PR" Twins' Klondike King and his son, "PR" Twins' Husky Stuff. "The keys we have found to making a dog act are: First, some well-bred American Eskimos, and second, patience, practice and consistency. When we see a group of well-behaved trick dogs, doing an act together, we know it's no accident...Anything is possible with the American Eskimo!...We can say from experience that the American Eskimo is a tough act to follow and we want to keep it that way."

FIRST ATTEMPTS TO FORM A CLUB

Several attempts were made to form clubs for the breed. Our research shows that the very first Eskie club may have been established as early as 1936. In that year, fanciers in the Louisville, Kentucky area formed the Louisville Eskimo Club. Mrs. Wright Duke served as President, Mrs. Bonnie L. Kane was Vice President and Mrs. T. H. Jackson was elected Secretary. The Club held at least one show. At this outing there were separate classes for males and females and divisions based on age: Puppies (under one year), one to two years; two to four years; over four years. The Dec. 1936 issue of *Bloodlines* reports that Elizabeth Duke's *Danny Boy III* was Best Male and Best in Show and Mrs. Wright Duke's *Suzanne* was Best Female. Sadly, this club did not survive.

'PR' McCroskie's Sandy, a Standard female, takes her babies for a stroll.

Another attempt at forming a club began in 1946. Myra Ramage (Mrs. W. R.) Ingram, of Montgomery, Alabama gathered local fanciers together to begin the Eskimos Refuge Club. The owner of Bethro-Anne Kennels, Mrs. Ingram was a tireless worker on behalf of the breed. Apparently, this group was successful. "Our American Eskimo Club is coming along nicely and the American Eskimo is gaining widely spread popularity in the south," Mrs. Ingram wrote. "I know that we will succeed in bringing this beautiful breed out in front."

We do not really know if the club held any shows, during 1946, but they may have. Mrs. Ingram reports on a "contest" to determine the "Most Outstanding American Eskimo of the Year 1946." Her *Ingram's Eskimo Boy Snowball*, who would be featured on the cover of *Bloodlines,* won the prize. Second place went to *Snowdrop Frosty,* owned by Mrs. K. G. Littlejohn, of Clearwater, Florida.

In 1947, it was decided that this southern club should be expanded. Renamed the National American Eskimo Club, Mrs. Ingram, who now lived in Tallahassee, Florida, began a nation-wide membership drive. Everyone who joined the club received a pin with the club's name and a picture of the Eskie. Official membership certificates, suitable for framing, were also sent. In addition, there were small stickers, with an Eskie drawing, which could be placed on a house or car window and larger stickers which were to be attached to kennel signs.

"The club's goal is to the advantage of the American Eskimo. We seek to protect you from the dishonest breeder and the people who will advertise their stock as 'eligible' (for registration). We have meetings in various cities from time to time, and thus

FIRST UKC AMERICAN ESKIMO BREED STANDARD (1958)

The American Eskimo is what could be called a miniature Samoyed and they are identical except for size. The small size of the American Eskimo is due to years of breeding down in size from the larger type dog. The American Eskimo in general appearance is a miniature of a working dog and should be strong and active and graceful. His coat should be heavy and weather resisting. He should have a short body, but neither too long nor too short. He should be muscular, allowing freedom with good chest expansion and well-sprung ribs, strong neck, straight front and exceptionally strong loins. The hind quarters should be particularly well developed, stifles well bent, any suggestion of unsound stifles or cowhocks severely penalized.

Disposition that of intelligence, alert, full of action, but above all, displaying marked affection toward all mankind.

Coat. The body should be covered with thick, close, soft and short undercoat with harsh hair growing through it, forming the outer coat which should stand straight away from the body and be quite free from any curl.

Head. One denoting power and wedge-shaped with broad flat skull, muzzle of medium length, a tapering foreface, yet not too sharply defined, ears not too long and slightly rounded at tips, set well apart, and well covered inside with hair. Eyes dark, set well apart and keen, with alert intelligent expression. Lips black. Hair short and smooth before the ears. Nose and eye rims black for preference, but may be brown or flesh colored. Strong jaw with level teeth.

Back. Medium in length, broad and muscular.

Chest and ribs. Chest should show broadness and depth. Ribs should be well-sprung, giving plenty of room for heart and lung action.

The *hind quarters* should be muscular, stifles well let down, cow hocks or straight stifles very objectionable.

Legs. Straight and muscular and of good bone.

Feet. Long, flattish, and slightly spread out. Soles of the feet well padded with hair.

Tail. Long and profuse, carried gaily over the back or side when alert. Sometimes dropped down when at rest, tightly curled or double hook is a fault.

Color. Most desirable pure white. White and biscuit cream, cream. Black or sable spots not desirable and should be disqualified.

Scale of points:

General appearance	20 points
Head	15 points
Coat	10 points
Size	10 points
Chest and ribs	10 points
Hind quarters	10 points
Back	10 points
Feet	5 points
Legs	5 points
Tail	5 points
Total	100 points

AKC SAMOYED STANDARD
(1958)

General Appearance— The Samoyed, being essentially a working dog, should be strong and active and graceful, and as his work lies in cold climates, his coat should be heavy and weather resisting. He should not be long in back, as a weak back would make him practically useless for his legitimate work; but at the same time a cobby body, such as the Chow's, would also place him at a great disadvantage as a draught dog. Breeders should aim for the happy medium, *viz.,* a body not long, but muscular, allowing liberty, with a deep chest and well-sprung ribs, strong neck, straight front and exceptionally strong loins. A full-grown dog should stand about 21 inches at the shoulder. On account of the depth of chest required, the legs should be moderately long, a very short-legged dog is to be depreciated. Hindquarters should be particularly well developed, stifles well bent, and any suggestion of unsound stifles or cowhocks severely penalized.

Disposition— Intelligence, alert, full of action, but above all, displaying marked affection toward all mankind.

Coat— The body should be well covered with thick, close, soft and short undercoat with harsh hair growing through it, forming the outer coat which should stand straight away from the body and be quite free from any curl.

Head— Powerful and wedge-shaped with broad flat skull, muzzle of medium length, a tapering foreface, not too sharply defined, ears not too long and slightly rounded at tips, set well apart, and well covered inside with hair. Eyes dark, set well apart and deep, with alert intelligent expression. Lips black. Hair short and smooth before the ears. Nose and eye rims black for preference, but may be brown or flesh colored. Strong jaws with level teeth.

Back— Medium in length, broad and very muscular.

Chest and Ribs— Chest broad and deep. Ribs well-sprung, giving plenty of heart and lung room.

Hindquarters— Very muscular, stifles well let down, cow hocks or straight stifles very objectionable.

Legs— Straight and muscular. Good bone.

Feet— Long, flattish, and slightly spread out. Soles well padded with hair.

Tail— Long and profuse, carried gaily over the back or side when alert, sometimes dropped down when at rest, tight curl or double hook is a fault.

Size and Weight— Dogs, 21 to 23 1/2 inches at shoulder, 50 to 67 pounds; bitches, 19 to 21 inches, 36 to 55 pounds.

Color— Pure white, white and biscuit, cream. Black or black spots to disqualify.

General Appearance	20 points
Head	15 points
Coat	10 points
Size	10 points
Chest and ribs	10 points
Hindquarters	10 points
Back	10 points
Feet	5 points
Legs	5 points
Tail	<u>5 points</u>
Total	100 points

The late Thomas Maxwell devoted his life to the breed. He helped to form the National American Eskimo Dog Association, served as its President for many years and was one of the first licensed judges.

get a chance to really get to know each other. Some member of the club plays the part as host or hostess in their respective city...At our meetings we held shows and outdoor exhibits, of the American Eskimo, and only UKC registered dogs of this breed are eligible for entry. Prizes are awarded as well as points. Prior to the opening of the show these prizes are donated by members. They can be in the form of a small amount of money or other small item of value.

"The club can do so much to bring our breed to the front. It is what we have needed for so long. Won't you join us for a good time and help us to promote our purpose and at last let the whole nation know what they have missed by not really knowing the American Eskimo, 'THE DOG BEAUTIFUL.'"

Apparently, Mrs. Ingram's nationwide campaign did not succeed. Her frustration can be seen in one of her letters to *Bloodlines*. "Our newly formed nationwide drive for new members...for the National American Eskimo Club is gaining slowly. I have wondered why so many of you have hesitated to join us." Despite Mrs. Ingram's passion for the breed and her commitment to establishing a national club, the effort failed.

In 1951, Mrs. J. F. Chandley and Mrs. B. H. Wood again made a second attempt to form a national club. By today's standards, Mrs. Chandley would be judged a commercial breeder, for there were nine breeds at her Gerald, Missouri kennels, including American Eskimos, Pomeranians and Samoyeds. She was, however, greatly concerned with quality. The club, she hoped, would encourage the breeding of top-quality dogs. Mrs. Chandley was concerned that dogs, whose only attribute was their white coat, were being foisted on unsuspecting and unknowledgeable buyers. Poor quality Eskies should, she felt, be sold as pets and not bred. She encouraged any breeders or owners who were interested to contact her. Sadly, the Chandley and Wood appeal apparently feel on deaf ears. As far as we know, no club was ever formed.

FIRST OFFICIAL STANDARD

During the 1950s, Dr. E. G. Fuhrman was the president of the United Kennel Club. He helped move the organization forward and was the first to fashion UKC breed standards. Consulting with breeders, he drew up standards for the American Eskimo and the Toy Fox Terrier, two of the UKC's most popular registered breeds.

The Eskie standard was written in 1958. Dr. Fuhrman should be complemented for this dramatic step forward, however, he labored under a major false assertion. No comprehensive study of the breed history had, as yet, been undertaken. Therefore, Dr. Fuhrman assumed that the Eskie was a direct descendant of the Samoyed. "The American Eskimo is what could be called a miniature Samoyed and they are identical except in size," the first line of the standard reads. In fact, as we shall see, in the accompanying sidebar, he adopted, in some cases, word-for-word, the Samoyed standard. We can see that statements, such as the allowance of brown or flesh-colored nose and eye rims, came directly from the Samoyed standard. It was unfortunate that these were included, for this fault haunts breeders, even today.

There is one glaring omission in this first standard. No specifications for size are included in the document. While size is allotted 10 points in the "Scale of Points," no size parameters are actually included. As we have seen, books of the time varied widely in their depiction of appropriate size for the breed. Both Harry Miller, in his 1950 book, and Jeannette Cross and Blanche Saunders, in their 1952 book, say that the height at the shoulder should be 18 inches and the average weight 16-18 pounds. That's an awfully low weight for an 18 inch dog. Still, other books portray the Eskie as weighing 25-35 pounds in weight. Today, we know that these differences are obvious reflections of the Standard and Miniature, but no books make reference to the breed being available in two sizes.

The famous Ch. Maxwell's Gidget, owned by Tom and Ruth Maxwell, was the world's first Champion American Eskimo.

We know that Dr. Fuhrman conferred with Toy Fox Terrier breeders when he molded the first standard for that breed. It's logical to assume, therefore, that he also con-sulted Eskie breeders of the time. We can speculate that there must have been such a wide variation in size that no agreement could be reached. Therefore, any specifics on the breed's size were, simply, omitted.

THE MODERN AGE

In the 1960s, fanciers began to band together to seriously improve the breed. They became interested in showing their dogs in conformation and obedience. On November 8, 1969, a group of dedicated fanciers met in De Soto, Missouri, to form the National American Eskimo Association. Later, the name would be changed to the National American Eskimo Dog Association. Present at that original meeting were: John L. Wilson (MO), Mr. and Mrs. Charles Vail (IL), Mr. and Mrs. Thomas Maxwell (MI), Benton Parks (MD), Mr. and Mrs. John G. Goske (MO), Mr. and Mrs. William Sankpill (MO), Mr. and Mrs. Lelan Carr (IL), Mr. and Mrs. George Stiedle (MO), James L. Wiley and his daughter Patria Sue (MO), Harry McKiney (MO), Mrs. Carolyn Brown (MO) and James Poe (MO). Also present were Dr. Fuhrman, his daughter Susan, and Sharon Shepherd, representing the UKC. John L. Wilson was chosen President and Treasurer, Mrs. Carolyn Brown was selected as the Vice President and Mrs. George Steidle served as the first Secretary.

The group voted to adopt the standard written by Dr. Fuhrman, but added two sizes to be used for show classifications. Initially, weight, rather than height, was used to set the sizes. Standard males were to weigh 17-30 pounds, while Standard females would tip the scales at 16-25 pounds. A miniature male was to weigh 12-16 pounds, while a Mini female should weigh 10-15 pounds.

There was a discussion about who was qualified to judge the breed. Dr. Fuhrman accepted Lelan Carr, James Poe, George Steidle, Mrs. Ruby Sankpill and Thomas Maxwell as the first licensed Eskie judges.

Mr. and Mrs. Thomas Maxwell, of Davison, Michigan, were among those attending that very first meeting. Thomas Maxwell (1924-1986) would prove to be an untiring promoter of the breed. He would later serve as President of the National Club, holding the office for many years. During his tenure, he did much to promote the organization of state Eskie clubs. He and his dogs appeared on television and helped to introduce many people to the breed. His first American Eskimo, *Ch. Maxwell's Gidget,* became the very first breed champion. His miniature, *Ch. 'PR' Maxwell's Zsa Zsa,* was the first miniature female to earn the championship title. These were only the first of many Maxwell owned champions, including three Grand Champions and one National Grand Champion.

Tom Maxwell traveled extensively, showing and judging Eskies. He took particular pride in helping newcomers to the breed. After shows, his motel room became a traditional gathering place for anyone wanting to "talk Eskies." American Eskimo fanciers owe him a debt of gratitude for helping our breed.

The National American Eskimo Dog Association continues to be a force in the breed. They hold annual specialty shows which are well attended. "National Grand Champions" are selected at these events and the competition, to achieve this coveted title, is always keen. Early National Grand Champions were given framed certificates, but the title was not officially listed on pedigrees. Several years ago, the U.K.C. changed this policy, allowing the title to become an

The Gr. Ch. 'PR' Hofman's Country Diamond, owned by Nancy and Darrel Hofman, scoring his first major win. 'Country' was the first Grand Champion on the Pacific Coast. His greatest contribution to the breed, however, is in the many Champion and Grand Champion children and grandchildren he produced. He can be found in the pedigrees of a great many of today's bloodlines.

A Tribute to Recent NAEDA

(Above) Nat. Gr. Ch. Gr. Ch. 'PR' Thunderpas Mighty Max *(Gr. Ch. 'PR' U-CDX Sweetwater Thunderpas x Gr. Ch. U-CD 'PR' Thunderpas Arctic Revel)*, bred and owned by Talitha Bell. *J. J. Allen photo*

(Below) Nat. Gr. Ch. Gr. Ch. 'PR' McKee's King Jacob *(Gr. Ch. 'PR' Cascade's Shasta-Snow CGC x 'PR' McKee's Ginger Bear)*, bred by Dean and Gloria McKee and owned by Gordon and Dottie Patterson.

(Above) Nat. Gr. Ch. Gr. Ch. 'PR' Jaybar's Outback Cody *(Gr. Ch. 'PR' Kort-Mar Sierra's Vegas x Ch. 'PR' JBar's Snoflash Lolipop)*, bred by Barbara Blackwood and owned by Sally Bedow. *Lindgren photo*

(Below) Nat. Gr. Ch. Gr. Ch. 'PR' Sierra's Blockbuster, bred and owned by Diana Allen. *Booth photo*

The Spitz in America

National Grand Champions*

(Above) Nat. Gr. Ch. Gr. Ch. 'PR' J-Bar McKinley Xplorer *(Gr. Ch. 'PR' Kort-Mar Sierra's Vegas x Ch. 'PR' JBar's Snoflash Lolipop)*, bred and owned by Barbara Blackwood.

(Below) Nat. Gr. Ch. Gr. Ch. 'PR' Sierra's Panda Bear *(Gr. Ch. 'PR' Sierra's Tehkoma Royale x Ch. 'PR' Richardson's Sierra Sun)*, bred by Diana Allen and owned by Charline Dunnigan.

(Above) Nat. Gr. Ch. Gr. Ch. 'PR' Stevens' Toybear Apollo *(Gr. Ch. 'PR' Tinker's Toy Bear x Ch. 'PR' Stevens' Snow Princess)*, bred and owned by Rosemary Stevens. *Eddie Rubin photo*

(Below) Nat. Gr. Ch. Gr. Ch. 'PR' Stevens' Diamond Sparkle *(Gr. Ch. 'PR' Tinker's Toy Bear x Gr. Ch., Int'l. Ch., RBKC Ch., SKC Ch., U-CD 'PR' Lucky's Tynee Tygrr CD, ARBA CD, ASCA CD, CGC)*, bred by Rosemary Stevens and owned by Lynda Gagnon.

*The above includes only those dogs who have earned their title since the U.K.C. began to officially list the title on pedigrees.

AKC Ch. & Gr. Ch. 'PR' Stevens' Gorbachev, owned by Sandy Tocco, became the first American Eskimo to earn an American Kennel Club championship. *Rich Bergman photo*

official part of the dog's name. Since that time, there have been eight National Grand Champions. They are: *Steven's Toybear Apollo, Sierra's Panda Bear, Thunderpas Mighty Max, Jaybear's Outback Cody, McKee's King Jacob, J-Bar McKinley Xplorer, Sierra's Blockbuster and Steven's Diamond Sparkle.*

THE ESKIE TODAY

The American Eskimo's horizons have expanded dramatically in the last few years. Indeed, the breed is becoming increasingly popular and has gained a reputation as a superlative house dog and companion, a glamorous show dog and a talented obedience competitor. In addition, Eskies are beginning to take part in many other activities, as well. Numerous organizations now admit the breed to their competitions.

The breed is, of course, still recognized by the United Kennel Club. Indeed, the numbers of dogs competing in UKC conformation and obedience events has risen dramatically. There are many champion and Grand Champion Eskies. (The first Grand Champion of the breed was *Richardson's Keta Shelton,* bred by Jennifer Shelton.) Eskies have earned the highest accolades in UKC obedience competition.

The National American Eskimo Dog Association has continued to prosper, as well. There are now 26 chapters in different states. Furthermore, the Eskie has been exported to several foreign countries.

During the 1980s, several organizations took note of the Eskie. The breeds' obedience prowess earned it a place in the illustrious Gaines Obedience Classic.

Now, the breed is eligible to compete on the regional and national level in this "superbowl" of obedience. The breed was also invited to participate in the prestigious "Tournament of Champions" co-sponsored by *Kennel Review* magazine and the Iams Company. Indeed, an Eskie won the Group at such an event.

It was the growing interest in international shows which led to the formation of the States Kennel Club. The Eskie is eligible to compete in all shows run by the organization. Standard size Eskies are shown in the Working Group, while Miniatures compete in the Nonsporting Group.

Clearly, the most significant event in the recent history of the American Eskimo is the breed's recognition by the American Kennel Club. Eskies have now begun to compete in AKC shows. There are three size divisions: Standard, Miniature and Toy. The breed is shown in the Non-Sporting Group. This marks an exciting new chapter for the breed. Now, American Eskimos are able to compete against thousands of dogs for Group and Best in Show awards.

As this book goes to press, the American Eskimo has made quite a splash in AKC rings. Many breeders, at first concerned about recognition, have now begun to actively show their dogs at AKC shows and trials. Initially, there was a scramble to see who could become the first official AKC champion of the breed. That honor goes to *AKC Ch. and UKC Gr. Ch. 'PR' Stevens' Gorbachev,* bred by Rosemary and Steven

AKC Ch. & Ch. 'PR' Kadoc's Lucky D.D., owned by Sandy Tocco, is believed to be the first American Eskimo to earn a Group placement in an American Kennel Club show. *Kitten Rodwell photo*

Stevens and owned by Sandy Tocco, of Lakeside, California. Ms. Tocco may have also captured another honor. Her female *AKC Ch. and UKC Ch. 'PR' Kadoc's Lucky DD,* won a Group Second, from the classes, on the second day the breed was eligible for competition. This may well be the first group for the breed.

Over the next few years, the American Eskimo is certain to gain many additional followers. One hopes that these new owners and breeders will thoroughly study the breed's background and conformation and seek to always maintain and improve the breed. One hopes, too, that this new exposure will not lead to over-commercialization.

And so, at last, we come to the present day. Our journey through the American Eskimo's history has been a long one, but one that we hope was interesting. From the dogs of Stone Age man to the valued watchdog of German farms, to the show rings of, first, the United Kennel Club and now the American Kennel Club, the American Eskimo has been fully accepted in the United States. He is still appreciated as a superb watchdog and a devoted companion, but he is now also an animated show dog and brilliant obedience performer. Current Eskie owners can point with pride to the breed's long and illustrious history. We find, in the American Eskimo, a dog who has always been esteemed as a partner to man.

SHARE! PUSS AND SHOCK.
Crust and Crumb, 1872

Chapter 9

Famous Owners

Throughout history, the American Eskimo, and the White Spitz before him, has been the companion of the rich and famous. Indeed, this dog has charmed some of history's most celebrated individuals. Famous artists, writers, scientists, rulers, musicians, composers, actors and industrialists have all owned these dogs. The breed's sparkling ways and charming countenance have added joy to the lives of many celebrities.

We have compiled this list of famous owners from German, English and American books, as well as newspapers and magazines. Perhaps you know of other historical or present-day owners we can add to the list. If so, we would love to hear from you.

Michelangelo Buonarotti (1475-1564) Universally acknowledged as one of the greatest of the Renaissance artists, Michelangelo created masterpieces in sculpture, painting and architecture. Modern artists still marvel at his ability to portray the human form with such beauty and elegance.

From 1508 to 1512, Michelangelo took on the enormous project of painting the ceiling of the Sistine Chapel. It depicts Biblical history, beginning with Genesis. This is said to be most intricate rendering in all of Western art.

The famous Italian book, *Il Cane (The Dog)* tells us that a white Spitz was Michelangelo's constant companion. The dog kept his master company while he painted his Sistine Chapel frescos. It is said that the Spitz lay on a satin pillow while Michelangelo worked.

Martin Luther (1483-1546) Known as the father of Protestantism, Martin Luther was a German theologian and major leader of the Reformation. The Lutheran religion was named for him. His principles were adopted by many other religious leaders and the movement he began changed the face of Western religion.

His dog *Belferlein* is mentioned in several of Luther's writings. He took great pleasure in watching his son play with the small dog. "And also for good little Belferlein," he wrote, "there will be a place in heaven someday!"

Sir Isaac Newton (1643-1727) A scientific genius, Sir Isaac Newton was the first of his profession to be knighted by the Queen. Most school children learn the story of how Newton, in 1671, discovered gravity as he sat beneath a tree and was bonked on the head by a falling apple. The tale, unfortunately, is not true. Nevertheless, he did formulate the theory of gravity and establish his three laws of motion. Newton was the first to accurately explain the cause and variation of tides, the way in which the Earth rotated on its axis and the relationship between the moon and the sun. He had an extraordinary impact on modern physics and celestial mechanics.

We don't know much about Sir Isaac Newton's dog. We do know that while he worked on his scientific findings, however, he was entertained by his Spitz *Diamond*. It is said that the dog bumped into the table where Newton studied, toppling a candle and setting several years worth of notes afire. Despite his frustration, Newton remained loyal to the dog. (While some writings depict Diamond as a Spitz, other say that the dog was a Greyhound.)

Carl Friedrich Abel (1723-1787) The famous German musician and composer, Carl Friedrich Abel is said to be the last of the masters of the instrument known as the viola da gamba. He played for the great Dresden court orchestra, but his greatest fame would come in England. In 1759, he went to England and became a chamber musician to the great Spitz fancier Queen Charlotte. There he wrote more than 40 symphonies. He lived with Johann Christian Bach (son of Johann Sebastian Bach) and, between 1765 and 1781, they gave the famous Bach-Abel subscription concerts, consisting of 15 concerts per year.

Carl Freidrich Abel was a close friend of the famed artist Gainsborough, who painted his in 1777. He exchanged this and two other paintings for one of Abel's viola da gambas.

Abel was very close friends with the artist Thomas Gainsborough (1727-1788) and his home was filled with the works of this master. Art historians believe that the famous *Two Fox Dogs*, painted in 1777, was done for Abel and depicts his pets *(see page 33)*. Abel appears with one of his dogs in the portrait *Carl Friedrich Abel*, also painted by Gainsborough.

King George III (1738-1820) and Queen Charlotte
This royal couple were the first British rulers known to own white Spitz dogs. Their love for the breed was so great that they inspired others to obtain dogs, even helping them to import stock from Germany. The story of their involvement, with the breed, is extensively discussed in the chapter on "The Spitz in England."

Richard Cosway (1742-1821) Considered one of the greatest of the English miniature painters, Cosway's tiny masterpieces were rendered on ivory. Most of his patrons were wealthy or prominent people of the time. Art historians praise his light touch and the great influence he had on the genre.

The famous painter George Stubbs (1724-1806) featured one of Cosway's pets in *Portrait of a Spanish Dog Belonging to Mr. Cosway*. This painting has also been listed as *Dog Chasing a Butterfly* and *A Spanish Dog*. This 1775 work is considered one of Stubbs' most charming paintings.

Wolfgang Amadeus Mozart (1756-1791) Mozart is widely considered the greatest musical genius the world has ever seen. He excelled in every musical genre which he tried. He had a phenomenal ear for music, often penning his compositions in their final form, without the need for revisions. This trait began early. As a 13-year-old, he heard *Miserere*, by Allegri, while on a tour of Italy. Though he heard it only once, he quickly jotted the entire piece down from memory.

Mozart is also considered the greatest child prodigy in history. He started to write minuets at five years of age and composed his first symphony when he was nine. His father, Leopold Mozart, was also a successful composer and skilled violinist. He passed his love for music on to his two children: Maria Anna, who played the keyboard and Wolfgang, who played both keyboard and violin. The Mozart children performed for audiences in Germany, France and England.

Mozart died when he was only 35. During his lifetime, he had produced an astounding 626 known works. He is credited with having an extraordinary influence on later composers, particularly Beethoven.

The letters of the Mozart family are filled with references to the Spitz family pet. She is variously referred to as *Bimperl, Pimperl, Miss Bimbes* or *Miss Pimpes*. It is clear that the dog lived in the house, as many of the letters state that the writer has taken the dog out for a walk. Furthermore, the Spitz seems to have been a favorite with the entire family.

A 1777 letter to Wolfgang says: "Miss Pimpes too is living in hopes, for she stands or sits at the door whole half-hours on end and thinks every minute that you are going to come. All the same she is quite well..."

Maria Anna Mozart wrote, in 1777: "Bimperl, I trust is doing her duty and making up to you, for she is a good and faithful fox dog." This statement has sometimes erroneously been translated as "fox terrier," rather than the commonly used "fox dog." It should be remembered that "fox dog" was a name applied, during this time period, to the Spitz.

Indeed, Maria Anna often included postscripts concerning the family pet in her letters. In a 1778 letter

Famed artist George Stubbs painted this *Portrait of a Spanish Dog Belonging to Mr. Cosway,* for the great English miniature painter.

Mary Darby Robinson (1758-1800) The English actress Mary Robinson led an interesting and colorful life. At 16 she married Mr. Robinson and, two years later,` gained fame when she appeared as Shakespeare's Juliet. In 1779, she played the part of Perdita in *The Winter's Tale*. This is when she caught the eye of the Prince of Wales and became his mistress. He showered her with gifts but, by 1781, the Prince had turned his attention to other women. Still, he must have cared for her since he granted her a yearly stipend of £500. She led a lavish lifestyle and her parties were the toast of England, attracting a wide variety of nobles and other celebrities. After the break-up with the Prince, Mrs. Robinson became the lover of General Banestre Tarleton, known

she wrote: "A kiss for Bimperl, who will by this time have forgotten me and will no longer recognize me." And again, later in the year, she tells Leopold: "I send greetings to Theresa (a maid) and a kiss to Bimperl. Is the warbler still alive?"

Bimperl seems to have been a favorite of Leopold Mozart too. A letter to Wolfgang, written in 1778, informs him that "Bimperl (sends) several thousand licks." On New Year's Eve, 1778, he tells him: "As I write this letter I am almost going crazy, for it is New Year's Eve, and, although the door is closed, the bell is ringing the whole time, Bimperl is barking, Ceccarelli is shouting and chattering, and people are deafening me with wishes for a Happy New Year, although they see that I am writing and that I am in a hurry, for the post is going off..."

Wolfgang Mozart's letters, too, shine with his affection for the dog. He writes from Munich, in 1777, "Please tell Nannerl not to give Bimperl too much to eat, lest she should get too fat..." and in 1780: "My greetings to all our good friends...Give Bimperl a pinch of Spanish tobacco, a good wine-sop, and three kisses..." A letter in December of 1780, closes with "A thousand kisses to Bimperl."

Authorities say that Mozart penned a musical aria to his Spitz. "You could never be disloyal to me, of that I am certain! Oh no, oh no, my Spitz!" Sadly, this aria was never completed.

The 1781 Gainsborough painting *Perdita,* shows Mary Darby Robinson and her white Spitz.

The George Stubbs painting Fino and Tiny *is one of several works which picture the parti-color Spitz who was a favorite of King George IV.*

as a British hero of the American Revolution. She later turned her attention to writing.

The Prince of Wales commissioned Gainsborough to paint Mrs. Robinson's portrait in 1781. He presented this to her as a gift. By her side is her devoted white Spitz, probably a present from the Prince, too. In her hand she holds a miniature portrait of her royal lover, painted by Joseph Meyer, another gift from the Prince.

King George IV (1762-1830) This British King is said, by many historians, to be one of the worst monarchs ever to sit on the throne. While King George III still reigned, his son, the future George IV, publicly allied himself with his father's enemies. As King, his policies led to open discrimination against Roman Catholics and Protestants who belonged to denominations other than the Anglican Church. While still Prince of Wales, he was notorious for his extravagant lifestyle and this often got him into trouble. In 1762, he entered into an illegal marriage. Parliament later insisted that he deny the marriage in return for paying his monumental debts. Subsequently, he married Princess Caroline, of Brunswick, but his shabby treatment of her outraged polite society.

Like his father and mother, King George III and Queen Charlotte, George IV owned and loved Spitz dogs. He is believed to have owned several. George IV spend copious sums on artwork, engaging many of the masters of the day to paint him, his horses, carriages and, occasionally, his dogs. A parti-color Spitz, named Fino, seems to have been a great favorite as he appears in two paintings by Stubbs. For dog fanciers, the most famous of these renderings is "Fino and Tiny," painted in 1791.

Johann Paul Friedrich Richter (1763-1825) This German writer used the pen name Jean Paul. He wrote several satirical essays and texts on poetry and education. He is best known, however, for his novels which were often humorous and quite witty. German literary historians credit him with developing the psychological novel.

Numerous comments about dogs can be found in Jean Paul's novels. He once wrote that he could not live without a Spitz. One of his dogs, named *Spitzius*

Spitz dogs were popular with most of the royal family during the late 1700s. A white Spitz, a Wolfspitz (or Keeshond) and another dog who may be either a black-and-tan Spitz or a Spitz cross are seen in the 1782 George Stubbs painting John Christian Santhague. *We are not sure precisely who owned these dogs because Santhague, the page pictured above, served in the households of the Prince of Wales, his brother Prince Frederick and, later, King George IV.*

Hofmann, was so beloved that Jean Paul was never seen without him.

Adrian Ludwig Richter (1803-1884) A German painter and illustrator, Richter was famous for his depictions of rural life. During his lifetime, he produced more than 2,000 woodcuts. For the canine historian, Richter's works are a treasure trove, for a dog is included in almost every illustration. The white Spitz is a common feature and Richter pictures the breed as a loyal companion, playmate for children and superb watchdog.

George Sand (1804-1876) This was the pseudonym for Amandine Lucile Aurore, one of the most colorful literary figures of the 1800s. She married Casimir Dudevant in 1822 and later divorced him. Under the laws of the time, she was forced to give up her entire estate, receiving only a modest yearly stipend, in return for the separation. Her outrage at this injustice was expressed in many of her popular novels. She became a free spirit and subsequently had affairs with many famous artistic figures of the day. Among these was the renowned composer Frederick Chopin. When Sand met Chopin, his career was in a decline. They took a trip to Majorca and then returned to Sand's country estate in France. These were the happiest days of Chopin's life and he produced a succession of masterpieces.

Sand had a charming Spitz which was a source of pleasure for the couple. So impressed was Chopin with the dog that he composed *Valse des Petits Chiens* in tribute.

White Spitz dogs were commonly included in the work of German painter/illustrator Adrian Ludwig Richter.

On her death bed, Queen Victoria petted her white Spitz "Fluffie."

Charles Dickens (1812-1870) Considered one of the greatest of English writers, Charles Dickens was a master storyteller. His novels portrayed the gritty life of industrialized Victorian England and displayed a sensitivity for the lower classes. Many of his masterpieces, *Oliver Twist, A Tale of Two Cities, David Copperfield, Great Expectations,* etc., are still required reading in English and American high school classes.

We know that Dickens loved dogs. He was fond of his daughter Mamie's pet, a white Spitz named "Mrs. Bouncer."

Queen Victoria (1819-1901) One of the greatest dog fanciers of all the British monarchs, Queen Victoria purchased a reddish Spitz dog in 1888. This led to a revival of interest in the breed in England. Unfortunately, it also led to the demise of the large white Spitz. The Queen did, however, retain a fondness for white Spitz dogs. One of her special pets was a dog named "Fluffie," who lay by her side on her death bed. The story of Queen Victoria's involvement with the breed is discussed in detail in the chapter on "The Spitz in England."

Henry Morrison Flagler (1830-1913) One of the wealthiest men in America, Flagler borrowed money and, in 1867, entered into business with John D. Rockefeller and others. The company they formed would become Standard Oil. Flagler is best known for his contributions to Florida development. He is one of those who made the state's tourist industry possible.

Henry Flagler probably knew the breed simply as the Spitz. It was recognized as the American Eskimo in the year that he died. There can be no doubt, though, as this photo illustrates, that it is the same breed we know today.

His Florida East Coast Railroad was the first to extend to Miami and Key West. He reportedly spent more than 50 million dollars in the Sunshine State, largely on a series of palatial hotels, including the famed Royal Palms.

We do not know the name of the white Spitz who was Flagler's favorite. The dog, however, was his constant companion, accompanying him on many of his travels around Florida.

Marie von Ebner-Eschenbach (1830-1916) The daughter of a count, this Austrian novelist is considered one of the premier women writers of her time. She sensitively depicted the life of both the poor and the aristocracy. She had a special affinity for children.

The Spitz must have been a great favorite of von Ebner-Eschenbach's for the breed figures prominently in two of the poems she penned. *Die Spitzin* *(The Spitz Bitch)* and *Der Fink (The Finch Bird)* demonstrate her familiarity with the breed.

Wilhelm Busch (1832-1908) This German writer and artist may well be the father of the comic strip. Before Busch's time, children's books contained illustrations, but they seldom correlated with the story. His *Max und Moritz,* originally published in 1865, was the first book which required the reader to look at both the text and the drawing to understand the story.

Max und Moritz was the inspiration for Rudolph Dirks' American comic strip *The Katzenjammer Kids,* first published in 1897. This strip was sometimes known as *Hans and Fritz,* the names which had been substituted for Max and Moritz. During World War I, there was so much anti-German sentiment that the strip was renamed *The Shenanigan Kids* and the German accents were toned down. Rumor has it that, had the war continued, the accents would have been changed to Irish.

German school children still enjoy the adventures of those two scalawags Max and Moritz. They can often quote lines from the stories, particularly those involving Widow Bolte and her unjust punishment of her loyal Spitz dog, who she believed had eaten her roasted chickens.

Spitz dogs are also featured in the Busch tales *Hans Huckebein* and *Die Fromme Helene*. He often drew parallels between the lively Spitz and the "Spitzbube." This is an affectionate German term for a "little rascal" or a naughty little boy.

King Edward VII (1841-1910) This son of Queen Victoria earned the scorn of his mother when, as Prince of Wales, he became known as a playboy. He also gained renown as an avid sportsman, a noted patron of the arts and a frequent traveler. His duties were largely ceremonial until he was almost 60 years old. Then, the Queen finally relinquished the crown. Though he served as King for only nine years, Edward was extremely popular in Britain and abroad.

While he was Prince of Wales, a large white Spitz was the treasured companion of the future king. The dog often accompanied him on his travels to many European resorts, including the spas found at the famous mineral springs at Baden-Baden, in Germany.

Kaiser Wilhelm II (1859-1941) Son of Frederick III and Victoria (daughter of Britain's Queen Victoria), Wilhelm II was King of Prussia and Emperor of Germany. Though intelligent, he was determined to rule on his own, but he lacked the experience, maturity and training to succeed. He is also said to have had an explosive and unpredictable personality. Advisers suggested that he make concessions which would gradually give more power to the German people, but he steadfastly refused.

During his reign, Germany made steady gains in industry. The country had not, however, been involved in extensive world colonization, like Britain and France. Eager to become a player, Kaiser Wilhelm II adopted an expansionist policy. His saber-rattling speeches alarmed all of Europe and were further intensified when he began expanding Germany's navy. Indeed, his strident tone did the seemingly impossible by uniting traditional enemies: Britain, France and Russia. His policies, as well as his backing of Austria-Hungary, led to World War I. His avid support of submarine warfare, even attacks on civilian vessels, drew the United States into the conflict.

Kaiser Wilhelm's absolute refusal to consider any peace proposals, finally alienated leaders of the Reichstag. In 1918, when the Armistice was signed, he fled to Holland, where he later abdicated the throne. He would live out his life in exile.

While his policies led his country to war, Kaiser Wilhelm II was a patron of purebred dogs and had an intense interest in the newly growing sport of dog shows. He actively supported several dog clubs, even contri-buting his own money to them. He was particularly fond of white Spitz and owned several of them. In retirement, the dogs went everywhere with him. In 1991, German dog fanciers unveiled a monument to Wilhelm II in Würtemberg, considered to be the cradle of German dog breeding. A similar monument was also erected in Holland. Both statues show the former ruler with his beloved Spitz.

A controversial ruler, Kaiser Wilhelm II was a great fan of all dogs, particularly the Great German White Spitz. In retirement, he was rarely seen without several of the breed.

Three-year-old Franklin Delano Roosevelt, future President, and his white Spitz *Budgy.*

Franklin D. Roosevelt (1882-1945) The 32nd President of the United States, Franklin Roosevelt was elected for an astonishing four terms of office. Born in Hyde Park, New York, of Dutch and English ancestry, young Franklin lived a wealthy and privileged life. In his early years, he was quite athletic. In 1905, he married his distant cousin, Eleanor Roosevelt, who was given away by her famous uncle President Theodore Roosevelt. In 1921, while vacationing at their summer home, in Canada, Franklin was stricken with polio. Despite the infirmity, as President, Roosevelt saw this country through both the Depression and the Second World War. He died only a few months before the Allied victory.

Most people think of Roosevelt with his Scottish Terrier, Fala. As a child, though, it was a white Spitz who was his constant companion. This dog, *Budgy,* was, in fact, his first pet.

Princess Ileana of Romania, later known as Mother Alexandra (1909-1991) The eldest child of King Ferdinand I and Queen Marie, Princess Ileana had a truly royal lineage. On one side of her pedigree, she was descended from England's Queen Victoria and, on the other, she was the great-granddaughter of Czar Alexander II, of Russia. In 1931, she married Archduke Anton von Hapsburg, of Austria, and went to live in a castle, outside Vienna. One of her sisters became

MAX AND MORITZ

From A Little Boys' Story in Seven Pranks (Prank Two)

In the first prank, those two rascals Max and Moritz kill Widow Bolte's chickens.

When the Widow Bolte recovered from the painful experience of losing her chickens, she thought that it would probably be best, quietly and in honor, to eat the chickens well-roasted.

The chickens, had on pretty days, scratched in the sand, in the backyard, then later in the garden, happy to be alive.

Ah, Widow Bolte weeps anew and her Spitz stands there with her, too.

pleasantly sizzling in the skillet.

Max and Moritz smelled them. "Quick, let's crawl up on the roof!" they said. Through the chimney, with pleasure, they see the chickens lying there, already without their heads and craws,

Just then, Widow Bolte takes a plate and goes down to the cellar to get a serving of sauerkraut, which she especially enjoys when it is heated.

Famous Owners

Meanwhile, on the roof, the boys are regarding the matter at hand. Thinking ahead, Max had brought along a fishing pole.

Schnupdiwup! In no time at all, a chicken is lifted up through the chimney. Schnupdiwup! Now number two! Schnupdiwup! Now number three! And now comes up number four! Schnupdiwup! "We've got you!"

Of course, the Spitz closely observed all of this and he barks: "Rawau, rawau!"

But they have already climbed down from the roof and have quite cheerfully gone away

Well, what a spectacle for us to see, for Widow Bolte came back just then. As if rooted to the ground, she stood there. Soon, she looked at the skillet. All the chickens were gone.

Spitz!" That was her first word! "Oh, you Spitz, you devil you! Just wait! I'll get you!"

With her hard wooden spoon, big and heavy, she works her Spitz over. The air loudly resounds with his cries of pain for such unjust punishment for he feels innocent.

In their hiding place, Max and Moritz are snoring, now fast asleep, beside the hedge. And from their entire chicken feast, only a leg remains.

83

Greece's Queen and another was Queen of Yugoslavia. Upon her father's death, her brother succeeded him as King of Romania.

The start of World War II, brought an end to Princess Ileana's peaceful Austrian life. Fearing the Nazis, she and her family went back to Romania, where they sat out the war. They were forced to flee again, in 1947, when the Communists came to power and compelled them to relinquish the throne. The family moved to Switzerland and, later, to Argentina.

The Princess had always been imbued with a sense of duty. In 1961, she entered religious service and was later given the name Mother Alexandra. She immigrated to the U.S. and founded a monastery, near Wurtemburg, Missouri.

Mother Alexandra died in 1991. "In clearing out her personal effects from the monastery," writes Bill Burmeister, in *Legends of Lawrence County, Volume II,* "it was noted that a small gold container on her bed stand contained a handful of Romanian soil which she had taken with her into exile. At that time, she said she wanted the soil to be buried with her. She is buried with her tiny handful of Romanian soil on the monastery grounds."

Like so many other members of the European royal families, Princess Ileana was well acquainted with the white Spitz. The love and tenderness which is shown in the photo included here depicts her deep attachment to the breed.

Maria Murdszenty (c. 1920s) Little is known about Maria Murdszenty. During the 1920s, and possibly into the 1930s, she was the prima donna, or leading woman soloist, with the famed Vienna State Opera. This opera and the Vienna Philharmonic Orchestra, which provides its music, are listed among the most renowned performing companies in the world.

While we may know little about this operatic diva, we do know that she was often photographed with her adoring white Spitz dogs.

Salvatore Bono (1935-). Better known as "Sonny," he rose to fame, during the 1960s, as a singer and songwriter. The duo of Sonny and Cher had many chart toppers, including their most identifiable song, "I Got You Babe." During the 1970s, the couple starred in a television variety comedy show. When the marriage broke up, Bono turned his attention to business. Among his ventures was a very successful Hollywood restaurant.

In 1987, Bono turned his attention to politics. In 1988, he was elected Mayor of Palm Springs and founded the Palm Springs International Film Festival. He was recently been elected to the House of Representatives, where he serves California's 44th District.

An American Eskimo named "Mo" shares the home of Sonny and his fourth wife, Mary, 33. He is a valued playmate for the couple's children, Chesare and Chianna. Mo has joined the jet set, commuting from the couple's townhouse in Georgetown to their mansion in Palm Springs.

Burton Gilliam (?-) His name may not be familar to you, but his face certainly is. Burton Gilliam has been in many of America's best loved motion pictures and television shows. The successful Golden Gloves champ was a Dallas fireman for 14 years before he hit the big time. Though he had no acting experience, he was

Most of the European royal houses were related by either blood or marriage. The German Spitz was a popular pet among monarchs. Romanian Princess Ileana cuddles her beloved Spitz. It takes only a glance at her face to tell how devoted she is to her dogs.

Well-known actor Burton Gilliam and Ch. "PR" Stevens' Magic Touch.

offered the co-starring role in *Paper Moon,* in which he played Floyd, the desk clerk. His performance caught the eye of Mel Brooks, who hired him to play Lyle, Slim Pickens' sidekick, in *Blazing Saddles.* Mr. Gilliam, in fact, has the first lines in the movie and earned much attention for his hilarious performance. He has also appeared in *Honeymoon in Vegas* (as the lead Elvis impersonator), *Back to the Future III, Gator, Fletch, Jinxed, Hearts of the West, Farewell My Lovely, The Getaway, Telefon, At Long Last Love,* and *Thunderbolt and Lightfoot* among others.

He has performed on more than 100 television shows. His TV movie credits include *North and South II, Hail to the Chief, The Jericho Mile, Dream West, Red River, Convicted, The Georgia Peaches* and *The Night That Panicked America,* as well as many others.

He has made over 125 guest star appearances on various series. From 1991-'93, he was frequently seen in the role of Virgil Mosley, on *Evening Shade.* In addition, he has appeared on *The Dukes of Hazzard, Soap, Knight Rider, The A-Team, Alice* and *The Fall Guy.* He also starred in the pilot *The Girl, the Goldwatch and Dynamite.*

Burton and his wife, Susan, are two time American Eskimo owners. Their first dog was "PR" Stevens' Princess Aasta, better known as "Annie," bred by Rosemary Stevens. She and a Shetland Sheepdog shared the Gilliam home until she died, of old age, in 1994. The two dogs were so close that the Sheltie would not eat after Annie's death. Burton and Susan were also devastated. They quickly phoned Rosemary and asked when her next litter was due. In the course of the conversation, Rosemary mentioned that she had a two-year-old dog she might like to place. He was an active, exuberant dog who was a bit much for Rosemary to handle. Soon Ch. "PR" Stevens' Magic Touch was happily ensconced in the Gilliam home. He made the transition easily and Magic and the Sheltie quickly became fast friends. Magic sleeps on the Gilliams' bed and Burton is obedience training him.

Jane Wiedlin (1950s or '60s -) Wiedlin is one of the founders of the popular all-girl rock band, the Go-Gos, which earned three gold albums and had a number of single record hits, during the 1970s. In 1984, she left the group, which subsequently broke up, to embark on a solo career. Wiedlin shares her home with two dogs, including an Eskie named "Kitty Igloo."

The Japanese Spitz may be a direct descendant of the American Eskimo. This is Aus. Ch. Lacebark Sno Anastasia, owned by Val Megyeri, of Australia.

This red-orange German "Klein," or "small," Spitz is closely related to the American Eskimo. *Photo courtesy of Peter Machetanz, Verein für Deutsche Spitze e.V.*

A head study of the rare Great German Black Spitz. This is Amor vom Butzibach, owned by Americans Bretta and John Anderton, who are working to save this color variety.

This impressive German White Spitz, Cherie vom Berg Sonnenhof, is owned by Ilse Lauermann.

Chapter 10

American Eskimo Relatives

As American Eskimo fanciers have learned more about their dogs, they have become increasingly curious about those breeds which are most closely related to the Eskie. While the Spitz family of dogs is a large one, there are still a few breeds which could be called "cousins" to our present breed. We have listed several of these relatives, including a couple that are now, sadly, extinct.

GERMAN SPITZ

"We need only step out into the street, and before long at all, we can catch glimpse of a genuine, pure German Spitz..." wrote Strebel, in 1904-05. Though those words were penned almost 100 years ago, the German Spitz remains popular throughout his homeland. The favorite of country, suburban and apartment dwellers, the Spitz is still esteemed as a watchdog and companion.

Those who have read the history chapters in this book, will already be fully aware of this breed's interesting background and the influence it has had on so many other breeds, including the American Eskimo.

The Verein für Deutsche Spitze, or Association for German Spitz Varieties, founded in 1899, is the national club for the breed. It has many affiliated chapters in German cities and helps those both there and abroad stay abreast of German Spitz activities.

In Germany, the breed is separated into five distinct varieties. These are:

1. Wolfsspitz (or Keeshond)
2. Great German Spitz (Grosser Spitz or Großspitz)
   15 3/4 to 19 3/4 inches
   Colors: pure white, jet black, brown (dark chocolate)
3. German Middle Spitz (Mittelspitz)
   11 1/2 to 14 inches
   Colors: black, white, orange, wolf-sable, brown (dark chocolate)
4. German Small or Miniature Spitz (Kleinspitz)
   9 to 11 inches
   Colors: same as for the Middle Spitz
5. Zwergspitz (Dwarf Spitz; same as the Pomeranian)
   not more than 9 inches
   all colors permitted

The rarest of all the varieties is the Great German Black Spitz. Once one of the most popular of all German Spitz, interest in the Great Black has been declining for some time. It is so rarely seen now, in Germany, that fancier Bill Ledbetter considers them extremely endangered and fears that this variety will become extinct.

American Eskimo fanciers, Bretta and John Anderton, of Ft. Walton Beach, Florida, have taken up the cause of the Great Black. The Eskie owners became aware of this variety when John was posted to an Air Force base in Germany. They were invited to attend one of the meetings of the Darmstadt chapter of the Verein für Deutsche Spitze. The couple was impressed with the hospitable welcome and joined the club.

The Andertons were very impressed with the medium and small sized black Spitz which they saw. However, they preferred a larger size dog and set out to find a Great Black. "It was at this point we realized how rare the large black German Spitz was," Britta says.

When they returned to the U.S., the Great Blacks came with them. Britta wanted to have the dogs registered with the AKC, but they could only be accepted as black Keeshonden. The Andertons are dedicated to seeing the Great Black recognized in this country. They have had one litter already and plan another. Additionally, they have been showing their dogs in events sponsored by the States Kennel Club and the American Rare Breed Association. Hopefully, their efforts will prove successful. It would be a terrible shame if one of the oldest and most impressive of the German varieties became extinct.

The Great German Black Spitz is now endangered. This is Wieta v.d. Beyenburg, owned by Bretta and John Anderton.

World-famed breeder Eÿke Schmidt-Rohde with a Great German White Spitz at a show in Frankfurt. Mrs. Schmidt-Rohde has been tireless in her efforts to promote the breed.

The German Spitz is recognized in all countries which are members of the Federation Cynologique Internationale. England has recently recognized the breed, too, although they consider the Keeshond (or Wolfsspitz) and the Pomeranian (or Zwergspitz) to be separate breeds.

JAPANESE SPITZ

The Japanese Spitz is gaining quite a following outside his homeland. The first European imports came to the Scandinavian countries, but interest has quickly spread to England, Italy, Germany, Australia and many other countries. The breed attracts attention no matter where he goes, not only for his sparkling good looks, but his charming personality, as well. Indeed, many of those involved with other Spitz breeds, have added one or more Japanese Spitz to their homes. Often, they've discovered that the dogs are so delightful in their ways, that they have turned their full attention to breeding this little "white Samurai."

The Japanese Spitz should be of special interest to American Eskimo fanciers. It is believed that the Eskie may, in fact, be one of the progenitors of the breed. The Japanese have not been able to give a definitive explanation for the appearance of this white Spitz in their country. Several theories exist to explain the roots of this breed.

Some Japanese believe that, during the "Taisho Period," of the late 1920s, a number of white Spitz dogs

The German Mittelspitz is the same size as our Miniature Eskies. This lovely dog is Gipsy aus dem Norden, owned by Mrs. Irmgard Fischer, of Germany.

This is the white Kleinspitz bitch Suse Edelweiss vom Haus Gohfeld, owned by William Ledbetter. Ledbetter, who was born in the U.S. and now lives in Germany, is a fan of all Spitz breeds and has added to our knowledge of the history of these dogs.

This lovely black German Mittlespitz is bred and owned by Birgit Moritz, of Bingen, West Germany.

This wolf-sable German Kleinspitz is about the size of a Toy American Eskimo. *Photo courtesy of Peter Machetanz, Verein für Deutsche Spitze e.V.*

arrived from foreign countries. Some of these animals came from the United States and Canada. About the same time, it is believed, the Samoyed also journeyed to Japan and was soon joined by the Russian Spitz via Manchuria. It is also thought that some German Spitz were brought to the country, from Poland. These dogs were all interbred and a new distinct breed emerged. The larger dogs became known as the "Samo" and the smaller ones were simply called the "Spitz."

The second theory ties the breed's importation to the great Japanese earthquake of 1923. Supposedly, a Canadian cargo ship was destroyed and a group of Spitz dogs, probably American Eskimos, were discovered in the wreckage. Then, in the 1930s, the Russian Spitz arrived in Japan. These two groups of dogs were interbred and the Japanese Spitz resulted. Advocates of this theory hold that no Samoyed blood was ever introduced.

The third theory holds that the breed is uniquely Japanese and has been in the country for centuries. Originally, advocates of this scenario speculate, the ancestors of the Japanese Spitz, came to the islands from the Arctic regions and prospered in their new homeland.

"I cannot believe that the Japanese Spitz and the American Eskimo are not somewhat related," says Lynne Robson, one of England's most successful breeders. "Everything about them is too much of a coincidence."

Records show that these Spitz dogs were being actively bred in the 1930s. It was not, however, until 1940s or '50s that the first standard was drawn up and the dogs were given the official title "Japanese Spitz." Today, the breed is well represented in Japan. While not as popular as the Akita or Shiba, he does have the support of a loyal group of fanciers. Many travelers to Japan have seen large numbers of these white dogs walking with their masters or cavorting with children.

We may never fully know the truth about the breed's origins, but it's obvious that the Japanese Spitz bears an uncanny resemblance to both the American Eskimo and the German Spitz. He has a well-built, compact body, with a broad and deep chest. His back is short and level and he has good tuckup. He is truly beautiful in motion, as he moves with light, lively steps. His skull is broad, with little stop, and narrows to a pointed muzzle, tipped by a black pigmented nose. His always erect ears are small, set high, and face forward.

Like the Eskie, the Japanese Spitz has a glorious, profuse double coat. The coat is particularly pronounced around the neck and shoulders, forming a ruff. The moderately long tail is set on high and carried curled over the back. The hair on the tail is quite long, giving a lovely finish to the dog. The ideal color is a pure white. Cream colored patches are seen occasionally, but are not desirable.

Size has been a controversial subject in recent years and the requirements vary from country to country. The Federation Cynologique Internationale standard,

These lovely Japanese Spitz are Ch. Ginkyo Almond Amai Rassan and Ch. Zuzushii-san von der Hausruckhöhe, bred by well-known author Britta Schweikl-Ecklmayr, of Austria, and owned by Mr. and Mrs. Zapf, of Germany.

which most countries use, allows males to be 12-16 inches at the withers and females to be 10-14 inches. The English have now reduced the top heights for the breed. Under their current standard, males must not exceed 14 inches and females 12 inches. The Japanese are worried about moves, from outside the country, which reduce the breed's size. They fear that the Japanese Spitz will be recast as a toy breed.

Lively, bouncy, intensely curious, extremely affectionate, deeply loyal, intelligent, spirited and proud...these are all traits which the Japanese Spitz embodies. No doubt, they will sound familiar to American Eskimo owners, as well. Lynne Robson was struck by the similarities when she read the first edition of our book, *The American Eskimo*. "One thing I had to do when I was reading your book was to keep reminding myself that I wasn't reading about the Japanese Spitz."

KEESHOND

The Keeshond (pronounced "caze-hawnd") is the largest of the German Spitz varieties. In Germany, he is called the "Wolfsspitz," but in Holland, Britain and the U.S. he is know as the Keeshond (the plural is Keeshonden).

Ludwig Beckmann, the esteemed German animal artist and authority, considered the Keeshond the oldest of all the German Spitz varieties. "The oldest variety which still exists is also the variety which stabilized into a constant form the earliest: our Wolfsspitz, which is also sometimes referred to as the coach driver's or river boatman's Spitz," Beckmann wrote in 1894-95, in *Geschichte und Beschreibung der Rassen des Hundes* (*History and Description of the Breeds of Dog*). "This variety is most frequently seen nowadays in the Western regions of Germany which border on Belgium and Holland, and in the northern Rhine regions...With regard to the inheritance of type, coat and color, this wolf-gray or wolf-sable variety shows the highest degree of uniformity."

For centuries the German Spitz had been known in neighboring Holland. There, the dogs served as watchdogs on farms and the barges which plied the Rhine River. On these small barges, or *rijnaken*, they guarded any stock to be traded.

Political events were to propel the German breed into prominence and to recast him as a symbol, in Holland. In the years shortly before the French Revolution many people in European countries rose up, demanding more freedom from their governments. In the 1780s, political strife broke out in the Netherlands. The Patriots, the group of the common man, were led by Cornelis de Gyselaar. He was better known by the nickname Kees. A dog lover, he owned a wolf colored Spitz dog. So identified did the dog become with the leader, that the breed would become known as Kees' dog, or Keeshond ("hond" is "dog" in Dutch). The opposition was led by the conservative Prince of Orange, who served as governor of the Netherlands. He was often seen with his pet, a Pug, and this became the symbol of state power. Indeed, the Pug was often

Val Megyeri poses with some of her Laceback Japanese Spitz. At her side are Ch. Tinto's Distinct Dream in White and Ch. Laceback Sno Toybear. Seated in front are Ch. Laceback Sno Anastasia, 12-year-old Ch. Kawaii Shiroi Aijin and Ch. Laceback Sno Spectacular.

In this country, the Keeshond is registered as a separate breed. This is Ch. Windrift Special Billing. "Tux" is owned by Harry and Vivian Toepfer.

featured with an orange ribbon about his neck. Both dogs were frequently seen in political cartoons of the day.

The conservatives ultimately crushed the upstart Patriot rebellion. Suddenly, it was not fashionable to be seen with the dog so identified with the party. It is reported that many of Keeshonden were killed. Some staunch supporters, however, quietly continued to breed their dogs. Some even kept their own records and pedigrees.

For over 100 years, the breed languished in obscurity. In the 1920s, the Baroness van Hardenbroek became interested in the historic breed. She searched the country to see if any of the old stock remained. On the farms in the countryside and on the riverboats, she found many excellent specimens. The Baroness succeeded in reviving the breed and helped form a club for them. In 1933, they were officially recognized by the *Raad van Beheer op Kynologisch Gebeid in Nederland,* the Netherland's Kennel Club.

The Keeshond first arrived in England in the 1920s. British breeding stock was based on imports from both Holland and Germany. Anti-German sentiment was rife in England, at the time, and every effort was made to distance the breed from its German roots. Initially, known as the Dutch Barge Dog, the name was later changed to the Keeshond.

The Keeshond was recognized by the American Kennel Club in 1930 and the foundation bloodlines came primarily from England. While not one of the most popular breeds, the Keeshond has always had a dedicated and loyal following in this country.

"...the Wolfsspitz is usually somewhat larger, robuster and more ruggedly built than the other two larger varieties," Ludwig Beckmann wrote. "(he) usually has a somewhat denser, harsher and even more profuse coat than the larger Blacks and Whites have."

This physical description still holds true. The Keeshond's good looks have made him a top contender in Group and Best in Show rings. His charming, loyal personality has made him a favorite with owners.

LOUP-LOUP

The French version of the Spitz is now, sadly, extinct. Up until the 1930s, however, he was quite well known. As in Germany, the breed was used as a watch dog. "The Great White Spitz, especially, was frequently used as a watch dog for stage coaches (in France) during the period prior to trains and railroads," wrote Ludwig Beckmann, in *Geschichte und Beschreibung der Rassen des Hundes (History and Description of the Breeds of Dogs),* published in 1894-95. In the 1867 book, *Le Chien (The Dog),* the French writer Gayot, says the white dogs were common guards on mail coaches and carrier vans.

The name Loup-Loup appears to have been first used by the naturalist Buffon. Gayot mentioned the *Chien de Poméranie* or *Lou-Lous de Poméranie* and the *Loup-Loup d'Alsace.* He believed that the Loup-Loup d'Alsace was a native French breed which had existed for centuries. Beckmann disagreed. He thought that all the dogs hailed from Germany and attributed the name *Lou Lous de Poméranie,* or "Little Wolf Dogs of Pomerania," to the fact that the wolf sable (or Keeshond) was originally the most popular of the varieties.

An article in a German magazine, published in 1882, describes the observations of a gentleman visiting the Jardin Zoologique d'Acclimation show, in Paris. "Six little Miniature Spitz are standing together and looking round carefully, so attentively with their

Sadly, the French breed, the "Loup-Loup," is now extinct.

clever, sparkling little eyes, the little pointed noses in constant motion, the little triangular-tipped ears held high and erect, each little fellow radiating in his entirety such dignity, such a ceremonious gravity, that you have to laugh, whether you want to or not. One of them, not much larger than a squirrel, wrangles and quarrels, snarling through the wire mesh of his box at one of his neighbors, a Bloodhound, who naturally takes no notice of his temperamental, furious little opponent. You feel *compelled* to take this audacious, saucy little guy and put him in your overcoat pocket, where his size would certainly not hinder his lodging capacity. "

By the early 1920s, French fanciers had begun to sort out the size differences. There were "Grand Lou-Lous," (about the size of our Standard American Eskimos), the Moyen, or medium sized, Lou-Lou (approximately equal to our Miniature Eskies) and the "Nain," or Toy Lou-Lou (about the size of the Pomeranian). Further divisions were made for color, with classes for whites, blacks and wolf-grays.

The introduction of the Samoyed caused great confusion among breeders. Some made crosses between the Grand Loup-Loup and the Sammy, believing that both were the same breed. This situation occurred, no doubt, because there was no club for the breed which could provide guidance. All Loup-Loups were categorized as *chiens d'agrément,* or "pet dogs," and came under the banner of the Société Français des Amateurs de Chiens d'Agrément.

In 1935, a specialty group, the Club Français du Loulou de Poméranie, was finally formed. It looked for awhile like the breed would thrive. Champion Prince Lulu, owned by Mr. de Fomier de Savignac, became a successful show dog and white Loup-Loups, particularly Grands and Moyens, became quite popular. But it was not to be. Other breeds caught the public's fancy and the Loup-Loup lapsed into obscurity.

POMERANIAN

"The elfin Pomeranian is a pixie in a long fluffy coat that makes him look like an animated puff-ball, bouncing joyously around his adopted home. He idolizes his household, but his real allegiance is to one person whom he adores best of all," writes Viva Leone Ricketts, in *All About Toy Dogs.* "He never gets too old to romp with friends and members of his household, and he lives to a ripe old age if he is not allowed to grow obese."

"No one ever possesses a Pomeranian," Ricketts writes in *The New Complete Pomeranian,* "for once a Pom has stared into your face with elfin look from adoring eyes, and has placed his feathery-light paw-print upon your heart, you are his to have and to hold forever after.

"Poms have a way of infiltrating your life and happiness in such a way that they become an integral and important part of the very warp and woof of your existence."

Pomeranians, known as Zwerg (dwarf) Spitz in Germany, have always been popular in the U.S. and England. *From The New Book of the Dog, by Robert Leighton.*

We have discussed the early history of the Pomeranian in the chapters on both "The Spitz in England" and "The Spitz in America." As we have seen, the craze for small dogs was the reason for the decline in the popularity of the large white Spitz.

Few breeds have remained so steadfastly popular as the delightful Pomeranian. He has captured the hearts of people round the world and, in this country, remains one of the top toy breeds. Always a first-class contender at dog shows, the Pomeranian has frequently topped this country's most prestigious events, winning many Bests in Show, including Westminster.

The Pomeranian standard calls for a weight of three to seven pounds, but lists four to five pounds as the "ideal" weight for a show dog. The breed is well known for its double coat. The outer coat is harsh in texture and should stand out from the body. The standard says that it forms "a frill or halo around him." One of the most intriguing aspects of Pom breeding is the tremendous range of colors found in the breed. Poms can be found in white, cream, black, brown, blue, orange and red. There are also shaded sables, black and tans and parti-colors.

In England, other United Kingdom countries and the United States, this toy Spitz is recognized as the Pomeranian and considered a separate breed. In Germany, he is known as the Zwergspitz or Dwarf Spitz and is considered a variety of the German Spitz. Holland uses a similar categorization, referring to the Pom as the Dwergkeeshond.

SEIDENSPITZ

Sometime in the late 1800s, a few German breeders decided to cross the Pomeranian, or Dwarf Spitz, with the Maltese. The breed they formed was known as the Seidenspitz, or Silky Spitz. These dogs conformed to the Pomeranian standard, except for the coat, which was closer in appearance to that of the Maltese. Soft and silky, in nature, the hair generally hung about six inches or so in length. The ears were shaved in order to enable them to stand, in Spitz fashion. Some fanciers also shaved the muzzle and lower legs, but most did as little trimming as possible. Average weight of the Seidenspitz was five pounds.

The German Spitz club, the Verein für Deutsche Spitze, never approved of the breed and did not recognize them. We do know, however, that some Seidenspitz were entered in German shows. The breed is pictured in a 1900 catalog from Arthur Seyfarth's kennel, in Kostriz/Thuringen. Several books from the 1920s and '30s picture dogs who were award winners.

Though the Seidenspitz was said to have an exceptional personality, the breed never really caught on. It is now extinct.

A rare drawing of a Seidenspitz. This now extinct breed was created by crossing the Spitz and Maltese. Though shown in Germany, the breed was never embraced by Spitz fanciers.

VOLPINO ITALIANO

The Volpino is the delightful Spitz breed which makes his home in Italy. The name "Volpino," is taken from the word "Volpe," or "fox," and aptly describes the foxy look of the head.

The breed has been known in Italy for hundreds of years. In the days before motorized transportation, the Volpino was the watchdog of choice for many farmers. He guarded the wagon when his master took his wares to market. While the farmer peddled his goods, the Volpino kept any suspicious characters away from the wagon.

During the 1700s, the breed was particularly popular in the west central part of Italy, Tuscany and the city of Florence. He was so well known in Florence that he earned the title Volpino di Firenze, or Florentine Volpino. He was also sometimes known as the "Dog of Florence." It was here that he became known as the preferred companion of wealthy women. Records show that the Volpino was sometimes referred to as "The Dog of the Quirinale." The Quirinale is one of the seven hills upon which ancient Rome was built.

We have received conflicting reports about the state of the breed in Italy today. Many books say that this is a tremendously popular toy breed. The esteemed German Spitz breeder, Britta Ecklmayr, interviewed Mr. Panciroli, one of Italy's three most successful breeders, for an article she wrote. According to him the breed is very popular, with more than 100 dogs registered annually.

Marco G. Piasentin, one of Italy's premier Japanese Spitz breeders, presents a different picture. He says that, during the mid-1900s, Italians gradually lost interest in their little Spitz. The situation was so bad that the breed became virtually extinct by the 1970s. A few dedicated breeders were determined, however, not to see this native breed disappear. Working with the Italian Kennel Club, they formulated a plan to revive the breed. Their work continues. According to Mr. Piasentin, there are fewer than 200 Volpini in all of Italy.

The Volpino still appears to be a favorite with upscale Italian women. German Spitz fancier William Ledbetter recently went on a trip to Lake Garda, in northern Italy, near Verona and Milan. "I saw lovely, beautifully dressed, wealthy Italian ladies strolling with their beautiful white Volpino Italianos along the shore of the resort lake." Seeing these dogs on the promenades, beneath the palm trees was, Mr. Ledbetter says, "a breath-taking sight!"

The outstanding Italian, French, Monte Carlo, German, European, World and Int'l. Ch. Zorro della Volpe Candida, owned by Roberta Marconi, of Italy, was the top Volpino Italiano in 1994.

The Volpini is not well known outside of Italy. They do make an occasional appearance at French shows and are just beginning to be seen in other countries. Recently, dogs have been exported to Germany, Austria, Switzerland and Holland.

The Volpino Italiano stands 10 to 12 inches at the shoulder and should weigh less than nine pounds. Pure white is the most common color, although red/orange dogs are permissible under the standard. A champagne color does sometimes occur, but is not desirable. The Volpino has the typical Spitz personality. He is lively, loyal and playful and bonds closely with his family.

Chapter 11

UKC
United Kennel Club Official Breed Standard

GENERAL APPEARANCE: The American Eskimo is a well balanced, typical model of a Northern working type dog. The body is proportioned and balanced. Back length from point of shoulder to root of tail should equal the height from pad to top of withers. The face is Nordic type with triangular ears which are slightly rounded at the tips and readily distinguished black points (nose, lips, and eye rims). Has an alert, smooth carriage. The coat should be thick, especially around the neck, forepart of shoulders and chest forming a lion-like mane. The rump and hind legs down to the hock are thickly coated forming the characteristic trousers. The ruff (mane) and long outer guard hairs are more prominent on males than females. The richly plumed tail is carried over the back. They should present a picture of natural beauty, alertness, strength and agility.

HEAD: One denoting power, being wedge shaped with broad, slightly crowned skull. Head size should be in proportion to body. The stop should not be abrupt but well defined.

MUZZLE: In proportion to head, medium in length, and covered with short, smooth hairs.

EARS: Should conform to head size, slightly rounded at the tips, triangular, held erect, set well apart and covered inside with hair. Ears should softly blend with the wedge shape head. Outer part of ears to be covered with short, smooth hairs, longer tufts in front of the ear openings. Color inside of ear should be pink or slight tinge of grey.

EYES: Should be slightly oval and not slanted. Should be black to brown, set well apart, with intelligent expression. Eye rims black but dark brown is permissible. Eyelashes should be white.

NOSE: Leather black to dark brown.

LIPS: Black to dark brown. Saggy flews are objectionable.

TEETH & JAW: Strong jaw with close fitting teeth meeting in a level to scissors bite. A full compliment of sound teeth is preferred.

NECK: Medium length and in proportion to body; strong, carried proudly erect, blending into the shoulders with a graceful arch.

BODY: Strong and compactly built but not too short coupled. Back length from the point of shoulder to root of tail should equal the height from the pad to top of withers. In the male, both testicles must be present in the scrotum.

CHEST & RIBS: Should be strong, showing broadness and depth. Depth of chest is at approximate point of elbows. Ribs should be well-sprung and begin upsweep behind the ninth rib to ensure adequate room for heart and lung action. Heart and lung room are secured more by body depth than width. Belly should be slightly tucked up immediately behind the ribs.

BACK & LOINS: Should be straight, level, broad and muscular. Loins should be well muscled and not so short as to interfere with easy rhythmic movement and powerful drive of the back legs. Females may be slightly longer in back.

FOREQUARTERS: Front legs should be parallel and straight to the pasterns, elbows close to the body and turned neither in nor out. Pastern should be strong and flexible to add spring to movement. Length of leg should be proportioned to body size for a total even balance. Shoulder should have a 45 degree lay back and be firmly set. Front legs well feathered on back side. Dewclaws may be removed at the owner's option.

HINDQUARTERS: Upper thighs are well developed and muscled. Stifles approximately 30 degrees lay off the pelvis, hocks well let down and sharply defined. Hind legs should be parallel when viewed from the rear in a natural stance, they should turn neither in nor out. Dewclaws are objectionable on hind legs and should be removed for dogs own safety. The hind legs should be muscular and of adequate bone to blend with body size. The dog should not appear clumsy or racy.

FEET: Should be oval in shape, compact, well padded with hair. Pads should be tough and deeply cushioned. Feet should neither "toe in" or "out" in a normal stance.

TAIL: Should be set moderately high just below top line, covered with long, profuse hair and carried over the back, not necessarily centered, when alert and when moving. Sometimes dropped when at rest. The tail bone should come to hock when down. Tightly curled or double hook is a fault.

COAT: The body should be covered with soft, thick, short undercoat, with a longer, guard hair growing through it forming the outercoat, and should be free from any curl or wave. There should be a noticeably thicker mane covering the neck area, forming the ruff. Length of the outercoat will vary from dog to dog. Quality is more important than quantity.

COLOR: Most desirable is pure white. Permissible are white with biscuit cream or cream.

MOVEMENT: The American Eskimo should trot, not pace. They should have a quick, agile stride that is well timed. The gait should be free, balanced and vigorous, with good reach in forequarters and good driving power in the hindquarters; when trotting there should be a strong rear action drive. Moving at a walk or slow trot they will not single track, or brush, but as speed increases the legs gradually angle inward until the pads are finally falling on a line directly under the longitudinal center of the body. The back should remain strong, firm and level.

DISPOSITION: Intelligent, alert and energetic, loyal, friendly, but conservative. Overly aggressive and overly shy dogs are penalized.

SIZE: Miniature: Males 12" up to and including 15". Females 11" up to and including 14". Puppy class **only**: minimum height could be male 11" and female 10".

Standard: Males over 15" and up to and including 19". Females over 14" and up to and including 18".

FAULTS: Flop ears, pink or white eye rims, pink nose, pink lips, overshot or undershot bite, roach back, camel back, razor back, straight stifles, cowhocks, splay feet, double curl in tail, tightly curled tail, curly coat, stilted gait, crabbing, crossing over in front, hackney action.

DISQUALIFICATIONS: Any color other than white, biscuit or cream. Blue eyes. Any alterations of dog. Viciousness. Dogs that are cryptorchid or monorchid, deaf or blind.

SCALE OF POINTS

General Appearance	15
Movement	15
Head	10
Coat	10
Chest and Ribs	10
Forequarters	10
Hindquarters	10
Back	10
Feet/Legs	5
Tail	<u>5</u>
TOTAL POINTS	100

Chapter 12

American Kennel Club Official Breed Standard

General Appearance

The American Eskimo Dog, a loving companion dog, presents a picture of strength and agility, alertness and beauty. It is a small to medium-size Nordic type dog, always white, or white with biscuit cream. The American Eskimo Dog is compactly built and well balanced, with good substance, and an alert, smooth gait. The face is Nordic type with erect triangular shaped ears, and distinctive black points (lips, nose, and eye rims). The white double coat consists of a short, dense undercoat, with a longer guard hair growing through it forming the outer coat, which is straight with no curl or wave. The coat is thicker and longer around the neck and chest forming a lion-like ruff, which is more noticeable on dogs than on bitches. The rump and hind legs down to the hocks are also covered with thicker, longer hair forming the characteristic breeches. The richly plumed tail is carried loosely over the back.

Size, Proportion, Substance

Size. There are three separate size divisions of the American Eskimo Dog (all measurements are heights at withers): Toy, 9 inches to and including 12 inches; Miniature, over 12 inches to and including 15 inches; and Standard, over 15 inches to and including 19 inches. There is no preference for size within each division. Disqualification: Under 9 inches or over 19 inches. *Proportion.* Length of back from point of shoulder to point of buttocks is slightly greater than height at withers, an approximate 1.1 to 1 ratio. *Substance.* The American Eskimo Dog is strong and compactly built with adequate bone.

Head

Expression is keen, intelligent, and alert. *Eyes* are not fully round, but slightly oval. They should be set well apart and not slanted, prominent or bulging. Tear stain, unless severe, is not to be faulted. Presence of tear stain should not outweigh consideration of type, structure, or temperament. Eye rims are black to dark brown. Eyelashes are white. Faults: amber eye color or pink eye rims. Disqualification: blue eyes. *Ears* should conform to head size and be triangular, slightly blunt-tipped, held erect, set on high yet well apart, and blend softly with head. *Skull* is slightly crowned and softly wedge-shaped, with widest breadth between the ears. The stop is well defined, although not abrupt. The *muzzle* is broad, with length not exceeding the length of the skull, although it may be slightly shorter. *Nose* pigment is black to dark brown. *Lips* are thin and tight, black to dark brown in color. Faults: pink nose pigment or pink lip pigment. The *jaw* should be strong with a full complement of close fitting teeth. The *bite* is scissors, or pincer.

Neck, Topline, Body

The *neck* is carried proudly erect, well set on, medium in length, and in a strong, graceful arch. The *topline* is level. The *body* of the American Eskimo Dog is strong and compact, but not cobby. The chest is deep and broad with well-sprung ribs. Depth of chest extends approximately to point of elbows. Slight tuck-up of belly just behind the ribs. The back is straight, broad, level and muscular. The loin is strong and well-muscled. The American Eskimo Dog is neither too long nor too short coupled. The *tail* is set moderately high and reaches approximately to the point of hock when let down. It is carried loosely on the back, although it may be dropped when at rest.

Forequarters

Forequarters are well angulated. The shoulder is firmly set and has adequate muscle but is not overdeveloped.

The shoulder blades are well laid back and slant 45° with the horizontal. At the point of shoulder, the shoulder blade forms an approximate right angle with the upper arm. The legs are parallel and straight to the pasterns. The pasterns are strong and flexible with a slant of about 20°. Length of leg in proportion to the body. Dewclaws on the front legs may be removed at the owner's discretion; if present, they are not to be faulted. Feet are oval, compact, tightly knit and well padded with hair. Toes are well arched. Pads are black to dark brown, tough and deeply cushioned. Toenails are white.

Hindquarters

Hindquarters are well angulated. The lay of the pelvis is approximately 30° to the horizontal. The upper thighs are well developed. Stifles are well bent. Hock joints are well let down and firm. The rear pasterns are straight. Legs are parallel from the rear and turn neither in nor out. Feet are as described for the front legs. Dewclaws are not present on the hind legs.

Coat

The American Eskimo Dog has a stand-off, double coat consisting of a dense undercoat and a longer coat of guard hair growing through it to form the outer coat. It is straight with no curl or wave. There is a pronounced ruff around the neck which is more noticeable on dogs than bitches. Outer part of the ear should be well covered with short, smooth hair, with longer tufts of hair growing in front of ear openings. Hair on muzzle should be short and smooth. The backs of the front legs should be well feathered, as are the rear legs down to the hock. The tail is covered profusely with long hair. THERE IS TO BE NO TRIMMING OF THE WHISKERS OR BODY COAT AND SUCH TRIMMING WILL BE SEVERELY PENALIZED. The only permissible trimming is to neaten the feet and the backs of rear pasterns.

Color

Pure white is the preferred color, although white with biscuit cream is permissible. Presence of biscuit cream should not outweigh consideration of type, structure, or temperament. The skin of the American Eskimo Dog is pink or gray. Disqualification: any color other than white or biscuit cream.

Gait

The American Eskimo Dog shall trot, not pace. The gait is agile, bold, well balanced, and frictionless, with good forequarter reach and good hindquarter drive. As speed increases, the American Eskimo Dog will single track with the legs converging toward the center line of gravity while the back remains firm, strong and level.

Temperament

The American Eskimo Dog is intelligent, alert, and friendly, although slightly conservative. It is never overly shy nor aggressive, and such dogs are to be severely penalized in the show ring. At home it is an excellent watchdog, sounding a warning bark to announce the arrival of any stranger. It is protective of its home and family, although it does not threaten to bite or attack people. The American Eskimo Dog learns new tasks quickly and is eager to please.

Disqualifications

Any color other than white or biscuit cream
Blue eyes
Height: under 9" or over 19"

Chapter 13

Reflections on the Breed Standard

During the years that I have been involved with the American Eskimo, great changes have taken place. When I obtained my first dog, in 1971, the Eskie was a dying breed. Bred for many years, solely as a pet, little attention had been paid to conformational considerations. A small band of dedicated followers had, only two years before, formed the first truly national club for the breed. Slowly, those of us who fell in love with the Eskie's many charms began to learn as much as we could about the breed, the bloodlines that were available and what qualities a good American Eskimo should possess. We showed our dogs, carefully planned our breeding programs and sought to improve the breed while maintaining its essential strengths.

The past decade has seen many changes for the breed. The Eskie has dramatically increased in popularity, attracting numerous new exhibitors and breeders. This upward trend is certain to continue now that the AKC has recognized the breed. I believe that the American Eskimo now stands poised on a great precipice. As the Eskie becomes better known, it seems logical that many more newcomers will be attracted to the breed. Some will have had experience in other breeds. One can only hope that they will become sincere and dedicated breeders and that the Eskie will not fall victim to the fads that have damaged so many other breeds of dogs. The Eskie must remain the same as he has always been. He is not a "designer dog," to be changed by whim or fashion. He is, most emphatically, not a scaled down Samoyed, a white Keeshond or a white Pomeranian. Let us hope that all breeders, novice and veteran alike, never lose sight of this.

In this chapter, I would like to share my views on the breed standard. Both the AKC and UKC standards for the Eskie go into a great amount of detail and I have no desire to merely rehash material which is covered elsewhere. Instead, I'll try to explain some of the points, emphasizing those that I consider particularly important. I would also like to address questions that I am frequently asked by those who are new to the breed. I hope, in this way, to give newcomers a picture of how most Eskie puppies grow and develop. *(See chapter 24 for more on this.)*

I make no claim to being an absolute authority on the American Eskimo. Some will agree with my views and others will take exception to them. That's fine with me. In my view, such divergences of opinion are healthy and the discussions that they provoke are learning opportunities for all of us.

THE TOTAL DOG

I firmly believe that all breeders should strive for what I call the "total dog." In the show world, it's often easy to get caught up in breeding for glorious coats, eye-catching heads and magnificent movement. Yet, we should all remember that the Eskie is more than a combination of purely physical attributes. Since the earliest times, Spitz dogs have been valued for their companionship and devotion to their owners and homes. They have been reliable and trustworthy, as well as entertaining and fun to be around. We, as guardians of the breed, must ensure that these traits are perpetuated and bred for, just as surely as we breed for white coats and properly carried tails.

In my view, a snarling, snapping, aggressive Eskie, no matter how beautiful, can never be a superb example of the breed. Likewise, a cringing, slinking, cowardly dog can never fulfill the watchdog duties which are an essential part of the Spitz heritage. In our quest for physical perfection, we can never lose sight of the importance of these qualities. We must not tell ourselves that we will accept undesirable temperament now and "breed up," in future generations, to improve it. No matter how successful our breeding program, most of our puppies will undoubtedly go to pet homes. We owe the general public, as well as the American

Eskimo itself, an obligation to breed only mentally sound dogs. If your Eskie flunks the temperament test, don't breed him!

Our breed has always been known for its vitality and good health. "Hale and hardy" are words often associated with this breed. We are fortunate that the Eskie does not suffer from the myriad of health problems seen in so many other breeds. Generally speaking, American Eskimo puppies are strong and easy to raise. As adults, Eskies often live to ripe old ages with few health problems. In my opinion, it's the obligation of breeders to continue this long-standing tradition. Dogs who suffer from heritable diseases should not be bred and those that lack the vitality and robust good health, which typify this breed, should be excluded from breeding programs. It may seem like a sacrifice in the short-term, but the long range benefits to the breed are just too significant for compromise.

Novices often obtain their first show dog, read the standard carefully and begin attending shows. Typically, they discuss the standard with other breeders, eager for any information they can get. They are likely to hear many divergent opinions, for breeders often stress different points in their breeding programs. Soon, they will be able to pick out faults and will begin fault judging the dogs they see. This is all a valuable part of the learning process. While it's quite easy to spot faults, it sometimes takes longer to be able to properly assess virtues. The dog with the least faults is not necessarily the most outstanding specimen of the breed. I've seen many novices who fall victim to simple fault judging and build their breeding programs around it. They select a stud to breed to in hopes of eradicating a single fault. They may well succeed but, in the meantime, they have introduced other problems. By all means, breed to compensate for faults, selecting not only an individual dog, but a whole line which is strong in this point. But, in doing so, search for an outstanding example of the breed—one who glowingly exhibits many virtues that you admire. It may take longer to find such a dog, but if you keep your eye on the "total dog," you'll have more success in your breeding program.

THE ESSENTIAL ESKIE

The word "type" is often bandied about among breeders and can be confusing to novices. This is because the word is used in several different ways. First and foremost, it refers to overall *breed type,* i.e., the qualities that typify the entire breed and distinguish it from any other. *The Complete Dog Book* says, further, that "type" is "the embodiment of a standard's essence."

We often hear that Eskies are *Spitz type* dogs. Dogs of this general type are characterized by upright ears and tails which curl over the back. This category

An outstanding Samoyed Am., Mex., Can. Ch. Silveracres Special Edition, owned by Ann Hamlin, Alta Kennels. *Ludwig photo*

Gr. Ch. 'PR' Stevens' Max-A-Million, owned by Kathy Cella. *Mitchell photo*

Though both breeds share certain similarities, there are distinctive type differences which differentiate the two breeds. The Sammy is a larger dog with heavier bone, a blockier head, a wider muzzle and a distinctly almond-shaped eye. The Eskie appears "foxier" in appearance with a livelier, constantly alert look.

includes the American Eskimo's close relatives—the German Spitz, the Keeshond, the Japanese Spitz, and the Volpino Italiano. It also includes such breeds as the Alaskan Malamute, Siberian Husky, Finnish Spitz, Akita, Shiba Inu, Karelian Bear Dog and many breeds which are rare in this country. Some authors include the Welsh Corgis, Basenji and the uncommon Telomian among this group, too.

You will also hear breeders talk about type in relation to *types within the breed*. This is most likely to occur during a discussion of Eskie heads. You will hear that some breeders prefer a *bear type*, while others like a *foxy type*. Years ago, one would occasionally see what was called a *wolf type*. It was not preferred then and has disappeared from the breed today. You may also hear breeders say that dogs are of a *Sammy type*, referring to the Samoyed breed.

Sometimes you will hear about *line types*. These are essentially bloodlines, or strains, within the breed. Thus, the person at ringside may say that such and such a dog is characteristic of my "Country line" or some other bloodline.

Breeders will, at times, have a discussion about *type versus movement*. This is a debate which takes place in many breeds. Some argue that excellent movement should take precedence over breed type and vice versa. I do not consider this an appropriate discussion. In my view, one of the essential properties of an American Eskimo is the breed's wonderful movement. Without sound movement, I consider an Eskie lacking in overall breed type.

Since the days when the first standard was written, Eskie breeders have taken particular pains to make sure that this document spells out what an American Eskimo should look like and how it differs from other breeds. This is particularly true in the case of the Samoyed. Those unfamiliar with the breed are often apt to think of the American Eskimo as simply a smaller version of this more popular dog. One early book on the Eskie goes so far as to claim that the breed is descended from the Samoyed. Nothing could be further from the truth. It's true that both breeds are white in color, have a "smiling" appearance, similar amounts of coat and tails which turn over the back. Yet, as you will learn, there are very many differences between the two breeds. The Eskie is typified by a "foxy," light and lively look, while the Samoyed is a larger, heavier and coarser dog, in comparison. The "foxy" look is an essential breed characteristic, which should never be forgotten. Those who are familiar with both breeds will also note a very big difference in the temperaments of the two breeds.

In recent years, there has been a movement to establish a line of Toy American Eskimos. The breeding

Nat. Gr. Ch. Gr. Ch. 'PR' Stevens' Diamond Sparkle, owned by Lynda Gagnon, demonstrates perfect balance and proportion.

of a toy version of the breed has been a highly contentious subject among Eskie breeders. Breeders of Toy Eskies must concentrate on reducing size while still maintaining the essential qualities of the breed. We must be certain that Toy Eskies are not mistaken for white Pomeranians. Breeding top quality Toy Eskies has proven to be quite a challenge as, when reducing size, we are apt to alter other breed characteristics and introduce new problems. Breeders of Toys should always keep in mind that their goal should be to produce exact replicas of the larger American Eskimo.

We should always remember that our first allegiance should be to preserving *breed type*. We must not jump on the latest bandwagon simply because it's fashionable. It's tempting to go along with judges who may be putting up heavily boned dogs, those of a certain size or a particular head type. After all, everyone likes to win. Yet, if we study the standard, learn about the breed's history and keep our eye on *essential breed type*, we will be helping to preserve the very qualities that make the American Eskimo the breed it is. We should all strive to breed dogs which are "the embodiment of the standard's essentials."

PROPORTION AND BALANCE

Anyone who reads the American Eskimo standards will quickly run into the words "proportioned" and "balanced." Everything about the Eskie is in proportion. He is a very natural dog, a study in moderation. American Eskimos lack the exaggeration seen in so many other breeds. A good Eskie is a symmetrical dog. Each part flows harmoniously and smoothly into the whole. Each individual part of the body is perfectly balanced with every other part. Thus,

Always look for proper balance and proportion when selecting puppies. This beauty is sired by Gr. Ch. 'PR' Shamroc's Mystic Rythm and out of Gr. Ch. 'PR' Shamroc's Jasmin Nytesong, owned by Brenda O'Sullivan.

an Eskie should have a head which is balanced with the size of his body. The proportions of the head itself—the breadth and length of the skull and muzzle, the size of the eyes and ears—should be in proportion, too. The length of the dog, from the shoulders to the rump, as well as the height from the shoulders to the ground and the size of the dog's bone should all be considered when assessing balance and proportion. This call for proper proportion is meant to guard against dogs who appear, on the one hand, coarse and clumsy, or, conversely, leggy or racy. Moderation, proportion and balance are always preferred over extremes.

Don't let the Eskie's thick, profuse coat interfere with your assessment of his proportion and balance. Use your hands to feel what's under the coat. For an experienced breeder or judge, his hands often become his eyes when evaluating a dog. Don't miss the opportunity to take a long look at your dog's conformation after you have bathed him and before he has been blown dry. Those shoulders that disappear beneath the heavy ruff, will now be easy to see. The ears, neck, chest, topline and underline will now be revealed to you in detail. You will quickly be able to determine the amount of bone your dog really has, now that the hair is wet. You will gain an appreciation of the terms balance and proportion.

HEAD

A good head is a pleasure to behold. It is a particularly important breed characteristic for it does much to stamp the dog as an American Eskimo. I like to see a powerful, wedge-shaped head with a broad, slightly crowned skull that conforms proportionately to the size of the body. Nothing can beat a happy, alert, bright-eyed, smiling Eskie. He simply radiates happiness, beauty and a zest for life. When you see a good Eskie head, you won't be able to resist the temptation to smile. In his characteristic fashion, he holds his head up, with a proud expression which says, "Hey, look at me, I'm king of the mountain."

Overall, heads have improved in the past twenty-five years. This is particularly true for Miniatures. Much improvement is still needed in Toy Eskies which are sometimes "apple-headed." With this fault, the skull is overly rounded and, often, the stop is too abrupt. The muzzle may also appear either too short or snipey.

Bring up the subject of the head types found in the Eskie, and you're sure to get a lively discussion going. There are foxy-type heads, bear-types and a type that is midway between the two. It's difficult to get breeders to agree on what constitutes each type—everyone has a different opinion! Regardless of the type you prefer, you should still see the bright-eyed, smiling, happy look which is so much a part of the breed. There is also a "Sammy"-type which most breeders shun. This is characterized by a large head, with a broad skull, definite almond-shaped eye and blocky muzzle.

You should beware that the interpretation of head type is often in the eye of the beholder. What one person considers a "foxy" type, may be another

It's hard to resist the appeal of an outstanding American Eskimo head as modeled by Nat. Gr. Ch. Gr. Ch. 'PR' Stevens' Toybear Apollo, owned by Rosemary Stevens.

EARS: Triangular, slightly rounded at tips, held erect, conform to head size. Short, smooth hair on outer ears; longer tufts in front of ear openings

SKULL: Broad, slightly crowned

EYES: Slightly oval, black to brown

STOP: Well-defined, not abrupt

MUZZLE: Medium length

NOSE: Black to dark brown

TEETH & JAW: Level to scissors bite; strong jaw

LIPS: Black to dark brown

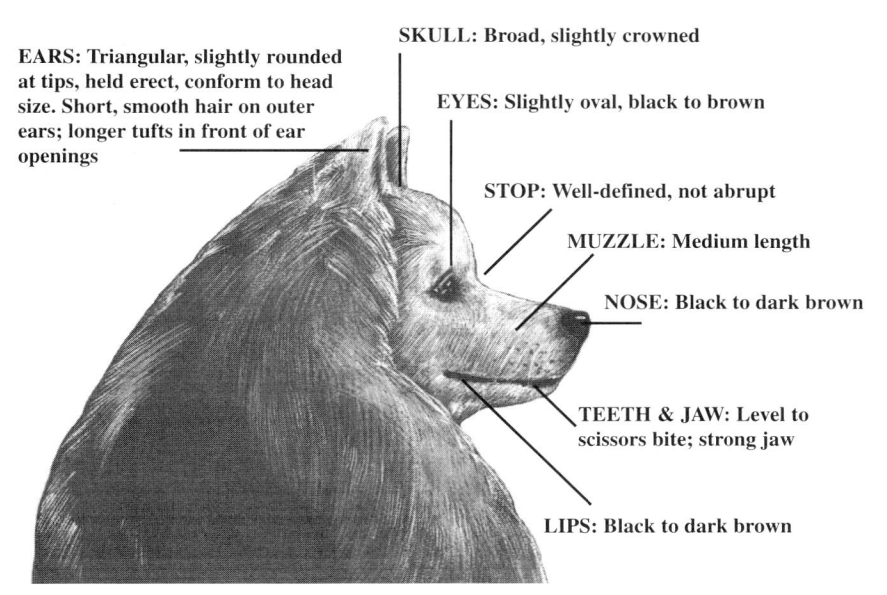

Linda Voight drawing

breeder's "bear" type. I once had a man who called me explicitly requesting a "bear" look. When he arrived, he selected a puppy that was just what he wanted. I considered the dog a "foxy" type.

Males usually have more impressive heads than females. Female heads are generally smaller and not as wide. They are apt to be a bit smaller, less wide and more refined. Most breeders die for a "doggy bitch," who has the same impressive head found on the male. The converse is not true. A bitchy looking male is shunned by most breeders and stands little chance in the show ring.

In assessing Eskie heads, it's important to keep in mind the age of the dog. Most American Eskimos, particularly Standards, don't finish fully developing until they are two or three years of age. Puppies go through a variety of stages, which breeders commonly call the "uglies," until they reach maturity. We generally say, during this time period, that Eskies are all nose, ears and legs. During this phase, your dog's head may appear narrow, long, and out of proportion to his body. You will be quite surprised at how it will correct once the dog matures.

One occasionally sees Eskies with overly wide heads. Generally, this is coupled with a too short neck so that the head appears to rest on the shoulders. This destroys the balanced look that we strive for in the breed.

Conversely, we occasionally see "Collie" heads, in which the dog has a long, narrow head. Often, heads of this type will also have only a slight, or no, stop. Such heads are always disproportionate to the rest of the body. Before labeling a dog as having a "Collie" head, though, be sure to consider the dog's age. Sometimes, this is just a growth phase, seen in the "teenage" years, and will improve with maturity.

Skull

The Eskie has a moderately wide skull with a slight crown. The crown is sometimes referred to as the "topskull." Oftentimes, due to a heavy growth of hair, the crown may appear flat. It is, however, easy to feel for the crown. Place the dog so he is facing you. Beginning at the stop, run your fingers toward the back of the head. You'll be able to feel the crown. You can also usually see it when you view the dog in profile.

Stop

The stop is the indentation, near the eyes, where the skull and the nasal bone meet. The proper Eskie stop is well defined, but not abrupt. An incorrect stop does much to mar the appearance of an Eskie. One will sometimes see a sharper stop in Miniatures and this is a common fault found in Toys.

It can be difficult to judge the stop on a puppy. As the head is developing, young Eskies often seem to have insufficient stop, yet, when mature, this often corrects itself and blends beautifully with the rest of the head.

Most breeders die for a "doggy bitch," who has the same impressive head, bone and coat found on a male. Such girls can beat the males at their own game. This is impressive Gr. Ch. 'PR' Shamroc's Jasmin Nytesong, owned by Brenda O'Sullivan.

This photo of Ch. 'PR' Stevens' Diamond Mystique, owned by Lynda Gagnon, clearly shows the wedge shape of the head.

At about three months of age, many Eskies start to get what we call a "puppy mask." They have longer hair on the forehead and this gives the impression of a predominant stop. Don't be misled by this illusion. Occasionally, one sees an adult dog who continues to carry this longer hair and you will have to feel to determine the degree of stop. Cup the Eskie's head in the palm of your hand. Take your two thumbs and run it over the stop, smoothing the fur back over the forehead. By doing this, you'll be able to properly assess the degree of stop.

Muzzle

The muzzle is the portion of the dog's head that extends in front of the eyes. This consists of the nostrils, nasal bone and the jaws. The ideal Eskie muzzle is neither too long, nor too short. The jaws should be strong. The lips should fit tightly and be black to dark brown in color. Personally, I like to see black lips. Pink lips are, in my opinion, a serious fault.

This four-month-old puppy clearly shows the "masking" effect.

A good head study of a Miniature. This is AKC Ch. & Gr. Ch. 'PR' Starlight's Karuk Star, owned by Donna Hays.

Thankfully, we do not see many muzzle faults in the Eskie. Snipey muzzles, those that are long, thin and weak, are a rarity. Breeders of Toys must guard against a too short muzzle. Saggy flews are mentioned in the breed standards, but not often seen in the show ring.

Ears

The ears should conform to the size of the head, being neither too large nor too small. Too be honest, I have never seen ears that are too small, though I have seen some that were too large. Most breeders would probably like to have smaller ears. In some bloodlines, one will find larger ears, but as long as they are still proportionate they fit the standard.

Gr. Ch. 'PR' Sterling Lakota Morningstar, owned by Rosemary Reseigh, has a distinctly feminine look.

A lovely head study of a male. This is Nat. Gr. Ch. Gr. Ch. 'PR' McKee's King Jacob, owned by Gordon and Dottie Peterson. *Olan Mills photo*

Proper ear set is very important to the appearance of the American Eskimo. We sometimes see ears that are set too close together. A far more common fault, however, is low ear set and this mars the dog's entire appearance. For me, this totally detracts from the true Eskie look. I can recall seeing a dog whose ears were set almost at the jaw line. "Bat ears," in which the ears extend out at an odd angle, are extremely objectionable, too. Low ear set is a fault that all breeders should certainly watch out for.

The amount of hair an Eskie has around the ears can contribute greatly to the appearance of ear size. Eskies have longer tufts of hair in front of the ear opening. They may also be heavily furred in back of and around the ear. Dogs who don't carry a lot of fur, often appear to have larger ears. In some bloodlines, the hair around the ear is thinner and tends to lie flatter. Such dogs often give the appearance of larger ears.

On the other hand, dogs with a wealth of fur often appear to have smaller ears. Try giving this smaller eared dog a bath, though, and the truth will come out. You'll be surprised at how large the ears really are and how much of a difference in illusion the hair makes. Those glorious puppy coats often carry a plethora of fur around the ears. This will take care of itself when the adult coat comes in.

The stage at which a puppy's ears come up

Some puppies, like little future Gr. Ch. 'PR' Stevens' Daisy Mae, carry a great deal of hair around the ears.

The amount of hair surrounding the ears can make them appear smaller, as demonstrated by Ch. 'PR' Stevens' Snow Queen, owned by Rosemary Stevens.

varies considerably. Generally, the ears come up on smaller dogs, such as Miniatures and Toys, sooner than on the larger Standards. The average age at which ears become erect is eight weeks to four months of age. I have known ears to take a full year to come up, but this is a rarity. If a dog's ears aren't up by six months of age, I, personally, would not breed the dog. Ears are such an integral part of the Eskie look, that I wouldn't want to introduce this problem into my breeding program.

The age at which the ear comes up depends on the skin and the strength of the ear. Run your hand over the ear to determine if the skin is thick and the cartilage is strong. Such ears usually have little trouble coming up. Dogs who have paper thin skin may have difficulty getting their ears up. Some puppies carry so much fur that it temporarily weights down the ears and takes them longer to come up.

Even within the same litter, ears come up at different times. One pup's ears are up, another has one ear up and one down and the third has both ears down. These sisters are 'PR' Aurora Razz-A-Ma-Taz, Lee-A and Kandi, bred by Ann DeTavernier.

A grown dog with flop ears. Though it mars the true Eskie look, this dog is a much loved pet.

The ears often go up and down during the teething process, at about four months. During this period, the dog is under stress. It's not unusual for both ears not to come up at the same time. One may be securely erect, while the other tips over at half-mast. The fallen ear usually comes up sooner or later but, in the meantime, it gives the Eskie puppy a comical appearance.

Flop ears are listed in the UKC standard as a "fault." In my view, they should be listed as a disqualification for they destroy the whole look of the breed. Dogs whose ears do not come up should, in my opinion, not be bred.

Eyes

Proper eye shape is extremely important to the Eskie look. It contributes mightily to that unique Eskie expression...that certain indefinable look that makes the breed endearing to us all. A dog with proper eye shape looks keen and alert and, at the same time, loving and gentle.

Both the AKC and UKC standards call for the eye shape to be "slightly oval." Some people believe that there is little difference between this slightly oval eye and the almond eye. To me, however, the slightly oval eye

As Eskies mature, they often go through a stage where they appear to be "all ears." This is five-month-old 'PR' Stevens' Bronco Billy, owned by Lisa Castelan.

is midway between the round and the almond eye. The Samoyed has a definite almond-shaped eye and this is one of the points that distinguishes the Eskie from that breed.

Some almond shaped eyes can become extremely slanty looking and this is something that should be avoided in the American Eskimo. Eyes that are too slanted lose the sparkle and the kind, laughing look that we expect to see in the breed. This can be very distracting. In the extreme, the overly almond shaped eye can have a squinty look that is totally inappropriate for the American Eskimo.

Proper Eskie eyes should not be fully round, nor should they be prominent or bulging. While seldom a problem in Standards, both Miniatures and Toys are apt to have rounder eyes. Prominent eyes are sometimes seen in Toys. Again, breeders should take care to ensure that the correct eye shape is maintained.

I must confess to being very concerned about the eye color that I see in today's Eskies. I've been harping on this for many years and it's a subject I feel very strongly about. To me, the American Eskimo is a pure white dog with eyes which appear to be coal black.

Both the AKC and UKC standards call for dark to medium brown eye color. Neither description is

The correct Eskie eye is "slightly oval," or midway between almond and round shaped. This is Ch. 'PR' Ann D's Mandolin, owned by Ann DeTavernier.

entirely pleasing to me. In my view, Eskie eyes should be *dark in color*. In fact, *the darker the better.*

One needs only to look at the German Spitz for guidance. Their standard calls for extremely dark brown eyes which appear black. Medium or light brown eye color is considered a fault and should be penalized severely.

I would like to see American Eskimo breeders adopt such a policy, too. Twenty-five years ago, when I began with the breed, very dark eyes were the norm. In recent years, we have seen a dramatic rise in the number of dogs with medium brown eyes. To me, this distracts from the Eskie look and I hope all breeders will pay close attention to this.

Amber colored eyes are a fault and dogs possessing them should not be bred. Blue eyes are a disqualification and should never be tolerated.

Along with eye color, I am also concerned about the eye rim pigmentation that I have begun to see. The American Eskimo is often referred to as a "white dog with black points." The black points refers to the pigmentation on the nose, lips and eye rims. The Eskie's eyes are one of the breed's most endearing features and they are set off by the pigmentation of the eye rims. Again, this is a quality that was better years ago and seems to have become altered today. One can only hope that this trend will not continue and that breeders will take note of its importance.

I have seen dogs with very black eye rims in which the pigment was 2/8 to 3/8 inch thick around the eyes. Such a look is strikingly beautiful and enhances the kind, gentle expression typical of the breed. Lately, we have begun to see dogs with less defined eye rims, giving the impression of being outlined by a thin eyeliner. I have also seen dogs who appear to have only a very thin pencil line. To be honest, I'm not sure why this is occurring, but I do hope breeders will take note of it and correct it before it's too late.

Some puppies are born with fully pigmented eye rims...a cause for rejoicing among breeders. They are also overjoyed when the pigmentation comes in right away on a whole litter. Dogs with pink or white eye rims or those with splotched color should be spayed or neutered and sold as pets. This is hereditary and such dogs should never be bred.

Dark eye rims are essential to the Eskie look. Note the pronounced black eyerims on the famous Gr. Ch. 'PR' Hofman's Country Diamond.

Both American Eskimo standards say that eyelashes should be white. For the life of me, I could never understand why this was included in the standard. I've never seen eyelashes of any color other than white! Still, it is an appealing feature of the breed and people will often comment on how beautiful those white eyelashes are.

Some American Eskimos have problems with eye, or tear, stain. Many breeders and judges consider the presence of eye stain to be very unsightly. The UKC standard for the breed makes no mention of eye stain,

Nat. Gr. Ch. Gr. Ch. U-CDX 'PR' Thunderpas Mighty Max, owned by Talitha Bell, has lovely dark eyes of the proper shape.

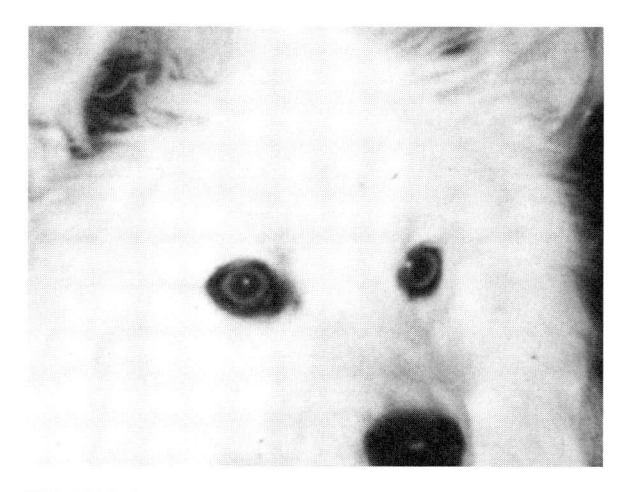

This Eskie has a lovely head, but the eyes are lighter in color than is desirable.

At 23 days, these puppies already have dark eye rims.

while the AKC standard says that "Tear stain, unless severe, is not to be faulted. Presence of tear stain should not outweigh consideration of type, structure or temperament."

In the chapter on Grooming Your American Eskimo, I'll discuss some of the medical reasons for eye stain as well as strategies for coping with it. Here, I would like to address the possible conformational reasons for which it occurs. Eye stain is sometimes seen in dogs with too round shaped eyes. In such instances, the lower eye rim may be more loosely attached making the eye more prone to watering and stain. Breeding for the proper eye shape, therefore, should be a consideration for all breeders.

Noses

Both standards specify that the Eskie nose should be black to dark brown. As far as I am concerned, the blacker the nose the better. One often sees brown noses on dogs with medium or lighter colored eyes. It goes without saying that Eskies should never have a pink nose. Years ago, I did see the rare pink or liver-colored nose, something which should never occur in Eskies. I have seen some dogs, purchased from pet shops, who had speckled noses. Such dogs are definitely pet quality and should never be bred.

Some confusion has arisen from the wording of the UKC standard for the breed. It specifies that the "leather is black to dark brown." The inclusion of the word "leather" is often confusing to novices and I am frequently asked about its meaning. "Leather" includes only the nose, not the skin just above the nose. The skin does not have to be black. Many Eskies have white or pink splotches here and they are in conformance with the standard. Some breeders don't like it and feel that it detracts from the look of the dog. Yet, as long as the nose itself (the "leather," if you will) is black, this coloring doesn't really matter.

When selecting a puppy, the rule of thumb should be: the blacker the nose, the better. Puppy noses may acquire pigmentation immediately or it may take

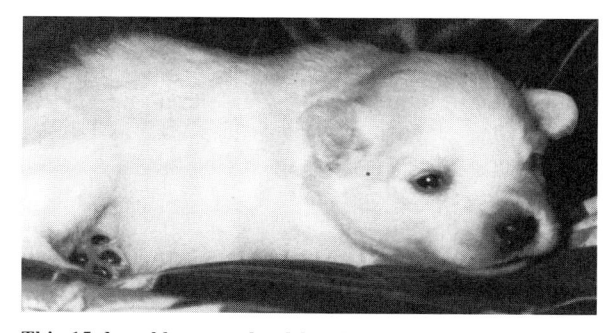

This 15-day-old puppy, bred by Kathy Cella, will have good pigmentation. Note the black nose and pads and the grey tinge on the eyerims.

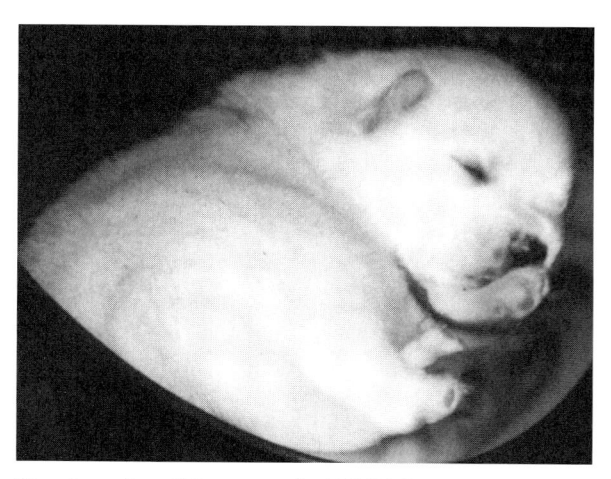

The pigment on little two-week-old 'PR' Star's White Wolf of Karuk, owned by Sherley Tooker, is already "running," or filling in. His nose will soon be black.

a week or two to fill in. Sometimes it takes longer. I like to see the pigmentation "running," that is the color continuing to move, even if just the slightest bit, every day. I like to see puppy noses fully pigmented by four months of age. In fact, the faster the color comes in, the better.

Because I think that black nose color is essential to the American Eskimo, I feel it should figure into breeding considerations. While dogs with splotched or pink noses should never be bred, I am also hesitant to breed dogs who were very slow to gain full nose pigmentation. If the dog is truly outstanding, in all other respects, I would make sure to select a mate with extremely black pigmentation, who exhibited color at a very early age.

The roof of the Eskie's mouth may be black, gray or pink in color. This really makes no difference. Some dogs are so heavily pigmented that it shows as black on the roof of the mouth. The tongue is pink. Healthy gums are a bright pink.

Sometimes Eskie's will develop what is called a "snow nose." This is not a pink nose, but a dark nose in which the pigmentation has temporarily lightened. You can usually tell a snow nose from a pink nose because black pigmentation remains around the base of the nose. Sometimes the eye rims will also be affected. Some bloodlines seem to be more prone to snow nose than others.

Snow noses can occur due to a variety of reasons. Weather is often at fault. Snow noses are often seen during periods of stress. Females typically get snow noses when they are in season or when they have puppies. Males often develop snow nose when a female is in season. Eskies with allergies or those who aren't feeling well are also apt to acquire snow noses. Dogs who enjoy digging may develop snow nose, too. It was hard for me to accept that loss of pigmentation could be the result of feeding and watering your dog from plastic dishes. I have, however, seen this for myself on several occasions. If your dog has difficulty with snow nose, it's best to use metal bowls.

Cases of snow nose can be very frustrating to show ring exhibitors. While the Siberian Husky standard makes allowances for snow nose, it is not mentioned in the Eskie standard and, so, has sometimes been penalized in the ring. I once had a dog shipped to me for showing. He arrived with a pink nose. It wasn't dark brown, it was pink and the shows were only a week away. I quickly phoned his owners. They couldn't believe it as the nose had been black when the dog left home. In three days, the dog's pigmentation was back to normal. He had a jet black nose and took Best of Show at both of the events in which he was entered. His snow nose had been caused by stress.

The impressive Gr. Ch. U-CDX 'PR' Thunderpas Sthrn Style, owned by Talitha Bell, has a temporary case of snow nose. It's easy to tell a snow nose from a light nose by looking at the base of the nose. You can clearly see that the base of this dog's nose is distinctly black.

Sadly, the stress of traveling to shows can often cause the onset of snow nose. I once had a judge disregard a dog solely because there was pink on the *inside* of his nose. We had been traveling for two days and this was a manifestation of stress. Within two hours, the inside of the dog's nose was back to its normal black. I showed the judge what could happen and he never again looked up a dog's nose when making a decision!

Bites

The AKC standard for the breed calls for a "scissors, or pincer" bite. According to *The Complete Dog Book,* "pincer" is another name for a "level" bite. The UKC standard calls for a "level to scissors bite." In a scissors bite, the outer side of the lower teeth touch the inner side of the upper teeth. This makes for the strongest bite possible. In a level bite, both upper and lower teeth meet edge to edge. Because the teeth do not mesh together strongly, this is a somewhat weaker bite. Dogs with level bites are also apt to have wearing away of the teeth as they age.

The scissors bite is the one most commonly seen on American Eskimos. In my view, it is the only correct bite. I have spoken with some judges who report that they are beginning to see a bite problem in the breed. Personally, I think the situation would improve if we would eliminate the call for a level bite in the breed standards.

I would be very hesitant to select a show puppy

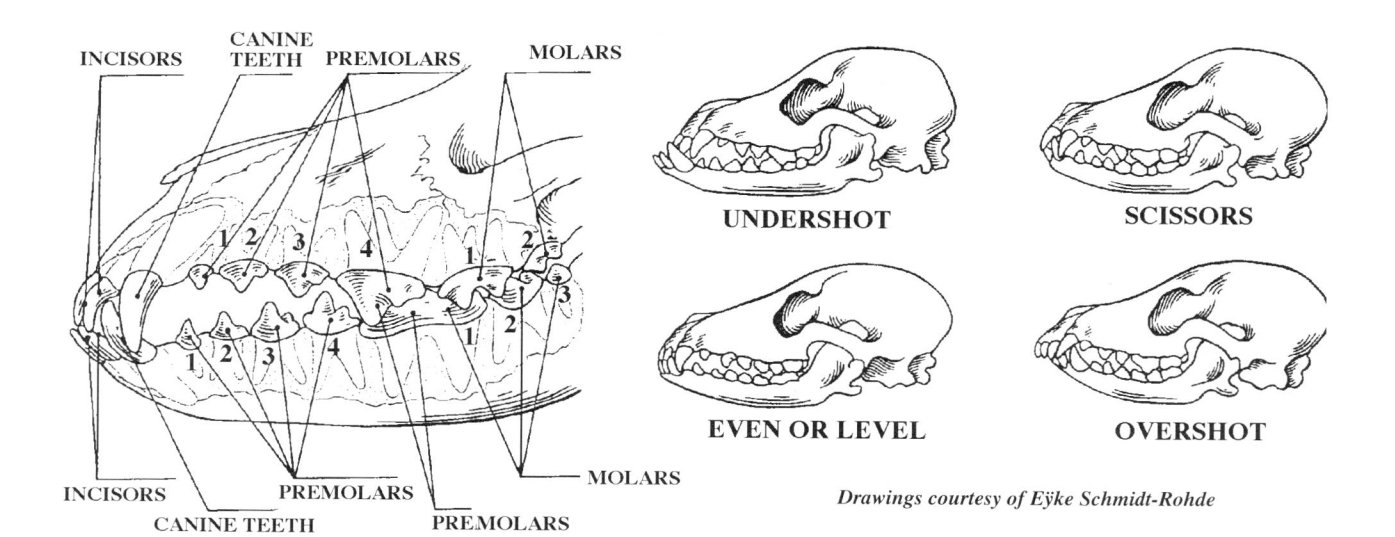

Drawings courtesy of Eÿke Schmidt-Rohde

with a level bite. I'd be afraid that this could develop into either an over or undershot bite. Like all breeders, I've seen puppies with marginal bites correct and turn out well. Naturally, I've also seen the reverse happen. Since the lower jaw often grows at a faster rate than the upper jaw, there have been instances when a puppy with an overshot bite develops a correct bite as it matures. Still, I would err on the side of caution and select a puppy with a scissors bite. The best time for assessing a bite in a puppy is when the second teeth come in. Like all breeders, I pray when placing a show puppy in a new home, even though I have never had a bad bite. While it doesn't happen often, it can be frustrating to see a good bite go wrong.

Bad bites can be more of a problem in Toy Eskies and, therefore, bear close watching. Breeding down in size can cause problems and, as we all know, many of the toy breeds have bite problems. Double rows of teeth can sometimes occur in other toy breeds and should be watched for. Toy breeders should be especially vigilant with regard to bites.

Bad bites are, of course, hereditary. Dogs with bad bites should not be bred. They should be spayed or neutered and placed in pet homes.

BODY

The American Eskimo is basically a square dog. The UKC standard says that the "length from point of the shoulder to the root of the tail should equal the height from the pad to the top of the withers." The AKC standard states that the length "from the point of shoulder to point of buttocks is slightly greater than height at the withers, an approximate 1.1 to 1 ratio." Either description conjures up the image of a square dog.

In my view, correct proportion should be carefully guarded. Both standards tell us that American Eskimos should have both strength and agility. Correct proportion is essential to achieving this dual commandment. Dogs with too much leg can appear racy, while those with short legs often give the impression of being clumsy. Likewise, dogs who are too short-bodied often appear overly chunky, a look which is totally inappropriate for the breed. Long-bodied dogs cannot fulfill the standard's call for a "compact" look.

In evaluating your Eskie's body proportions, it is important to consider both the dog's age and the amount of coat he carries. Remember, Standard sized Eskies don't mature until they are two to three years of age (usually closer to three years). Miniatures and Toys mature earlier. Dogs of all sizes can look slightly longer as they go through the maturation process.

The American Eskimo is a square dog, as Ch. 'PR' Jan's Diamond Lil, owned by Jan Palmer, clearly shows.

American Eskimos, of any

Miniatures mature more quickly than Standard-sized Eskies. Ch. 'PR' Shamroc Snofr Lil Bit O'Magic, owned by Charles and Linda Cummings, appears together though he is only nine months of age.

age, can appear short-legged if they carry a profuse coat. Do not be misled by this illusion. Feel under that coat to determine the actual leg length. Better yet, wet the dog down so you can actually see leg length and proportion. You will often be surprised to discover that the dog who appears short-legged is actually well-balanced.

Again, Eskies are basically square dogs and should neither be too long nor too short. The AKC standard says that the American Eskimo should not be "too cobby," meaning too short-bodied. This is not a fault we commonly see in the breed.

Long-bodied Eskies are also incorrect. We seldom see males who are long in body, but it is apt to occur in females. Indeed, the UKC standard says that females "may be slightly longer in the back." This statement has allowed Eskie breeders to excuse greater length in bitches. Often they will tell you it's the sign of a good brood bitch. Personally, I would like to see bitches held to the same standards as dogs with regard to length. After all, the American Eskimo is basically a square dog. I freely admit that my first Eskie, beautiful in every other way, was too long in body.

Many breed standards, in past years, allowed longer bodied bitches under the rationale that they would have room to carry more puppies. Males were the dominant forces in the show ring and were shown more often than bitches. Regrettably, it still takes a truly outstanding bitch (often a "doggy bitch") to capture top honors. Lesser males are often placed over better bitches. In the past 25 years, though, we have seen a change. Breeders are placing much more emphasis on producing good show bitches. Therefore, we should, in my opinion, hold bitches to the same high standards we use for males. It's easy to say that we will allow longer bodies on bitches, but we must remember that they contribute 50% of the genes in any breeding. There's no guarantee that that longer back won't show up in males, as well as females.

Bone

Many people ask what amount of bone an American Eskimo should have. The standards are largely silent on this issue. The AKC standard states that the breed should have "adequate bone." The UKC standard addresses the subject only under "hind legs," which it also says should have "adequate bone." For the confused novice, this does not provide much guidance.

I firmly believe that both breed standards should state that the Eskie has "moderate" bone. I'm afraid that the use of the word "adequate" may convey a false impression. Like almost all of the Spitz breeds (the Chow is an obvious exception), the American Eskimo is a study in moderation. Bone should not be so slight as to give a spindly-legged appearance. Neither should it be so heavy that the dog appears clumsy.

You will see a variation in bone size in American Eskimo bloodlines. In the show ring, we occasionally see dogs who are simply too light in bone. This detracts greatly from the overall appearance. In recent years, I've begun to see a growing number of dogs who are overly boned. This is incorrect for the breed. The UKC standard tells us that the breed should move with a "quick agile stride." The AKC standard also stresses agility. This is lost in heavily boned specimens.

As with length of leg, one must also take coat

The Eskie should have moderate bone. This Miniature male is Ch. 'PR' Snobird's Anchor Man, owned by Judy Jones.

into consideration when assessing degree of bone. Some dogs carry tremendous coats and the legs can be very thickly coated. Often, in show grooming, the hair on the leg is brushed up which makes the bone appear thicker than it really is. I can recall seeing one dog who appeared to have very chunky bone. It was too much bone for my taste. Imagine my surprise when I saw the same dog, out of coat, and discovered that his bone size was in perfect proportion. Again, feel to determine the actual size or look at the dog when he's wet or out of coat.

Neck

A proper neck contributes greatly to an American Eskimo's appearance. Of medium length, it should be strong, carried proudly erect and have a graceful arch. It's also important that the neck blend smoothly into the shoulders.

The neck is important, not only for the elegance and style it lends, but because it is a tangible, practical indication of good shoulders. We must remember that the neck is the bridge between the head and the body. Thin, weak, spindly necks usually make an abrupt change as they segue into the shoulders. Short, thick necks also move abruptly to the shoulders and are apt to cause the dog to carry the head horizontally, rather than proudly erect. This detracts greatly from the breed's appearance.

One of the American Eskimo's most glamorous features is the ruff around the neck. Like the mane of a lion, it is instantly impressive. A good length of neck, with the important graceful arch, shows this characteristic feature to best advantage.

When gaiting, most Eskies hold their heads up and this is the ultimate in the show ring. Good, strong neck muscles are necessary for this to occur. An Eskie, moving around the ring, head held high, is very impressive. The dogs have an interested, alert, happy look. They simply command attention. Dogs with this attitude fairly scream, "I'm here and you can't deny me the win." Even after all these years in the breed, I find it breathtaking.

In recent years, I have begun to see more dogs with big blocky heads and short necks. The two qualities seem to go together. With these "no-necks," as I call them, the head seems to sit directly upon the shoulders. There is no graceful arch, nor does the neck blend smoothly into the shoulders. As far as I am concerned, this is a particularly glaring fault and one that breeders should work to eliminate.

Shoulders

Evaluating shoulders can be one of the most difficult tasks for the novice. Even some veteran breeders have trouble properly assessing shoulders. Indeed, the rather technical sounding language of the breed standards does not provide much hands-on assistance in explaining what to look for in good shoulders. This is particularly true with a coated breed, in which determining the degree layback can be difficult.

You must make a hands-on examination of the shoulders to determine their placement. Feel for a smooth, continuous line, extending from the neck, past the shoulder blades, without a rise or dip. If your Eskie has this preferred conformation, chances are he has very good shoulders. There should never be an abrupt break where the neck and shoulders join. Similarly, a dip in the back, behind the shoulder blades, usually indicates insufficient layback. The ideal shoulder layback allows the dog to extend his front legs with maximum reach.

A good length of neck, with an arch, contributes to elegance and style and helps to showcase the breed's ruff. This is Gr. Ch. 'PR' Winterset Willow, a Miniature, owned by Lila Bean.

Though it may be difficult to understand the construction, special care should be taken in breeding for good shoulders. They contribute greatly to proper movement. Admittedly, it can be very challenging to breed for good shoulders. While you can often improve a faulty rear in a single generation, it usually takes much longer to improve bad shoulders.

Chest and Ribs

Both standards tell us that the American Eskimo's chest should be broad and deep with well-sprung ribs. The UKC standard goes on to specify that the ribs should "begin an upsweep behind the ninth rib to insure adequate room for the heart and lung action. Heart and lung room are secured more by body depth than width."

The Eskie's chest is moderately wide. When viewed in profile, the forepart of the chest (sometimes called the brisket), should extend approximately to the elbows. Inadequate depth in this area makes the Eskie appear to be unduly leggy, as though he were perched on stilts. When viewed from the front, the chest should be wide enough to enable the legs to stand parallel to each other.

The well-sprung rib cage, called for in the standard, is neither too narrow (slab-sided) nor too wide (barrel-chested). The proper oval shaped rib cage greatly enhances endurance. From above, the ribs should spring out from the spine and have a broad look. The circumference of the chest will narrow somewhat behind the elbows. This allows the dog clearance in bringing his front legs back.

The barrel-chest cannot expand as freely when the dog exerts himself. This fault is often accompanied by an overly wide front. In motion, the barrel-chested dog cannot get his front legs back behind him. Instead, they hit the chest and cause interference. In order to avoid this, the elbows are forced out. Barrel-chested dogs often have too much width between the shoulder blades.

The slab-sided dog is apt to be short on endurance, too. The lungs, contained in the rib cage, must be able to expand as the dog runs. If there's not enough room for this to occur, endurance is hampered.

In assessing chest width, one must again take age into consideration. During the "teenage" period, many dogs may appear too narrow in front. Yet, when they fill out, the chest may be perfect. In general, I think that American Eskimos have improved in this regard over the years. I can recall seeing barrel-chested and out-at-the-elbows dogs years ago, but we don't often see them today. On the rare occasions it does occur, you are more likely to see it in Miniatures. Most of the narrow chested dogs I see, are simply the result of immaturity.

Front Legs

The front legs should drop straight from the elbows to the feet. They should be the same distance apart at the elbows as at the feet. For this to happen, the chest must be moderately wide. When the chest is too wide, the legs are usually forced out at the elbows. This fault impairs movement and gives a very coarse, clumsy look. It should, in my view, be heavily penalized.

Gr. Ch. 'PR' Stevens' Max-A-Million, owned by Kathy Cella, has a good front.

A too narrow chest allows the dog to bring his elbows together under his body. This, too, should be faulted in the show ring. East west fronts, French fronts and Chippendale fronts all occur when the legs turn outward below the pasterns. This loose, unsound movement is occasionally seen and should be faulted.

Both the AKC and UKC standards call for "strong and flexible" pasterns. The AKC standard adds that the pasterns should have a "slant of about 20 degrees." While there is a slant to the pasterns, this should be *slight*. In fact, the pasterns should appear *almost* upright. This slight slope helps cushion the feet and absorb shock. It also provides the pasterns with a slight "give," or springiness.

Dogs who are too straight in the pastern often knuckle over. In this condition, the leg appears to double forward under the weight of the dog.

An American Eskimo should never have a pronounced slant to the pastern. This excessive slope is known as "down in the pasterns." It indicates a weak condition which serious hampers agility. Unfortunately, I have begun to see a number of dogs of late who are down in the pasterns. This is a serious, ugly fault that breeders should continually strive to eliminate.

Back

The American Eskimo should stand squarely, with his weight evenly distributed on all four legs. His back is straight, broad, level and muscular. When we look at the entire body, we can see why a strong, level back is essential. The spinal vertebrae act as a bridge, which supports the head and neck, as well as the weight of the ribs and body organs. They connect the forequarters to the hindquarters. Therefore, it is essential that the back be strong and taut.

The UKC standard says that the loins "should be well muscled and not so short as to interfere with the easy rhythmic movement and powerful drive of back legs." The AKC standard specifies that it be "neither too long nor too short coupled." The loins, also called the coupling, are the area between the last rib and the hindquarters. The dog who is too short in the loin will lack flexibility and agility. The dog who is too long in the loin will be loose in the back, thereby diminishing the transmission of power generated by the hindquarters.

Most judges seriously fault dogs who do not have level toplines. In addition to the inefficiency it indicates, they mar the American Eskimo's appearance. Sway or dippy backed dogs should be severely faulted. Roach backs, in which the back curves upward, are also to be faulted. The camel back, in which the back is arched like that of a one-hump camel, are also to be faulted, as are razor backs.

The belly of the American Eskimo is slightly tucked up. This gentle rise adds much to the appearance of elegance and agility. However, more is not better. Too much tuck-up gives a Greyhound appearance. This

A strong level back is important in the Eskie. Note the topline of AKC Ch., SKC Ch. & Gr. Ch. 'PR' Thunderpas Astraea CD, owned by Patrea Pabst.

is generally coupled with an excessive arch or roach of the loin and, often, a low tail set. The tuck-up is usually visible even in dogs with a heavy coat.

Rear Legs

The American Eskimo has a strong, muscled rear. When viewed from behind, the legs, hocks and feet should be straight. The hocks must always be perfectly upright. They should point neither in nor out. Cowhocks, in which the hocks turn inward toward each other, is a fault which should be penalized. This is an area in which the Eskie has improved over the years. I seldom see cowhocks on dogs in the ring anymore, although a few judges have reported finding dogs with this fault.

Most Eskies are nicely muscled in the rear. This is a very active breed and Eskies, by nature, tend to jump, or "spring," up and down on their rear legs. They love to be on their hind legs and they use them often. My friend Rosemary Stevens calls them "springalators." I often say they bounce up and down like "Peter Pan." In puppies, it's not uncommon to have the muscle (sometimes called "muscle mass") develop more quickly in one rear leg than the other. If this proves to be a problem, you can massage, or knead, the other leg to improve it.

To improve the amount of muscle, some Eskie breeders will exercise their dogs. Running in the sand, on a beach, is an excellent form of exercise. I know of other breeders who have their dogs run up and down stairs. Normally, this extra exercise is not necessary, though, since the breed is so active.

The stifles (the dog's equivalent of the human knee) are moderately angulated when viewed from the side. Since the rear is the source of the dog's drive and

American Eskimos should have moderate angulation as seen on Gr. Ch. 'PR' Shamrock's Dybrk Shandale, owned by Brenda O'Sullivan. Note that Shandale's front and rear angulation match.

power when moving, this moderate angulation allows the Eskie to step out with a free and easy stride. Ideally, the degree of rear angulation should exactly match that of the front angulation. The overly angulated rear often tends to be weaker and gives the dog a crouched appearance in the rear.

Straight stifles are equally faulty, for they restrict a dog's movement. The straight-stifled dog moves with a stilted, stick-like action. Watch a Chow Chow move in the show ring and you will see a ready example of the effect of the straight stifle on movement. Straight stifles impede agility and are, therefore to be faulted.

This dog's stifles are almost straight.

I must take a moment to emphasize a point that is very important for all breeders. *The American Eskimo should be moderately angulated.* This is a central characteristic of almost all the Spitz breeds (the above mentioned Chow Chow is a notable exception). Over angulation in an American Eskimo is wrong. Sadly, this is not specifically mentioned in the UKC standard. The AKC standard says that the hindquarters are "well angulated." I don't know why this was included, but it is wrong for the breed. I fear that there are those who will begin to breed for "well angulated," rather than "moderately angulated" rears and this key aspect of the breed will be changed. I urge all breeders to select for moderate angulation only.

Feet

Often, people make the mistake of overlooking the feet. And yet, poor feet can spoil the American Eskimo's overall appearance and hamper his endurance. Thin, splayed feet will mar the look of the most beautiful dog. Fortunately, we don't often see this fault in Eskies. When it does occur, it's most likely to be due to environmental factors.

Both breed standards call for the Eskie to have an "oval" foot. Some have made the mistake of thinking that this calls for a "hare" foot. In this type of foot, the two center digits appear significantly longer than the outside and inside toes of the foot, with less arching to the toes. The feet appear longer. This type of foot is usually seen on sight hounds. It provides greater leverage and makes for more speed, but is also more fatiguing.

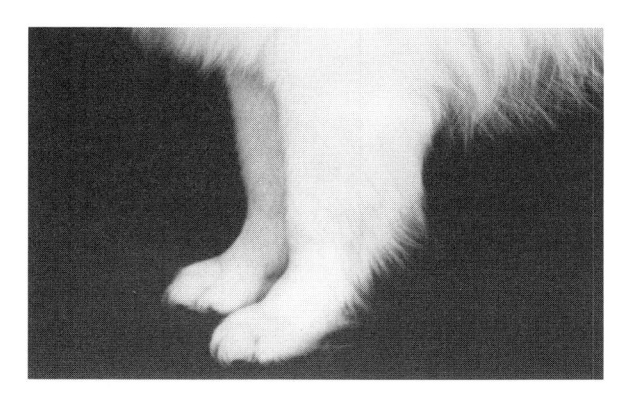

Down in the pasterns is a fault in Eskies.

The cat foot is round and compact with well-arched toes which are cupped closely together. This type of foot conserves energy, takes less effort to lift and is more efficient.

The proper American Eskimo foot, the oval called for in the standard, is midway between these two types. The toes are not as tightly cupped as you would find in one of the sporting or scent hound breeds. They are, however, closer to the cat foot than the hare foot. Most of the feet that I have seen on American Eskimos, my own included, come much closer to being cat feet than hare feet.

The AKC standard includes the curious statement that the "toenails are white." To be honest, I'm not sure where they got this. I've discussed this situation with many, many breeders and all concur. The Eskie's toenails may be white, but black nails are also routinely seen. Recently, several new buyers, interested in exhibiting in AKC shows, have passed over outstanding prospects simply because they had dark

Gr. Ch. 'PR' Snowfire's Goodlovin Sam, owned by DeAnn Lee, has good feet and pasterns.

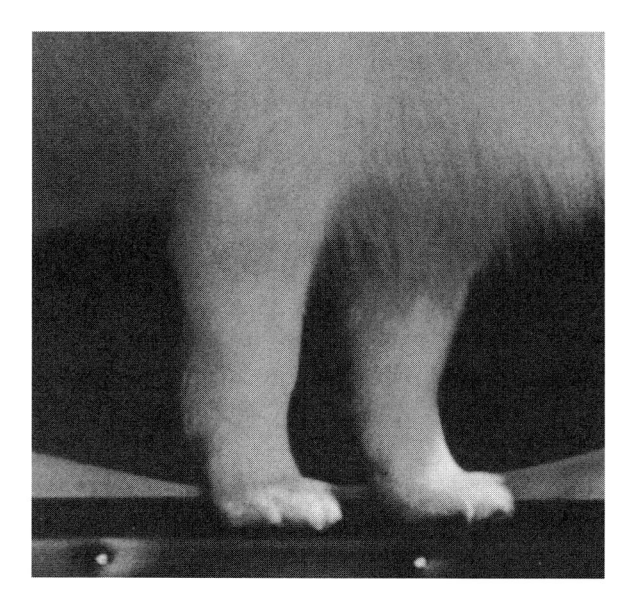

Good bone, feet and strong pasterns, as seen on Donna Hays' AKC Ch. & Gr. Ch. 'PR' Starlight's Karuk Star.

nails. The color of an Eskie's toenails should not matter at all. Further, it's possible that toe nail color may be correlated with dark pigmentation, a factor we should do everything in our power to encourage.

Most Eskie breeders trim around the feet and under and between the pads. Many dogs grow unsightly tufts of hair around and under their feet. These can pick up burrs, grass seeds, etc., which may irritate the dog and cause problems. The hair under the feet can also reduce the dog's traction, making it difficult to properly assess movement. Trimming has the additional advantage of offering a neater appearance in the show ring.

Both breed standards allow for the removal of front dewclaws at the owner's option. The AKC standard goes on to state that "if present, they are not to be faulted." I was one of the people who fought to get the UKC to include this option in their standard. One of my females continually caught her front dewclaw in my screen door. She did this almost every day of her life. She would often twist the claw, injuring it and sometimes getting it infected. I heard of many other people who experienced similar problems. The discretionary removal is a very sensible option.

The UKC standard says that dewclaws are "objectionable on the hind legs and should be removed for the dogs own safety." The AKC standard says that they "are not present on the hind legs." We don't see rear dewclaws much anymore, although they were more common years ago. You would see them on one or two puppies in a litter and, often, it would be on only one leg. Breeders seem to have successfully eliminated them.

Tail

The gloriously coated tail, set moderately high and carried forward over the back, is one of the key characteristics of an American Eskimo. It adds much to the dog's beauty. The AKC standard says that the tail should be carried "loosely over the back," while the UKC standard adds that it is "not necessarily centered."

I like to see a dog with a long, profuse coat on the tail. An Eskie with scant tail coat looks terrible. Thankfully, we don't usually see this unless the dog has blown its coat. Some dogs have real "plumes," or "pom-poms" on their tails and these are truly striking.

Eskie tails are often carried down over one side of the hip. In the show ring, dogs sometimes naturally hold their tails on the hip side facing away from the judge. This can be infuriating if the dog chooses not to cooperate when you flip the tail to the judge's side.

The correct American Eskimo tail is a little different than some other members of the Spitz family. Keeshond and Pomeranian tails are tightly curled and lie flat against the back. The Norwegian Elkhound tail is very tightly curled and centered. The proper Eskie tail is more loosely carried and, in most cases, lies over the hip.

The American Eskimo tail should not be double-curled. I call this a "donut," and it is seen in the show ring and should be faulted. You will also see what some breeders call "pigtails." When you run your finger along the tail and reach the end, the muscle is so tight that it literally grabs your finger. This is only occasionally encountered.

A glorious tail is a key characteristic of the breed. This lovely bitch is AKC Ch. & Gr. Ch. 'PR' Thunderpas Apollo's Gaea, owned by Rosemary Stevens. *Photos Today photo*

Miniatures often have a more profuse, standoff coat than Standard-sized Eskies. Note the beautiful coat on Ch. 'PR' Krystal Chanci, owned by Tammy Nichols.

It is important for the American Eskimo to hold his tail up in the show ring. A dog who continually keeps his tail down will be penalized, and rightly so. This is a key characteristic of the breed and, therefore, very important. Even the best of dogs can become moody and decide not to bring their tail up, on occasion. Many exhibitors walk out of the ring, cursing under their breath, about their dogs' failure to get the tail up. It often robs them of an otherwise deserved win. Usually, though, a dog will at least bring his tail up when moving. When at rest, the tail may be down.

Dogs who are nervous, intimidated or skittish, will often glue their tails to their bottoms. This is one of the reasons that socialization is so important in this breed. Similarly, a dog who isn't feeling well may fail to keep his tail up. Occasionally, one sees a dog who is overly relaxed or bored in the show ring. He seems to think he's in his own backyard and there's no reason to show off. The overly relaxed dog's tail, however, usually pops up when he is called on to gait. Dogs who get their tails up, when moving, are generally not penalized.

A thickly coated, well carried tail is a joy to behold and one of the breed's crowning glories. It bespeaks a bold, confident, alert nature. Breeders should take great care to select for proper tails for an incorrect tail positively mars a American Eskimo's appearance.

COAT

The American Eskimo has a thick, double coat. Closest to the skin, we find the very dense undercoat. Growing through this are longer guard hairs which make up the dog's outercoat. This type of coat affords maximum protection, for it allows a space of air to be trapped between the under and outer coats. This provides thermal protection. We can see this principle applied in the manufacture of double-paned windows for houses. Here we find two layers of glass with an airspace in between them. This type of construction helps to insulate houses from winter wind and cold, and also the heat of the glaring sun. Like those insulated windows, the Eskie's coat affords him the maximum in protection from the elements.

The amount of coat an American Eskimo carries depends on many factors. Climate has an effect on the degree of coat which will be seen. Dogs in northern climates often carry thicker undercoats with more profuse outercoats. This can sometimes give them, all other things being equal, a decided advantage in the show ring. Quality is always more important than quantity.

The amount of coat a dog carries is also due to heredity. This is one of the considerations a breeder usually takes into account when planning a litter. You should be aware, however, that it's easy to breed for more coat and more difficult to work to eliminate structural defects.

Some dogs develop allergies which affect the quality and amount of coat. Overall health also has an influence. Parasite infestations can wreak havoc with a coat. Dogs who suffer from other health problems may not carry profuse coats, either.

There are variations in the texture of American Eskimo coats and this can be very difficult to describe

A pronounced ruff, or mane, is a key characteristic of the breed. Males, like U-CD 'PR' Stevens' Toybear Sir Guy, owned by Charles and Linda Cummings, have a profuse ruff. *Linda Cummings photo*

This dog has a profuse overly soft coat, lacking in undercoat. He has a number of other faults, too, including flop ears. Dogs with many faults can occur in any litter. This dog's pedigree is composed of Champions and Grand Champions. While he may not be a show dog, his owner adores him and wouldn't sell him for a million dollars!

in words. We sometimes see dogs with what I call a "layered look." Such coats are not overly long, but they are remarkably thick. They have a wonderful plush feel to them. This is more apt to be seen in females.

There are also coats which have a "cottony" texture. This type of coat is quite thick and sometimes prone to mat. When bathed, the cottony coat also retains water. During shedding periods, the coat often peels off in sheets.

Males carry more coat than females. They also have the pronounced ruff about the neck that is so typical of the breed. Generally, the coat, like the dog, does not reach full maturity until about three years of age. The older the dog, the more coat he or she usually carries. However, the texture will often change as the dog matures. Miniatures and Toys come into their full coats at a younger age than Standards. Indeed, Miniatures and Toys often carry a more profuse coat with a greater tendency to stand off from the body.

The American Eskimo puppy coat is wonderful. It's soft, cuddly and very profuse. You will often find variations among the puppy coats in a litter. Be advised, just because a puppy carries a heavy coat, this doesn't mean that he will have a profuse coat as an adult. Most Eskies lose that wonderful, full puppy coat at about four months of age. How we all hate to see it go! There can be variations at the age when a puppy first blows its coat, however. My Gr. Ch. LilBit Country didn't blow his undercoat until he was one year of age. And, wouldn't you know it, it happened enroute to a Canadian show. By the time I arrived at the show site, I had a naked dog! LilBit turned out to be a very heavily coated dog.

Too much coat isn't usually a problem in Eskies, as long as the coat is properly composed of both an undercoat and outercoat. Too much long outercoat, without sufficient undercoat, is undesirable. We occasionally see dogs with too short coats or very little undercoat, but these usually come from pet shops. There doesn't seem to be too much of a problem, in the breed, with a silkier-type coat, either.

It's been years since I have seen curly or wavy coats. When such defects are likely to occur, you most often see them at the base of the tail. I saw more wavy-coated dogs 25 years ago. You seldom see them today. I also saw a dog with a curly coat, which fell in ringlets, in my early years in the breed. This dog was purchased from a pet shop.

Both the UKC and the AKC have taken pains to ensure that the American Eskimo remain a natural breed. Trimming, therefore, is largely verboten. One should never take scissors to the whiskers or body coat. The feet, however, may be trimmed for neatness and to improve traction.

COLOR

The American Eskimo is a pure white dog. Both standards, however, allow for white with biscuit cream, or cream colored dogs. The AKC standard goes on to say that the presence of "white with biscuit cream should not outweigh consideration of type, structure or temperament." Any color other than those mentioned is a disqualification under both standards.

The vast majority of Eskies exhibited in the show ring are pure white. I suppose it seems strange to say that there can be variations in the color white, but it's true. We see dogs who have a very bright white color. There are also dogs who have what I will term, for want of a better phrase, "off white" coats. This is a true white, but it lacks brightness. Some Eskie's have what I call a "pristine" coat. In this type of coat, there are sparkles which give a glittering, shimmering appearance. Not all Eskies have this coat but, when you see it, it is very attractive and not easily forgotten.

The biscuit cream and cream color is actually an off shaded buttery white. When these markings occur, they are most likely to show up at the tips of the ears and the base of the tail. Personally, I believe that such markings should be present on the tips of the coat only. They should *never* form actual round spots. If the marking is on the tip of the coat, you should be able to separate the hairs and find that the base of the hairs are white. This advice was passed on to me a number of years ago by someone who had bred Eskies for thirty years. It has stood me in good stead and I haven't had problems with color in my dogs.

On puppies, you will sometimes see a vague cream tipping on the ears or the head. These markings will often disappear when the first coat comes in and sometimes before. If you see actual spots, it's likely that these will remain when the dog matures. Spots, or coloring on the back, may well remain also.

The standards say that cream and biscuit cream are acceptable. Again, I dislike actual spots of the color. Some dogs are more heavily marked with cream and this often shows up as freckles on the head. This has proven a great source of embarrassment to me on more than one occasion. With all the sniffing of strange dogs that occurs at shows, one Eskie will occasionally urinate on the head of another. Naturally, we rush to wash this off before we go into the ring. Several times, I've informed the owner that his dog's head needs cleaning, only to be told that these are instead markings. Though it is certainly permissible under the standard, I don't personally find it attractive.

As I said, most Eskies seen in the show rings are pure white. I can recall, however, seeing an otherwise fine dog whose coat was entirely cream. It was distracting and judges were loathe to put the dog up. On rare occasions, I have also seen dogs with darker marks. These were an orangish or rust color. Freckles which appear all over the head and/or face are also very unattractive.

It goes without saying that it is never permissible to dye the dog's hair in order to obscure his true color. I know of several instances when this has occurred. We must remember that the true purpose of the show ring is not to garner awards. It is evaluate future breeding stock. This purpose is subverted when faking and trickery is employed.

This Miniature is Gr. Ch. 'PR' Snobird's Staker's Sebastian, owned by Judy Jones.

This is Gr. Ch. 'PR' Lucky's Pippin, owned by Choi Quay, a Standard-sized American Eskimo.

SIZE

In UKC shows, American Eskimos compete in two size classes. Standard Eskie males stand over 15" up to and including 19". Females are over 14" up to an including 18". Miniature males should be 12" up to and including 15". Mini females are over 14" and up to and including 18". The AKC includes a further class for Toys. These should measure from 9" up to and including 12". The AKC also includes a disqualification for dogs under 9" or over 19". While Toy Eskies can be registered with the UKC, they may not compete in shows.

There is and always has been a great deal of inconsistency in American Eskimo size. This is a heritage passed down from the German Spitz and will probably always be with us, to a certain degree. It is essential, therefore, that we pay close attention to size.

There are many breeders who try to specialize in one size only. I have always concentrated on Standard sized dogs and the vast majority of the dogs I have produced are indeed Standards Yet, even I have, on occasion, seen inconsistency. In one litter, I had six puppies. Four turned out to be Standard, while two were Minis. Most of the Standards males we see competing today are about 16 1/2 to 18 1/2" at the shoulder. Most Standard females are about 15 1/2 to 17 1/2 inches. It's unusual for a Standard Eskie to go oversize, but it can happen. Oversize dogs, of course, cannot be shown.

There has been a marked improvement in Miniatures over the years. Many Mini breeders select dogs who are closer to the top of the Mini height requirements. By doing so, they feel that they will produce dogs who are true Miniatures of the Standard.

They do produce Standard sized dogs in Mini litters. Some breeders are working to achieve Mini only lines.

The introduction of the Toy American Eskimo has been the cause of more heated debate and rancor than any other subject I can recall in my 25 years in the breed. The vast majority of breeders were not in favor of the move to establish this size range. They didn't feel that dogs of this size could carry on the essential qualities of the breed. They would not have the hardiness, vitality and strength for which the breed has been known. Already we are seeing some of this. The Eskie has always been known for its suitability as a children's companion. Yet, recently, some Toy breeders have refused to sell to homes with children because their small dogs were too fragile for such placements. The altering of the American Eskimo into some type of "hot-house" dog which needs special handling is abhorrent to most breeders. There is also a genuine concern among many breeders that there will be a trend toward ever smaller dogs, eventually culminating in "tea cup" sized Eskies.

Time will tell if the Toy American Eskimo is here to stay or proves only to be a passing fad. Those who wish to purchase a Toy should be aware that many of these dogs go oversize and must be shown as Minis. It's very difficult to breed a dog which combines very small size with all the qualities of the Standard sized Eskie. We should always remember that the Mini and the Toy should be scaled down versions of the Standard sized dog. Faults, such as apple heads, round eyes and prancing movement are more likely to occur in Toys and are never correct. Toy breeders, therefore, face tremendous challenges in producing dogs which live up to the breed standard in all other respects.

In AKC shows, Toy Eskies are allowed to compete.

Chapter 14

Understanding Correct Movement

It's always a pleasure to see a good moving American Eskimo. Movement is very important in this breed and has always been prized. I like to see an Eskie that moves out, head and tail up, alert and beautiful. A good moving Eskie is light on his feet. Indeed, he moves as light as a feather. Heavily boned dogs, with large bodies, just can't achieve this degree of lightness. Currently, Standard sized Eskies have the best movement. Some Miniature breeders have managed to consistently breed good moving dogs and others should work hard to achieve this ideal. Toy sized Eskies are relatively new in the history of the breed so it's difficult to assess movement from a widespread perspective. Toy breeders should, however, work to ensure that the "tippy toe" kind of action, found in some toy breeds, does not become routine for this variety. Likewise, the hackney action, which can seem so flashy in the show ring, is also inappropriate in any size Eskie.

It is often said that movement is the truest indicator of good conformation. There is something to be said for this, as gaiting is a good measure of overall soundness. Proper gait just isn't possible without proper conformation and structure. Many faults, that may not be apparent when the dog is posed, come quickly to light when the dog is moved. If you went to purchase a used car, you would not be content to merely look at it, no matter how close your examination. You would insist on taking the car for a test drive because you'd be more likely to feel or hear some defect. Likewise, when the dog moves, you may well see some fault that had previously escaped your attention.

In the show ring, the gait is examined from three angles. The judge will look at the dog from the side, in profile, as he gaits around the ring. He will also look at the dog from the rear, as he moves away from him, and from the front, while the dog approaches. This gives the judge a balanced view of the dog from every angle and allows him to best assess the Eskie's movement. The dog will be expected to "trot," which is the canine's most efficient and natural gait. When a dog walks, three feet are always in contact with the ground. When a dog trots, only two feet touch the ground at the same time. The trot is called a two-beat lateral gait, in which opposing diagonals move together. In other words, the right front foot moves at the same time as the left rear foot, and the left front and right rear feet move together. Good physical structure is very important when a dog trots for, in this mode, he must rely on speed and balance.

Profile Movement

The gait, as seen in profile, is the most difficult for the novice to assess. That's because so many interrelated parts of the body can be seen at the same time. The judge will be looking for a free and easy gait. He'll check the topline to make sure that it stays level when the dog moves. A dog whose back bobs up and down is not an efficient mover. He's wasting his effort with up and down, rather than forward motion.

Balanced angulation is essential to good movement, when viewed in profile. An American Eskimo whose front and rear angulation are equal, will have the proper rhythmic gait. Though an Eskie may have poor angulation (too straight in the shoulders and stifles) his gait will appear more balanced than the dog with mismatched angulation. His gait, however, will not be as efficient and free as the properly angulated dog. The length of his stride will be correspondingly shorter and he'll have to take more steps to cover the same distance. He will lack the beautiful, smooth stride, with good reach and drive, that is so desirable.

Let's think for a moment about the way an automobile operates. Generally, the rear wheels provide the propulsive power that drives the car forward. The front wheels set the course of direction. If your front wheel should sink into a mud hole, the propulsive power of the rear will probably be sufficient to dislodge the

All American Eskimo breeders prize good movement. This superb example of good Eskie movement is demonstrated by Nat. Gr. Ch. Gr. Ch. 'PR' Stevens' Toybear Apollo, piloted by his breeder/owner Rosemary Stevens.

vehicle. If the rear wheels should bog down, however, it will be much more difficult to free the car. If you should suffer a sudden blowout when you're on the highway, you'll have a much easier time controlling the car if one of the rear tires goes flat than if a front tire is affected. Since the front tires are so instrumental in controlling direction (steering), a blowout of a front tire, particularly at high speed, creates a dangerous situation. A blowout on the rear may temporarily affect control, but you will likely be able to safely maneuver your car to the side of the road.

Now, let's consider the dog's body as an efficient, car-like machine. His legs act much like the wheels of our car. The dog generates his power from the rear. Without strong muscular thighs and sufficient angulation, he won't be able to develop the power necessary to effortlessly propel him forward. His front legs, just like the car's front wheels, are responsible for changes in direction. They must have the angulation to enable the dog to make rapid turns and changes of direction. When the dog is ready to stop, the front legs and shoulders must be powerful enough to absorb the initial impact. With proper flexibility and balance, the dog can pull up suddenly, abruptly and appear to "stop on a dime."

The judge hopes to see free and effortless movement. He'll be paying attention to the dog's length of stride. He wants to see the rear legs reach well under the dog, then straighten out, driving the dog forward, and follow through vigorously. This long stride will provide the maximum in power. He will want to see the front legs reach smoothly forward from the shoulder, without breaking the straight line from shoulder to foot. The foot must then hit the ground smoothly, drive backward and follow through, although the front follow through should not extend as far as the rear. It's important that the front legs be able to keep up with those driving rear legs. If the front stride does not match that of the rear, it causes interference. This, of course, makes for an inefficient gait and impedes forward movement.

The feet must clear the ground cleanly. The dog should never appear to be tripping over his feet. However, they should *just* clear the ground. Neither the front nor rear feet should be raised abruptly upward. A dog who raises his feet is wasting energy, which should always be directed forward, rather than upward. If a dog raises his front feet high, this is referred to as "hackney" action. A dog who flings or kicks his feet upward while gaiting, breaks the clean forward motion we want to see. This inefficient motion tires the dog unnecessarily.

Rear Movement

The judge will want to examine your dog's movement from the rear, to ascertain if his hindquarters move properly. As the dog begins to move, he will be in a slow trot. At this slower speed, his rear feet should move straight forward. In a dog with a good rear, the hocks (sometimes called the rear pasterns) will be exactly vertical and moderately apart. If the dog moves with his hocks too wide, he will have a waddling, duck-like action. If the hocks are too close, particularly if they brush together, they will interfere with the

Since this Miniature Eskie is out of coat, we are better able to assess the movement. Note the front extension and rear drive. See how the feet *just* clear the ground, making for maximum efficiency. You can also see that the topline remains level while gaiting.

Without a full coat to hamper our view, we can see that the front legs extend in a straight, unbroken line from the shoulder to the ground. You can also see that, as the speed increases, the dog begins to single-track.

necessary free and easy movement. Either fault robs the dog of power. The hocks should not turn inward, which indicates cowhocks. Sometimes a dog who is minimally cowhocked will have escaped the judge's attention on individual examination. However, as the dog moves, the judge will be able to see that telltale convergence of the hocks. Similarly, the hocks should not turn outward. While this type of action is rarely seen, it should nonetheless be penalized.

As the dog picks up speed and moves into a fast trot, the placement of the feet will change somewhat. As speed increases, the dog has to adjust his foot fall in order to maintain balance. Therefore, he inclines his feet inward so that they converge on a center line under his body. This convergence is dubbed "single tracking" because the dog's front and rear feet will hit a single centered line. This phenomenon can best be seen on a sandy, damp beach where the dog's pads will leave an imprint. It's also possible to observe this in snow of the proper texture. The next time the opportunity presents itself, try trotting your dog on one of these surfaces. You'll be able to clearly see this center line, single tracking movement as the dog trots.

As we have said, in the fast trot the legs will incline inward. There should be no deviation, however, in that straight unbroken line from the hips to the feet. The feet should still reach straight forward, hocks straight, with no side to side motion. In the good moving dog, with proper angulation, the judge will be able to see the pads of the rear feet on the follow through. This shows the judge that the dog moves powerfully, gets his feet well under him and follows through fully. It's a visible testament to the dog's rear drive.

Front Movement

The judge will also want to see the dog's movement from the front. This is the most complicated and interrelated part of the dog's structure. Therefore, the list of front faults is extensive and too lengthy to be included here. In the very slow trot, the dog's legs should drop straight from the elbows to the feet and be parallel to each other. Just as in the rear action, as the dog's speed increases, his front feet will converge on that imaginary center line.

Front movement is dependent on numerous factors. In addition to correct shoulder lay back, the construction of the rib cage is vitally important. The judge will look for interference in the elbow action. If the dog has a barrel chest, he'll have to swing his elbows wide to avoid the chest. This horrid fault will be immediately apparent. The judge will also be looking for any unusual looseness in the front movement. He will quickly detect any crossing over or weaving of the front legs, which would point to a loosely constructed shoulder. Also objectionable is "crabbing," sometimes called "sidewinding." With this action, the dog's front moves in a line and he throws his rear out so that it travels in a different line. This may be caused by a body which is too short or a rear which is more angulated and powerful than the front.

The judge will look at the feet and pasterns, to be sure they reach straight forward. The front feet should neither turn inward nor outward.

A heavily coated Mini demonstrates rear drive, although it's obscured somewhat, in this photo, by the coat. Note that the hocks remain straight when the dog moves. The black pad of the dog's foot is beginning to become visible and, a second later, would be seen more clearly. This is a key to good rear drive.

A properly moving American Eskimo is truly beautiful. With his head and tail held high, he steps out alertly and lively, with a quick, agile stride. He should move straight forward in an efficient manner. All of his body parts join to give him a harmonious, synchronized action. Once we understand the complexities of movement, it is truly amazing to see everything come together to produce that wonderful effortless gait. Good movement in an American Eskimo should be treasured and cherished, for it is a sure indicator of a balanced, well-made dog.

"Love for Sale," Rosemary Stevens' sign proclaims. When choosing a breeder, look for someone who is dedicated to the breed.

Study the standard carefully when selecting a show prospect. This gorgeous ten-week-old puppy, owned by Charles and Linda Cummings, grew up to become Gr. Ch. 'PR' Wildwynd Shmroc Mystc Nytebreez. *Charles Cummings photo*

It's hard to resist the charm of an American Eskimo puppy. This beauty is future Gr. Ch. 'PR' Krystal Silver, owned by Tammy Nichols. *Olan Mills photo*

Your American Eskimo will be with you for many years, so it pays to take time in selecting your dog. This happy guy is "Gus," aka Gr. Ch. 'PR' Snobird's S-Ka-Pades, owned by Rosemary Reseigh.

Chapter 15

Selecting an American Eskimo

Buying your first American Eskimo is exciting. You've probably met an Eskie owned by someone else and can't wait to have one of your own. It's better to slow down, however, and give some hard thought to your purchase. After all, the American Eskimo is a long lived breed and this dog will be with you for many years. It's best not to dash out and buy the first cute puppy you see. The more that you learn about the breed, the better your chance of finding a dog that will suit your needs and provide you with years of companionship and joy.

WHAT DO YOU WANT?

What part will the dog play in your life? Are you looking for a pet that will be a wonderful companion? Many Eskies come to be regarded as "one of the family." Do you have children in your home? Perhaps you are buying an American Eskimo that will serve primarily as your children's companion. Have you always dreamed of having a show dog? Dog showing is a wonderful hobby and, of course, it's more fun to win than lose. Will you want to breed your dog? If so, quality will be a consideration. You won't want to buy a dog with a serious fault if you plan on eventually showing or breeding. Do you want a standard sized American Eskimo or would a miniature be more to your liking? All of these things will have to be taken into consideration.

A responsible breeder can be a great help to you in locating just the right dog. In order for him to do this, however, you'll have to be honest with him. Tell the breeder what you want. Remember, the breeder has invested time, effort and money in his dogs. His concern for them extends far beyond the money he will receive. No breeder wants to hear complaints and no buyer wants to be disappointed with his purchase. With cooperation, both of you can be satisfied. You'll have the dog that suits you and fulfills your needs, and the breeder will know that his dog has found a loving home.

WHERE TO BUY

Where can you locate a breeder of American Eskimos? There are a variety of ways to find a breeder. By perusing your local newspaper, you may be able to locate a nearby breeder. You can also contact the United Kennel Club (100 E. Kilgore Rd., Kalamazoo, MI 49001-5598). They will be glad to provide you with a list of American Eskimo clubs and breeders. The American Kennel Club (5580 Centerview Dr., Raleigh, NC 27606 or 51 Madison Ave., New York, NY 10010) will also provide you with a list of dog clubs in your area and may have the names of Eskie breeders.

A number of dog magazines carry American Eskimo advertisements. *Dog World* is the most widely circulated dog magazine in the world and includes ads, as well as valuable articles and information on both UKC and AKC shows. *Dog Fancy* is a national magazine which also includes ads and information. *Dog Fancy* publishes an annual magazine, *Dogs USA*, which includes the ads of many Eskie breeders.

If you are looking for a dog for show or obedience, you will have to decide if you wish to participate in UKC or AKC shows or both. An increasing number of fanciers are participating in shows offered by both organizations. Those interested in the UKC, should definitely subscribe to *Bloodlines*. You'll find information on shows, articles concerning Eskies and, of course, advertisements from serious breeders. The AKC publishes *Pure-Bred Dogs, The American Kennel Gazette*. The *Gazette* includes many articles and may include some advertisements from breeders. You can subscribe to a supplement to the *Gazette*, known as the *Events Calendar*, which provides lists of all shows, obedience trials and other events and includes the addresses of show superintendents and blank registration forms.

If there's a show in your area, by all means, plan to attend. You will have the opportunity to see dogs from a variety of kennels and will be able to determine what you like. American Eskimos have competed in UKC shows for many years, so you are apt to find the largest number of dogs exhibited at their events. Entries at AKC shows are growing rapidly, though, so it's quite possible you will be able to see Eskies at their events.

American Eskimos are occasionally seen in pet shops. Generally, it's best to steer clear of pet shop puppies. Since most reputable breeders refuse to sell puppies to pet shops, you're likely to pay a high price for a poor quality pup. In addition, the pet shop will only be able to provide you with sketchy information on the breed. You're far better off dealing with a breeder who knows the Eskie and is committed to the breed. If a problem should arise, the breeder will be there to assist you.

If you are fortunate enough to locate a breeder in your area, definitely make an appointment to visit his home or kennel. Do your own overall evaluation. Is the kennel clean? Do the dogs look well cared for? Be aware that most Eskie bitches lose their coat and look unkempt when they produce a litter. You may want to ask the breeder for a photo which shows the bitch in proper coat. If you plan to breed your Eskie, ask the owner if he exhibits his stock in shows. Watch the breeder and see how he relates to his dogs. Look for a breeder who is knowledgeable, takes pride in his dogs, and obviously loves them.

If you cannot locate a breeder within driving distance, don't despair. Many breeders are willing to ship a dog to you. Since you won't be able to meet the breeder in person, nor see his dogs, don't hesitate to ask questions. Request photos of the dog. Even via long distance, the breeder will be glad to help you.

ESKIES AND CHILDREN

Dogs and children have a unique rapport. In fact, owning a pet can be a very special experience for a child. A dog can provide a youngster with unconditional love and a deep sense of friendship. Psychologists have recently discovered that dogs and children develop especially close bonds. By using dogs, they have managed to reach many emotionally disturbed and withdrawn children. Dogs also aid in developing the growing child's character. By caring for and training the dog, children learn responsibility. The dog/child bond also helps to instill a sense of understanding, kindness and compassion.

If the dog is to serve as your child's pet, there are some factors that must be borne in mind. No matter how desperately the child wants an American Eskimo, parents must remember that dog ownership is a family venture. As a parent, you have ultimate responsibility for the dog. You must teach the child how to care for and handle the dog properly. If the child forgets to feed the dog, then you must willingly step in. You must be prepared to care for the dog without resentment. If you don't want the dog every bit as much as your child does, then don't make the purchase.

PURCHASING A PET

While most breeders hope to have a whole litter of show quality puppies, this rarely happens. It's far more likely that there will be pups in each litter who lack some fine point required for success in the show ring. Such "pet quality" puppies are usually available at a lower price. This can be a boon for the person seeking a companion. While the puppy may not have what it takes to be a show winner, he still comes from the same stock as his more illustrious brethren. He's been reared in the same way and received an identical amount of love and care.

Just because your puppy is labelled as "pet quality" and costs less, this does not mean that he's inferior. Indeed, the difference between a show and pet

Kids and Eskies form special bonds. This is Nicole Pettit with 'PR' Shamroc's Chilly Dawg.

quality puppy may not be outwardly discernible. A puppy with a slight underbite may appear to be equal or superior to his champion brother. This fault, however, will prohibit him from winning in the ring, and so he is sold as a pet and should not be bred. This does not in any way impair the dog's ability to function as a wonderful companion. The pet quality dog is every bit as intelligent and loving as his show quality littermates.

In purchasing a pet, temperament will be of prime importance. By closely observing a litter, you'll see indications of future temperament. Spend some time watching the litter at play. See how they interact with people, including their breeder. Chances are you'll be able to spot the most aggressive pup, the quiet one and the one who's most attentive. You want a sensible puppy with a stable personality. You should be aware that American Eskimos are somewhat aloof and do not always go willingly to strangers. Sit down so you are on the puppies' level, rather than lifting them into the air. Give the puppies time to relax and come to you. Avoid the puppy that is overly shy or who struggles and growls when you pick him up. Pet owners often say that their puppy "chose them." That's not a bad way to go.

SHOW AND BREEDING STOCK

A show quality puppy is one who conforms to the standard and can be expected to win in the show ring. It can be tricky to pick future show winners. The only guaranteed way to be assured of getting a show quality dog is to purchase an older dog who's already out there consistently winning. Still, if you have your heart set on a puppy, there are some points to bear in mind. Familiarize yourself with the standard, learn what you like and choose a breeder whose stock appeals to you. A breeder who's been working with his bloodline for years, and knows how his stock matures, will have a good idea which puppies will grow into superior Eskies. He will have the advantage of knowing how the puppy's ancestors matured and what they looked like at a young age.

Expect to pay more for the show quality puppy. You may also find that the show quality pup is slightly older. The breeder may well have recognized his potential and held him until a show home could be found. Since the breeder has more invested in the puppy, he'll ask a higher price.

In choosing the show quality puppy, there are certain things you'll want to see. It's obvious that the dog should not have any points listed as faults in the breed standard. A good head, sound legs, a strong topline, a properly carried tail and good movement are musts. Be sure that the puppy's eyes are black. Look closely at his pigmentation. The eyerims, lips and nose should be black. If these areas are partially pink, speckled with black, the dog will probably mature with proper pigmentation. Avoid the dog whose pigmentation appears white. When he's full grown, he probably won't have the black points so desirable in the breed. Some puppies will have their ears entirely up, at eight weeks. Others will have their ears partially erect. If the pup's ears aren't completely up, look for strong ear leather. Take a look at the coat. Some puppies will have a cream colored cast on their heads. This usually disappears as the puppy grows. The coat should appear thick and lustrous. In addition, look for that "something extra." A dog which exudes that indefinable "class" will generally go far. If you are looking at a group of show quality puppies and there's one you just can't take your eyes off, pick him.

There are additional points you should keep in mind. You want your American Eskimo to be capable of producing healthy, strong puppies of good quality. Look for the dog who comes from a long line of healthy dogs. Females should descend from a line of bitches who whelp easily and freely. Finally, look for the names of males and females, in the pedigree, who have a reputation for producing top quality offspring. If your Eskie comes from a long line of males and females who have produced champions, he's most likely to continue the tradition.

AMERICAN ESKIMO REGISTRATION

The American Eskimo has been registered with the United Kennel Club for over 80 years. Recently, the breed was also recognized by the larger American Kennel Club. This has led to some confusion on the part of both buyers and breeders. Should they register their dogs with only one Club or both? Out of allegiance to one group or the other or political considerations, some people urge one course of action only.

I would strongly urge breeders and buyers to register their dogs with both organizations. While this may be a little more expensive, it will allow for the maximum flexibility. The breeder may be interested in only UKC shows, but some of his puppy buyers may decide to try their hand at AKC events, too. Or, while the original purchaser was interested in only UKC events, the dog may eventually be sold to someone who takes an interest in AKC shows or trials. To be fair to everyone, dual registration is highly recommended.

There is one other cautionary note which should be included. Some Eskies are advertised with "UKC" registration papers. The buyer soon discovers that the dogs are not, in fact, registered with the United Kennel Club, but by an organization called the

"Universal Kennel Club." This group has no relation to the United Kennel Club and dogs registered with the Universal Kennel Club cannot be registered with either the United Kennel Club or the American Kennel Club. This is a case where the buyer should most definitely beware!

UKC REGISTRATION PAPERS

Make sure that you receive the United Kennel Club registration papers when you purchase your dog. In the 1930's, the UKC registered the "PR," or "Purple Ribbon" designation with the United States Department of Commerce. Dogs with six generations of purebred ancestors, three generations of which are registered with the UKC, earn "PR" status. All Eskies now carry the "PR" designation.

The back of the green Registration Certificate, or the "Bill of Sale," should be filled out at the time of purchase. The seller will fill in the date, his city, state and zip code, and sign the form. You should fill in your name, address and phone number, and affix your signature. If you wish to change the dog's name, now is the time. While the dog's name can be changed, his registration number always remains the same. Don't be surprised if the breeder insists that you include his kennel name as part of the dog's official registered name. If you're dealing with an out of town breeder, who will be shipping the dog to you, he will probably fill in the Bill of Sale for you. Be sure to sign your name and send the form to the UKC You will receive your permanent purple registration papers, complete with a pedigree, in four to six weeks. A knowledgeable breeder will be glad to answer your questions about UKC procedures. If you have any other questions, contact the UKC

Be leery of buying a puppy if the breeder does not have the registration papers. If the papers have not yet arrived, and you really want the puppy, take a few precautions. Make up your own Bill of Sale giving the puppy's birthdate and stating that he is eligible for registration. Ask for the names, registration numbers and birth dates of both the sire and dam. Both you and the breeder should sign this paper. If you have this information, and don't get your papers, you will be able to turn to the UKC for assistance. They will judge your circumstances on a case-by-case basis and may be able to help you register the pup.

AKC REGISTRATION PAPERS

When you purchase a puppy, you will receive a blue form entitled "AKC Dog Registration Application." On the front of the form, you will see the name of the breed, the birth date and the sire and dam's names. The registration numbers of the sire and dam will be listed to the right of their names. A month and year will appear in parenthesis following the registration numbers. This indicates the month that the parents' names were first entered into the AKC Stud Book and is useful for tracing pedigrees. You will also see the name of the breeder and the name and address of the litter owner. On the right side of the form, you will find the litter registration number and a box where the sex of the dog should be filled in. There is also a space for circling the color of the dog. Be sure to fill in the name you have chosen for the dog. The purchaser has the right to pick the name, although some breeders prefer to do this themselves or to incorporate their kennel name. If you have your heart set on a particular name, be sure and discuss this with the breeder.

On the back of the form, there will be places for the date, name and address of the breeder or breeders and their signature. At the bottom of the paper, there will be space for your signature, name and address. You should fill this in. Include the required fee (it will be listed on the front of the application) and send this off to the AKC at the address listed. Remember, it is illegal under AKC rules for someone to charge you extra for the registration papers on the dog you are purchasing.

If you are buying an older dog, he has probably already been permanently registered with the AKC. You will receive the white AKC papers, which specify the breed, the dog's registered name and number, color and information on his parents. You cannot alter the dog's name. The back of the form is similar to that of the puppy form and should be filled in by both you and the seller. You should receive your new papers in approximately three weeks.

If you are purchasing a pet, you may find that the dog is being sold with what's called "Limited Registration." This means that your dog is registered as a purebred and can compete in obedience, agility or any other dog sports. He cannot, however, be shown or bred. LRs are usually utilized by serious breeders who sincerely care about their breed. They don't want to see faulty or unworthy dogs perpetuated and believe that only those of highest quality should be bred. Dogs with LRs are often less expensive. If your puppy should mature into an excellent specimen of the breed, you may be able to have the "Limited Registration" reversed. It will take a letter from the breeder, however, to do so. There is one glitch in the system of which you should be aware. The Canadian Kennel Club and some other foreign kennel clubs, may not register dogs which have LR papers. If you live in another country and intend to show in obedience, it would be wise to check with the AKC before accepting an LR dog.

It's best not to buy a dog unless the seller presents the AKC papers to you. If he tells you they are delayed in the mail and he will forward them to you as soon as they arrive, you should protect yourself by getting some information. Ask him to give you a bill of sale or a written statement which includes the following: 1. the breed, sex and color of the dog; 2. the dog's date of birth; 3. the registered names of the dog's sire and dam (preferably with their registration numbers) and 4. the name and address of the breeder. Should the seller fail to provide the papers: write to the AKC (5580 Centerview Dr., Raleigh, NC 27606) and ask for help. They will review your case on an individual basis. But, remember what the AKC says: "When papers are not available at delivery, it is a red-flag warning sign to exercise extreme caution."

BREEDER'S TERMS AND CO-OWNERSHIPS

If you are looking for a show dog, you may find that he comes with breeder's terms or is offered only on a co-ownership basis. Before entering into such an agreement, make absolutely sure that you understand the specifics. And, don't take such agreements for granted. You and the breeder may have different interpretations of what is entailed. It is, therefore, imperative that you set out the details in writing and that both you and the breeder sign the agreement. This will save a great deal of heartbreak. Many promising friendships have ended because of disputes over such deals. The UKC and AKC are constantly asked to arbitrate such squabbles and, unless it affects a violation of rules, will not do so.

Both males and females may be offered on breeder's terms. Sometimes the breeder would like to retain stud privileges on an outstanding male or one with exceptional potential. They are usually selling the dog only because they do not have room to keep it themselves. Don't be afraid to ask questions. Do these stud privileges last for the life of the dog or only for a specified time? Will you be splitting all stud fees the dog generates? Will the dog be used exclusively on bitches owned by the breeder or is he entitled to use them on other bitches, too? Are you expected to show the dog? If so, who will foot the bill or do you share such expenses? What happens if you decide to move away or sell the dog?

Bitches are sometimes sold on breeder's terms, too. You may be offered a lower purchase price for taking the dog with such an arrangement. The breeder may want a puppy back from the bitch's first litter. The price may be half the litter or the money from the sale of one or more puppies. The bitch is usually co-owned until the puppies or money is delivered. Be sure you

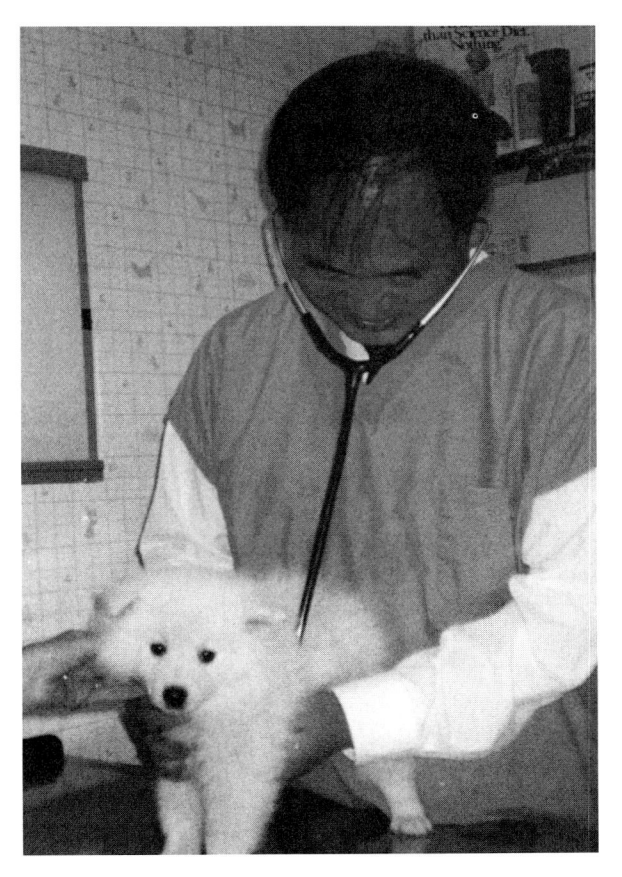

It's important to have your new puppy checked out thoroughly shortly after purchase. Dr. Kim checks out one of Rosemary Stevens' puppies.

know how long the agreement is in effect. Does it apply to only one litter or all litters the bitch may have? Are the costs entailed with the litter (the stud fee, medical attention, food, advertising, etc.) borne equally or are you expected to pay them all? Who gets to select the stud—you, the breeder or is it by mutual consent? Is the bitch to be shown? Who pays the bills for this? What happens if the bitch puppy does not live up to her potential and turns out to be a pet? What happens if you decide to sell the bitch?

Breeders terms and co-ownerships are tempting because they allow the beginner to obtain top-quality stock that might not otherwise be offered. It can be a benefit to the breeder, too, since it allows him to continue his breeding program even though he has no room to keep other dogs. Just be absolutely sure you understand the agreement before you take the dog.

SELECTING A HEALTHY PUPPY

Of course, you want to select a healthy puppy. Even though you aren't a veterinarian, there are some indicators you can check. Look for an overall healthy appearance. The pup's eyes should be clear and bright, not runny. His coat should look healthy and free of any rough patches or bald spots. Lift up the lip and look at the gums. They should be bright pink. Avoid the puppy with white gums, as he may have a severe case of worms. Look at the ears and make sure that they are clean, with no waxy buildup. If the puppy continually shakes his head, he might have a case of ear mites. Avoid the pup who sneezes or coughs. Watch the puppies play and see if they appear frisky and alert. These are good overall indicators of health.

Ask the breeder to write out the dates when the puppy received its shots. If he gave the vaccinations himself, ask for the type of vaccine used. The breeder should also tell you when the next shots are due. Most reputable breeders will allow you to take the puppy to a veterinarian for examination. Ask how long you have to take the puppy to the vet. Most breeders will allow you 24 hours. If it's a weekend, of course, extra time should be granted. Make certain that the breeder will return your money or allow you to select another animal if the dog fails the vet's examination.

Ask the breeder how often the dog is fed and what feed he's been using. Even if you intend to change the dog's feed, it's best to keep him on the diet he's accustomed to for the first few days. You can then introduce the new food gradually, by mixing it with his current diet. This will help to eliminate digestive upsets. It's also a good idea to find out when the dog had his last meal. Stop by the grocery or pet store and pick up the food recommended by the breeder. Ask the breeder for enough food for the next feeding. If you are purchasing the dog on a weekend and fear that you won't be able to locate the appropriate food, offer to pay the breeder for several days supply.

Now that you finally have your American Eskimo puppy, take him home and enjoy him. He'll soon worm his way into your heart and you won't be able to imagine how you got along without him. You'll quickly discover why owners become sold on this breed.

Chapter 16

Caring for Your American Eskimo

American Eskimos are beautiful, devoted and endearing companions. Most people who have owned an Eskie (or been owned by one), will consider no other breed. We are indeed fortunate that our breed is blessed with good health. While problems can occur in individual dogs, of course, there are no widespread health or genetic problems associated with the Eskie. Since these dogs become important family members, we are also fortunate that they are long lived. It's not unusual for Eskies to reach the age of 12-15 years. To insure that your American Eskimo lives a happy, healthy, full life, you, his owner, need to care for him sensibly. With proper care, you'll be able to enjoy the companionship of your Eskie for many, many years.

SETTING THE RIGHT TONE

If your American Eskimo is to become a pleasurable companion, it's necessary to establish the right tone in your relationship from the very beginning. Eskies, particularly young puppies, are adorable. Beneath that cute exterior, however, can lie the heart of a tyrant. Even the smallest puppy can be amazingly willful. New dog owners are often apt to give in to their demanding youngster. You may think it's amusing to watch your Eskie puppy growl and attack someone's pants leg. When he's full grown and the person he attacks is a small child or your frail, elderly grandmother, it's going to seem less charming. From the very beginning, strive for a well mannered and well trained dog. It's possible to be kind, generous and loving with your dog, without being indulgent and spoiling him unnecessarily.

To achieve this, it's best to decide that you will discipline your pup from the day you get him. Your Eskie must know that you love him and you will be kind to him. However, he should also know that you are the boss and when you give an order it is not to be ignored. You'll be perfectly happy to lavish him with affection, but only when he pleases you and acts correctly. You will not tolerate a dog that's "spoiled rotten." Be patient, be firm and be consistent. Your dog will come to understand what's expected of him.

PROTECTING YOUR ESKIE

While your Eskie is a rugged dog, you must safeguard him. This is particularly important when he's a puppy. Adult dogs will have learned what you consider on and off limits, but puppies are intensely curious and you will have to look out for them.

Puppies are wiggly and unpredictable. You need to understand this and exercise caution. You must take care that your puppy doesn't fall. Young puppies can leap from your arms in the wink of an eye, and a spill may result in injury. Be sure to hold your Eskie close to your body with a firm grip. If he's sitting on your lap, keep a cautionary hand on him. Puppies will learn to evaluate heights as they mature. Don't place your Eskie puppy on a couch or chair until he's large enough to jump there himself. It should go without saying that it is never correct to pick up an Eskie puppy, or adult, by the scruff of his neck or by his front legs. Instead, place one hand between his front legs and, supporting his rear legs with your other hand, lift him smoothly and gently.

If your home has slippery floors, do not permit your Eskie to play vigorously on this surface. This is particularly important when you have a young puppy. He could dislocate his hips, stifles or shoulders at this tender age.

If you have stairs in your home, keep your puppy off them. As your Eskie matures, you can allow him access to the stairs. It's best, however, to train him to use them safely. Place the dog on the top step and urge him down two or three steps. Take it slow. Within a few days, he'll be capable of managing the stairs.

Swimming pools can also pose a serious hazard to young puppies. Young puppies should be kept far away from swimming pools, unless they have a secure covering. Be sure to check the cover, periodically, to insure a tight fit. When your puppy gets older, you can teach him to swim. Before leaving the pool uncovered, make sure your dog has the ability to swim its length. You must also make certain that your dog knows where the steps are located, so that he can get out when he's through swimming.

Puppies are, by nature, inquisitive. Just as you would with a human baby, you'll have to teach your puppy not to put everything into his mouth. Try to make a tour of your home, searching the floor. That straight pin or rubber band could cause considerable damage to your puppy's stomach. Make certain your Eskie does not have access to any cleaning agents. Decorative figurines or breakable ashtrays should be placed out of reach, too. It's also best to remove house plants from the puppy's vicinity. Many house plants are poisonous. Be certain your puppy doesn't chew on telephone cords or electric wires. Be patient, be firm. While the puppy may drive you to distraction, he'll soon learn what's expected of him.

WHERE WILL YOUR ESKIE SLEEP?

The grown Eskie will generally select his own spot for sleeping. It may be a favorite chair, a warm spot by the fireplace or he may want to share your bed. For the puppy, however, you should provide a bed of some kind. This is best until your Eskie is fully housebroken and can be trusted. There are a variety of dog beds on the market and they range from the simple to the elaborate. However, it's best to avoid wooden or wicker beds. Puppies have a tendency to chew on these materials, while teething. Metal beds, with foam rubber mattresses, covered in a washable fabric are quite practical.

You may want to purchase a dog crate, such as the ones used by the airlines for shipping dogs. This will allow your dog to have his own private place, where he can feel secure and safe. The crate will come in handy if you plan on taking your dog to shows, or traveling with you. Miniature Eskies will be most comfortable in a number two sized crate, while a number three sized crate is ideal for Standard sized Eskies. To insure proper ventilation, you may wish to drill additional air holes in the crate.

FEEDING YOUR ESKIE

Dog owners today are truly blessed to have, at their fingertips, an amazing array of scientifically balanced dog foods. You may choose to feed your American Eskimo a dry dog meal, a canned food or a semi-moist feed. Most breeders recommend a dry kibble. Puppies should be fed one of the feeds specifically formulated for them. No matter which kind

Many Eskies love to swim. 'PR' McKee's Princess Alexandra and Nat. Gr. Ch. & Gr. Ch. 'PR' McKee's King Jacob enjoy a dip with Gordon Patterson. Pools can pose a hazard and you must protect your dog.

of food you select, you should examine the label to make sure that it's "nutritionally complete." This will insure that your dog gets the proper blend of protein, fats, vitamins and minerals.

American Eskimos thrive on a variety of diets. Over the years, most breeders have experimented and determined the diet that best suits their dogs. Ideas about the proper diet for an Eskie vary. This simply illustrates that there is more than one way to feed a American Eskimo and still maintain his condition. Unlike people, most dogs thrive on monotony. They are creatures of habit. Once you find a food that is palatable to your dog, it's best to stick with that food, rather than continuously switching brands. Encourage your dog to develop good feeding habits. Ideally, he should eat his food within minutes of your setting it out for him.

Breeders are often asked how many times a day an American Eskimo should be fed. Growing puppies need twice as many calories as an adult dog. Depending on the puppy's age, he may require two to four feedings a day. It's best to check with the breeder, or your veterinarian, and follow their recommendations. Adult dogs need only one or two meals per day. Most dogs appreciate regularity. It's best to feed them at approximately the same time every day. This is one of the best ways to instill good eating habits.

The American Eskimo owner should guard against handing out tidbits to his dog. It's awfully hard to convince your Eskie that he's not entitled to share in your midnight refrigerator raid. If you're munching on something, while watching television, your dog will, undoubtedly, try to convince you that he wants a snack, too. Instead, purchase dog biscuits and parcel out a couple per day. They'll help to keep your dog's teeth clean and won't add empty calories. You can, of course, provide your dog with bones. Just remember, poultry and chop bones can be dangerous. Poultry bones, particularly, are likely to splinter and lodge in your dog's digestive tract.

Be sure to provide your dog with plenty of fresh, clean water. Ideally, he should have water available to him whenever he's awake. However, it's best to avoid allowing your dog to drink too much cold water after a hard play period. Give him a small drink, and when he's quieted down, offer more.

HOUSEBREAKING YOUR ESKIE

Most owners prefer to train their dogs, from an early age, to eliminate outside in the yard. Apartment owners, however, sometimes prefer to have their dogs paper trained. For others, paper training may be an interim measure. If a puppy was purchased during winter, and the harsh weather makes it unsuitable to take him outside, paper training may be employed until the weather improves. Whichever method you use, you'll want to begin housebreaking as soon as you bring your new dog home.

One of the important factors in housebreaking a puppy is vigilance. You want to catch the puppy before he has an accident. If you note your dog beginning to squat, say "No" in a harsh voice. This will usually stop him momentarily. It will enable you to pick him up and place him on the paper or carry him to the yard. If the puppy has an accident and you're right there, scold him. Take him immediately to his paper or the yard so that he learns to understand that this is what you want. If you discover that he's had a previous accident, just quietly clean it up. It will do no good to castigate him for an accident made an hour before. Hitting the dog with a rolled up newspaper is, likewise, not necessary or very effective. When the dog does his duty, either on the papers or in the yard, praise him profusely. You may feel stupid praising a dog for going to the bathroom, but it is beneficial. Your compliments of "good dog" will get the message across.

While housebreaking your dog, it's best to restrict his range within the house. Confine him to the kitchen, for instance, if you can't supervise his movements. If he is loose in the house, make certain to keep an eye on him at all times. That way, you'll be able to intervene if he starts to have an accident. Watch your dog closely and learn his habits. Many dogs will sniff the floor or turn in circles before they begin to eliminate. This can serve as a good warning for you. Tell the dog, "No," scoop him up and carry him outdoors or to his paper.

There will be certain times when your dog is most likely to relieve himself. You should take him out first thing in the morning and last thing at night. You'll also want to take him outside or to the paper after each meal or after he's been drinking water. Dogs are often most prone to relieve themselves after a play period.

By taking your dog out at these critical times, you'll avoid most accidents.

If you are paper training your Eskie, begin by spreading newspapers over a large area of the floor. Try to determine precisely where you want the papers to lie. You don't want to continually move them and confuse the dog. If, for some reason, you find it necessary to shift the papers to a different location, do this gradually. Day by day, slide the papers closer to the desired spot. All papers containing bowel movements, should be removed as soon as possible. It's often beneficial, however, to leave a paper spotted with urine. This will entice the dog to return to the spot. Gradually, as your dog consistently uses the papers, you can remove some of them. You'll no longer need to cover such a wide area.

Housebreaking a dog can, at times, prove frustrating. However, American Eskimos are naturally clean dogs. Most Eskies will learn what's expected of them in short order. Some dogs will be housebroken in a matter of days. Occasionally, one will run across a dog who takes weeks to become trustworthy. Don't despair and don't become discouraged. Screaming and yelling will only make the whole situation more tense. Just follow the rules outlined above and stick by them.

LEASH BREAKING

Most American Eskimos are easy to leash break. Occasionally, however, one can get a stubborn dog who objects to having anything around his neck. This type of dog can be trained. It will just take a little longer and

Many breeders like using a crate to help housebreak their puppies. This is future Ch. 'PR' Desert Storm's Hylander, owned by Doug and Esperanza Kaz. *Doug Kaz photo*

require more patience. Your dog may be fully lead broken after only one session. A headstrong dog may require a week or more of work.

It's advisable to introduce your Eskie to the leash gradually. A lightweight, one piece show lead is best for leash breaking, but you may also use a nylon slip (choke) collar and regular leash. Place the leash or collar around your dog's neck. Call his name and talk excitedly to him. Try walking him back and forth. Talk to him all the while, telling him how good he is. You may want to snap your fingers or make little clicking noises. You'll soon learn what is best for keeping your dog's attention. Remember, you must make this fun. If your dog follows you, praise him enthusiastically. Repeat this for a few minutes each day for the next week.

If your dog objects to walking on the leash, you'll have to take the training a little more slowly. Sit down on the floor with your dog. Place the leash on him and spend a few minutes playing with him. Try letting him run around with the leash on. Be sure to keep a close eye on him. You don't want him to get wrapped around the leg of a chair or caught on something. Pick up the end of the lead. Follow the puppy around, holding the lead, while he explores. Stop and encourage the dog to come to you. If he refuses, kneel down and tap your fingers on the floor. This will usually attract his attention and get him to come. Should he still refuse, very gently pull him to you. Once he gets to you, pick him up, cuddle him and tell him how wonderful he is for responding. Now, try walking again. If your dog should balk, you'll have to begin all over again. You might try turning and walking away from the dog. Most dogs will quickly follow you. Some headstrong dogs will firmly plant their feet and refuse to move. One occasionally encounters a dog who leaps about like a bucking bronco. He spins in the air and won't keep all four feet on the ground. For this type of dog, persistence is the answer. Just keep giving him short sessions where you make it clear that you expect him to walk. Sooner or later, he will realize that you aren't going to give up.

YOUR ESKIE'S HEALTH

Your Eskie will need periodic veterinary visits to safeguard his health. Routine vaccinations will help

Socialization is important. The Kaz's took four-month-old future Ch. 'PR' Jan DK's Winterfest Jubilee to a club meeting.

to protect him. All dogs should be vaccinated, on a yearly basis, for distemper, hepatitis, leptospirosis and parvovirus. You may also wish to have your dog immunized to prevent kennel cough, or parainfluenza. Check with your veterinarian to determine if there are any diseases prevalent in your region and if a vaccine is available to protect your dog. Thanks to modern vaccines, many highly contagious diseases are almost a thing of the past. Your American Eskimo will also need a rabies vaccination. Check with your vet to determine how often this should be given. Some states require yearly inoculations while others stipulate that vaccination should be given once every three years.

Lyme disease has become a problem in areas with large deer populations. If you live in an area with confirmed cases, you may wish to have your dog innoculated against this bacterial infection. If your Eskie is exposed to many other dogs, as in show situations, you may want to have him vaccinated for bordetella. This bacteria contributes to kennel cough.

Heartworm is prevalent in areas where mosquitos are common. A simple preventative medication, given daily or monthly, will prevent infestation. Daily dosages can be given either by pill or a liquid may be used in the food. Those who live in warm climates, usually give the medication year-round, while those in cold climates, may opt to dose their dogs only in summer.

It's a good idea to take your dog to a veterinarian once or twice a year for a general routine examination. Such periodic check-ups will help to detect any problems, before they become serious. Take along a stool sample so your vet can examine it microscopically for worms. If your vet finds evidence of worms, he can supply you with the appropriate medication. He may also want to do a blood test to be sure that your dog does not have heartworms.

By feeding your Eskie properly, caring for his health and grooming him regularly, you'll insure that he stays in prime condition. Consistent training and discipline will help him to become an ideal companion. Be sure not to forget the most important ingredient of all...LOVE, and lots of it! American Eskimos thrive on love and attention. By building a close rapport with your dog, he'll become your true friend.

Chapter 17

Grooming Your American Eskimo

The American Eskimo's coat is his glory. A healthy dog, with a well groomed, pristine white coat, is a beautiful sight. For all his great wealth of hair, however, the American Eskimo is surprisingly easy to groom. This is a natural breed, and professional trimming or grooming is not necessary.

It is the composition and texture of the Eskie's coat that makes it so easy to maintain. The undercoat is soft, short and thick, while the outercoat is composed of longer guard hairs. This double coat serves to insulate the Eskie from both heat and cold. The length of your Eskie's coat may vary, somewhat, with your local climate. Dogs kept in harsh winter climates tend to grow thicker, more profuse coats. Interestingly, in summer, the Eskie's coat also provides valuable protection. The white color reflects, rather than absorbs, the rays of the sun. Even in the hottest climates, the coat of the American Eskimo should *never* be shaved.

Your Eskie will feel and look better if he is groomed regularly. During grooming sessions, you will have an opportunity to closely observe your Eskie's condition. Often potential medical problems can be detected, before they become serious. You will be able to see cuts or growths, feel abscesses or lumps beneath the skin, spot broken or ingrown nails, smell strong ear odor and see tartar buildup on the teeth. Burrs or thorns can be removed promptly, before they cause trouble. If, despite the best of care, your American Eskimo's coat looks lackluster, dry or brittle, you should check with your veterinarian. It may be that your dog has an internal condition, such as worms, that is affecting the coat.

PUPPY GROOMING

American Eskimo puppies have a beautiful, fluffy, fast growing coat. It's best to acquaint your new puppy with the grooming routine, soon after you get him. Your little Eskie will quickly adapt to the routine and come to enjoy it. There are a few important rules, however, for grooming pups. First and foremost, be gentle. By handling him carefully and being patient with him, he will learn to look forward to your grooming sessions.

Never groom your Eskie when you are tense or upset. While this is an important rule for Eskies of any age, it is especially crucial with puppies. Speak to the dog, as you groom him, in a calm tone of voice. Keep those first grooming sessions short. Encourage the dog to stand still as you groom him. And last, but certainly not least, tell your Eskie how good he was, when you are through with the sessions. Remember, Eskies thrive on praise. Telling the pup that he's very good, and looks beautiful, will please him to no end. You may even want to conclude the session with a small tidbit, as a reward. Soon, your dog will look forward to the routine as a special time you spend together.

WHAT WILL I NEED?

A few simple tools are all that's required to groom your American Eskimo. First, and foremost, you will need a good *bristle brush* that's comfortable to work with. A *wide-toothed comb* is a must. It's also best to purchase *shedding and dematting tools. Blunt-nosed scissors and/or thinning shears* can also come in handy. All of the above can be purchased through dog supply catalogs or at your local pet shop. A hair dryer is a real help. It's not necessary to buy one of the heavy duty types generally recommended for dogs, unless you have many Eskies to care for. A small, yet sturdy, hand held blow dryer will suit your purposes. You will need a good *shampoo, preferably with a whitening additive.* You will also find that a *coat conditioner* is helpful. Your grooming box should include *cotton balls, a styptic pencil, mineral oil, baking soda, cornstarch or baby powder* and *nail clippers.*

You will need a convenient work place. It's best if the grooming surface provides non-slip footing for the dog and is at a comfortable height for you. This will save wear and tear on your back and give you better control over your dog. You can purchase a specially designed, folding grooming table, with a rubber mat surface and a grooming arm. The owner with just a few dogs, however, can get along well without this. Some Eskie owners do their grooming on the top of their clothes washer or dryer. If this is your choice, a piece of indoor-outdoor carpeting will give your Eskie better footing. I have used the top of my number three sized kennel or crate with success.

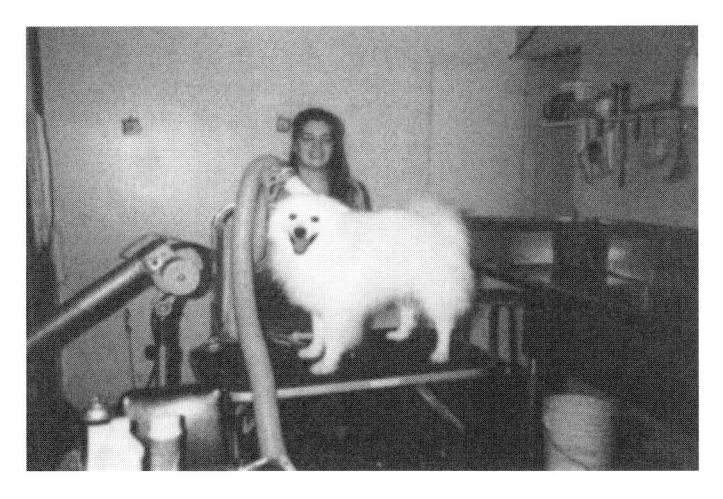

If you introduce your American Eskimo to grooming from the start, he will learn to enjoy the process.

BRUSHING

Regular brushing is the most important part of your grooming routine. Eskies should be brushed at least once a week, and twice a week is preferable. This will require a session of approximately fifteen minutes, if the dog is brushed regularly. A proper brushing will help to stimulate and clean your Eskie's coat.

Thorough brushing is a must. While it's tempting, particularly if you are in a hurry, to skimp on the brushing, don't! You will not achieve the desired results by just glossing over the surface. That marvelous, glowing finish is achieved by consistent and diligent brushing. You must be sure to brush right down to the skin. It's best to brush slowly, gently and methodically, so that you get every hair on the dog. Heavy handed treatment will only serve to remove the undercoat. I generally brush the coat down first and then back-brush the coat up toward the head. This gives the dog a fluffy, downy appearance.

While brushing, pay special attention to the particularly dense areas of the coat. The ruff, or mane, must be thoroughly brushed to prevent matting. After you've brushed the ruff, you may wish to follow up, by combing it with a wide-toothed comb. This will insure that there are no mats and will remove any loose hair. Special attention should also be paid to the hair on the hind legs, called the trousers, and the tail.

When you've finished brushing your Eskie, use the comb on the hair around the ears and armpits. These areas are prone to matting, and you will often find small knots or snaggles. If left unattended, these can develop into clumps or mats. Be gentle when combing these areas, as the coat is finer in texture.

REMOVING MATS

Hopefully, with regular brushing, your American Eskimo will not develop mats. However, even the best cared for dogs can get briars, thorns or burrs caught in their coats. At such spots, mats are likely to form. When working on mats, you must be patient. Removing mats can be tedious, time consuming work. Talk lovingly to your dog and offer him a tidbit. By all means, keep a firm hand on him, so he doesn't jump off the grooming table.

There are several methods for dealing with knots and mats. Each owner will have to decide what works best for him. Small knots can usually be teased out with the fingers. For larger mats, you may want to use talcum powder or olive oil, and slowly work out the mat, with your fingers. A dematting tool, sometimes called a mat splitter, together with your wide toothed comb, can be useful when dealing with stubborn mats. Take your time and pull a few hairs at a time away from the mat. You can also purchase a detangling preparation, from catalogs, supply houses or pet stores. This preparation can be sprayed on, so the area is fully saturated. Allow

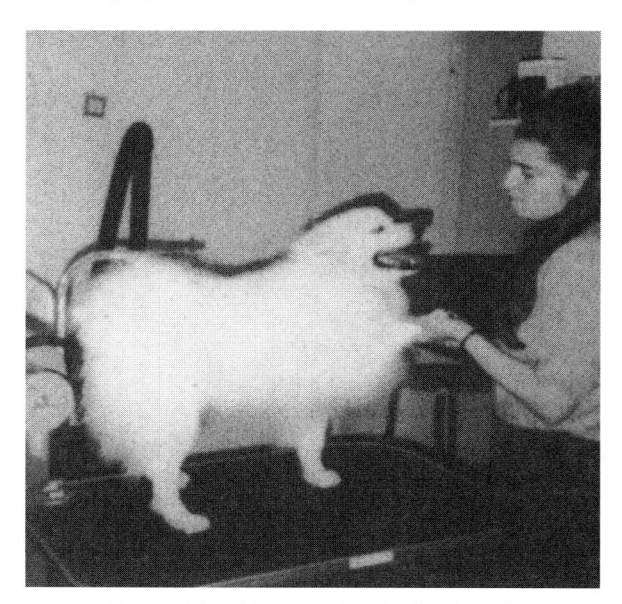

Frequent brushing is the key to a lovely coat.

AKC Ch. & Gr. Ch. 'PR' Kaz Cntry Western Harmony, owned by Doug and Esperanza Kaz—a new approach to bathing?

the saturated area to sit for a few minutes, before trying to remove the mat. For badly matted areas, it's sometimes necessary to make several applications of the detangling formula. Never yank at a matted clump as this is very painful to the dog.

If you still can't work the mat free, you can use scissors. Using blunt nosed scissors or thinning shears, snip as small an area as possible. Be sure to snip along the grain of the hair. Using your comb, begin working on the area. Never cut across the mat or cut it completely off. Your Eskie will end up with a moth eaten appearance.

If burrs or thorns have become tangled in your Eskie's coat, saturate the object and the hair around it with petroleum jelly, baby oil or olive oil. Then, work it free with your fingers and the comb. Nail polish remover can help to remove gum or sap from an Eskie's coat. Do take care, however, and don't allow the remover to touch the dog's sensitive skin.

Make absolutely certain that your dog has been thoroughly brushed before bathing. Knots, tangles and mats must be removed before shampooing. If not, they will clump together and become more firmly set and almost impossible to remove.

SHEDDING

A well groomed American Eskimo sheds surprisingly little. Many factors, however, can affect the degree of shedding. Generally, Eskies kept as house dogs shed more than those who spend much of the time outdoors. Stress also affects the degree of shedding. Physical problems, including allergies, can result in coat loss. Having a litter usually causes most females to shed, or "blow," their coats, and some also shed several weeks after they come in season.

Most American Eskimos blow their coats once a year. Males shed only once annually, while females may shed more often. Usually this occurs in summer, but it can often be influenced by the length of daylight in your area. The coat comes out in great handfuls, and your house will be filled with tufts of snowy hair. To eliminate this, it's best to get rid of the dead hair as quickly as possible. Much of the nuisance of shedding can be eliminated, if the owner will comb out the loose hair when he first notices that the dog is beginning to blow coat. Comb your dog frequently during the shedding period, to remove all the dead hair. Bathing, with warm water, will also help to loosen the dead hair. Again, be sure to give your dog a thorough brushing before bathing.

Your Eskie will look many pounds lighter after shedding. Indeed, you will be surprised at how his appearance changes. For several weeks, you may feel like hiding the naked looking dog. Have no fear, the coat will return. Generally, it takes about two to four months for the American Eskimo's coat to return to its full glory.

BATHING YOUR ESKIE

We often say that the American Eskimo has a "self-cleaning" coat. This is because the texture of the coat naturally repels dirt. When regularly brushed, it is possible for many Eskies to go months without a bath. Most Eskie owners bathe their dogs every two or three months. Show dogs, however, depending on the show schedule, may need more frequent shampooing, to keep them pristine white. Too much bathing is best avoided, as it dries out the skin and strips the coat of its natural oils. These oils are largely responsible for the coat's self-cleaning quality.

Remember, give your American Eskimo a thorough brushing and remove all mats or tangles, before bathing. While Eskies can be washed outdoors, with a hose, in warm weather, most breeders prefer to bathe the dogs in a tub. Place a rubber mat, or a towel, in the bottom of the tub to insure good footing. Many dogs become frightened, and difficult to control, when their feet begin to slip on the ceramic surface.

If at all possible, purchase a shampoo which contains a whitener. These are readily available through pet supply catalogs or at pet stores. If you are unable to locate such a shampoo, you can purchase laundry bluing at your grocery store. This is added to the final rinse water. You will also want to get one of the many good coat conditioners on the market today. Only by experimentation will you be able to tell which works best on your Eskie's coat.

The American Eskimo is a double coated breed. It's difficult to get water to penetrate through the undercoat, all the way to the skin. Doubtless, this served the Eskie well when he lived in a northern climate, but it can be frustrating when you are trying to bathe him. Using lukewarm water, wet your dog thoroughly before applying the shampoo. Be sure not to get water or shampoo into the ears or eyes. Some people like to place a small plug of cotton in the ears, and a drop or two of mineral oil in each eye.

Apply the shampoo to the coat, lathering the entire body. Work the lather in thoroughly, starting at the head and working your way towards the tail. Be sure not to forget the belly, the armpits and the undersides of the thighs. If you wish, you may allow your Eskie to stand in an inch or so of water. This is helpful, especially if his feet or pasterns have become muddy. They will have the chance to soak clean, while you are working on the rest of the coat. Shampoo your Eskie's face last. Lather the suds between your palms and gently wipe over the muzzle.

Now, it's time to rinse the dog. If your Eskie is particularly dirty, don't hesitate to rinse him, reapply the shampoo, and rinse again. Begin rinsing at the ears and neck, working down the back. Be sure to rinse thoroughly, until you see no traces of suds. Add the coat conditioner and give your Eskie a final rinse. If you are using laundry bluing, add three or four drops to the rinse water and shake it before applying it to your dog. Drain any water that remains in the tub. Now, let your Eskie have a good shake, to get rid of excess water. If he doesn't shake, blowing gently in his ear will usually do the trick.

Take your Eskie out of the tub. Gently towel off the excess water. It's really better to blot the coat dry, rather than rubbing it, which may inadvertently cause tangling. On warm, sunny days, some owners will let their American Eskimos dry naturally, in the sun. You must, however, be absolutely certain that your dog is not exposed to drafts.

Most breeders prefer to blow dry the Eskie's coat. Blow drying should be done while the coat is still damp. Place the blow dryer on the low setting. Aim it at a section of the coat and, with the brush in your other hand, brush up and towards the head. This is usually called backbrushing. Work the coat in sections, using light and easy strokes. The use of the blow dryer is the best way to get that light, airy look that is so extraordinarily beautiful.

DRY CLEANING

Between baths, it is possible to keep your American Eskimo looking clean and white, with a "dry cleaning." This consists of applying a cleansing agent to the coat, and thoroughly brushing it out. Dry cleaning is excellent when your Eskie has soiled only one spot on his coat. For old dogs, prone to chilling, a thorough dry cleaning can be sub-stituted for a regular bath. This method of grooming is also valu-able with puppies and will remove dirt from their coats when a buyer phones unexpectedly and wants to look over the pups.

There are many agents that can be used to dry clean your Eskie. I prefer corn starch, which does an excellent job and is inexpensive. Baby powder and talcum powder can also be used. Of the two, baby powder is preferable. In addition to doing a fine cleaning job, it leaves the dog nice and sweet smelling.

It's often difficult to bath one dog, but four puppies! A very brave Nadine Pettit washes puppies from her 'PR' Shamroc's Chilly Dawg's litter.

Dry clean your Eskie outside, or place a large towel or sheet over your work surface. The dry cleaner should be liberally sprinkled onto the coat. You must make sure that the coat is thoroughly dry, or else you have a sticky mess on your hands. Rub the cleaner in and allow it to remain on the coat for awhile. This gives the cornstarch, or powder, a chance to absorb any dirt or dust in the coat. Now, begin vigorously brushing your Eskie. At first, it will seem as though you are sending smoke signals. Keep brushing until all the powder has been removed. You'll be surprised at how sparkly white your American Eskimo looks.

CLIPPING NAILS

Your American Eskimo needs periodic trimming of his nails. Generally, a once a month clipping is best. Some dogs, particularly those kept on rough surfaces, will wear their nails down naturally. Most dogs,

Great care should be taken to soak the coat thoroughly, all the way to the skin.

however, will need to have their nails clipped. It's important to keep them clipped back, because nails which are allowed to grow long will cause the feet to splay.

Most breeders use a guillotine type clipper. Some dogs strongly object to having their nails clipped, and you may want an assistant to help you. If your dog puts up a struggle, you might try to shield his eyes, so that he doesn't see the actual clipping. This sometimes helps. Try your best to determine exactly where the quick (vein) in the nail ends. By looking closely at each nail, you will see the pink blood vessel. Place the nail clipper over the nail and cut just before the vein. If you should, accidentally, cut into the vein, just apply a little styptic powder or use a styptic pencil. Each time you cut the dog's nails, the vein will recede slightly. Therefore, the more you clip the dog's nails, the shorter they can be kept.

CLEANING THE EARS

Each time you brush your Eskie, it's best to clean his ears. Fortunately, with their upright ears, American Eskimos rarely have ear problems. The inside of the ear can become dirty, though. I prefer to clean the ears with a cotton ball, moistened with a little mineral oil. Under no circumstances should you probe deeper into the ear than the eye can see.

DENTAL CARE

While you are grooming your Eskie, you'll want to check his teeth. Routine cleaning of the teeth will help to avoid dental problems and prevent the buildup of tartar. I prefer to use a gauze pad and baking soda, for cleaning my Eskies' teeth. It is also possible to use a small toothbrush and doggy or human toothpaste. Start with the outside surfaces of the teeth. At first, this may be all your dog will allow you to do. As he gets used to the procedure, you can clean the inside surfaces of the teeth, too.

It's best to accustom your dog to teeth cleaning, from the time he's a pup. Dogs who are not used to the procedure, do not like having their teeth cleaned. It's best to do the cleaning, gently, quickly, yet thoroughly. Be sure to lavish your dog with praise, when you're through. If your American Eskimo has a heavy tartar accumulation, you will have to take more drastic measures. Purchase a metal tooth scraper. These are available through many dog supply catalogs. When scaling the teeth, try not to scrape too vigorously. You want to remove the tartar, but you don't want to chip the coat of enamel covering each tooth.

Be sure to have your veterinarian check your Eskie's teeth once a year. He can spot any trouble areas and recommend treatment. In the meantime, hard bones and dog biscuits will help to prevent the accumulation of tartar.

EYE STAIN

Many American Eskimos experience no problem with eye stain. For others, however, it is a persistent and unsightly problem. Eye staining is a common problem in many coated, white breeds. There are many reasons that eye stain can occur, and pinpointing the root of the problem may lead to an effective treatment Some dogs are prone to allergies, and excessive tearing of the eyes may be one of the symptoms. Dogs with too round eyes often have a more loosely attached lower eye rim (called the haw). This type of eye is more prone to watering and stain. Eye stain will also result when the tear duct becomes blocked or if hair grows into the eye rim. If your dog is plagued by excessive tearing, it's best to consult your veterinarian.

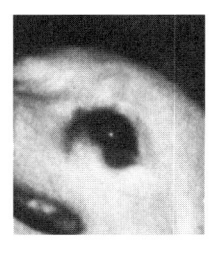

This dog has a serious case of eye stain, which is common in white breeds.

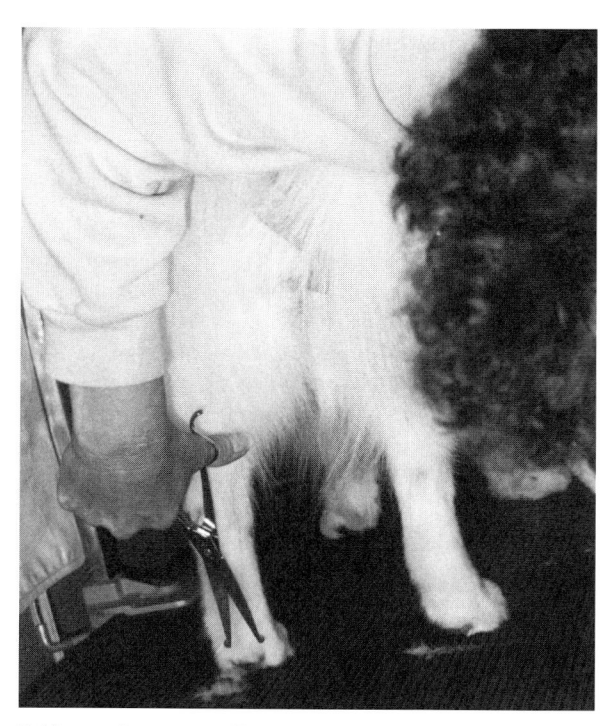

Eskies are shown naturally, with no trimming or shaping allowed. The only exception is tidying up the hair around the feet.

He may be able to detect the problem and prescribe appropriate treatment.

You can try to control the tearing, by applying vaseline to the area beneath the eye. This is sometimes helpful and will help the tears to roll off, rather than sinking in and staining. If your dog stains easily, moisten a cotton ball with warm water and attend to the eyes daily. *Blot up* the tears. *Do not rub* them away. You may want to try shaving off the badly stained hair. This, combined with daily cleaning of the area, may take care of the problem. The new hair will grow in white. However, if you have not discovered the root cause of the problem, the hair will quickly become stained once again. Some breeders have found that a daily application of cornstarch helps to prevent staining.

GROOMING YOUR ESKIE FOR THE SHOW RING

There's nothing more beautiful than a ring full of American Eskimos, groomed to perfection. You will quickly see why this breed has been christened "The Dog Beautiful." The United Kennel Club's rules are very specific, regarding show ring presentation. Absolutely no altering of the coat is permitted. The Eskie is not trimmed and the whiskers are left intact. The AKC standard specifically says that "THERE IS NO TRIMMING OF THE WHISKERS OR BODY COAT AND SUCH TRIMMING WILL BE SEVERELY PENALIZED. The only permissible trimming is to the feet and the backs of the rear pasterns." You may wish to tidy up the hair around your Eskie's feet. Some American Eskimos grow unsightly tufts of hair around and under their feet. This can prevent your Eskie from getting good traction and can make it very difficult for the judge to assess his movement. These hairs are also likely to get dirty or muddy, and to pick up grass seeds.

If you plan on showing your American Eskimo, you must devote time to grooming him properly. Cleanliness is most important and thorough brushing is a must. The difference between a meticulously brushed and a superficially brushed dog is certain to show. It takes diligence to give the coat that nice beautiful finish.

Shows are an excellent place to learn more about grooming. Individual Eskies will have varying coat textures. Some coat conditioners and products will work better with certain types of coats. Don't hesitate to discuss grooming products and procedures with other Eskie owners. Most are more than willing to take the time to discuss coat preparation, for the show ring, with you.

Chapter 18

The Stud Dog

Great care should be taken in the selection of a stud dog. Whether you are purchasing a male for your own use or planning to pay a fee for the use of an outside dog, much thought should go into the choice. The male American Eskimo can have a tremendous impact on the breed. While a female will have only one, or at most two litters a year, a male can be bred many, many times. He can pass on his good qualities, as well as his faults, to a great number of offspring. Indeed, a very popular stud, used for many years, can have a far-reaching impact on the breed.

What should you look for in a stud dog? Just because a male is a registered purebred, he is not automatically qualified to be a stud. Even those interested only in breeding pets should still be guided by the standard and attempt to produce typical American Eskimos. A male intended for stud usage should be a good representative of the breed. While he needn't be a champion, he should, nevertheless, excel in the basic breed virtues and have no glaring faults. A male who has blue eyes, unacceptable color, a poor coat, flopped ears or a bad bite should not be used for breeding. A dog who is structurally unsound would also be a poor candidate for stud use. Size should also be a consideration. Standard sized American Eskimos should measure 15"-19", Miniatures should be 12"-15" and Toys should be 9-12". Dogs who deviate from these height specifications, generally, should not be bred. It's best to breed Standards to Standards, Miniatures to Miniatures and Toys to Toys rather than intermingling the sizes.

You'll want to make sure that the male has both testicles. A cryptorchid male, or one with no testicles, will be sterile. A monorchid male (one with only a single testicle descended), however, may well be fertile. Monorchidism is a disqualification in the breed ring and, since the condition may well be hereditary, you should avoid the stud with only one testicle.

Pedigree is of great importance when you're deciding on a stud. The pedigree should reflect a background of careful breeding. Since the stud dog passes on the qualities transmitted to him by his ancestors, it will help if you can learn as much as possible about the dogs named in the pedigree. Look for a balanced breeding, with good dogs on both sides of the stud's pedigree. It may be tempting to use a dog sired by "Grand Champion 'PR' Mr. Wonderful," but if his mother was "'PR' Little Miss I Have Every Fault" then you are just as likely to get puppies resembling the mother as you are Mr. Wonderful.

The real "proof of the pudding," with a stud dog, is how well he can produce. The effectiveness of a stud dog should be measured by the quality of his progeny. It's a sad fact of life that some spectacular show winners never sire progeny as good as themselves. Conversely, some less flashy dog may consistently produce outstanding offspring. If you are using an outside stud, try to obtain as much information as possible about the quality of the American Eskimos he has produced. If you are using one of your own studs, keep detailed records and photos of his offspring. Check back with puppy buyers and try to see (in person or in photos) how the puppies matured. This way you will be able to see if your dog is living up to his potential as a stud.

While physical qualities are undeniably important, don't forget to look for a dog that excels in temperament. A dog passes on not only his conformation, but also his mental characteristics. An Eskie who is markedly shy or overly aggressive is not typical and makes an unsuitable stud dog. You must remember that the majority of your puppies will probably enter pet homes, where temperament will be of prime importance.

Last, but certainly not least, you want a dog who is healthy and vigorous. It's best if he comes from a background of long-lived, healthy dogs. You also want a dog who is a reliable breeder. While a dog's reliability as a stud is often molded by his early breeding experiences, the dog that is uniformly healthy and hardy is most likely to consistently have a good sperm count.

The foundation dog at Brenda O'Sullivan's Shamroc Kennels is Gr. Ch. 'PR' Jay-Be's Regal Apollo, pictured at ten years of age.

Bitches bred to such a vigorous dog are more likely to become pregnant and deliver strong puppies.

Your male should have a simple blood test to determine if he has the serious and highly infectious canine brucellosis. This bacteria is found in semen and urine of dogs who have this unfortunate condition. Generally, you will not see any outward signs which is why blood testing is so essential. Brucellosis is transmitted sexually and, since there is no cure, dogs having this bacteria should not be bred.

All breeders hope that they will have a prepotent stud. This is a male who is dominant for his virtues and can overcome the faults of most bitches. He can be used with success on a wide variety of bitches. Such studs can quickly make a name for a kennel and contribute much to its success. You are indeed fortunate if you discover that you own such a dog. A truly prepotent male comes along rarely, so take advantage of him if you are lucky enough to own one. Don't hesitate to seek the services of a prepotent stud owned by another breeder.

RAISING THE STUD DOG

Experienced breeders have learned that healthy, hardy dogs are most likely to be active, vigorous studs. A good, well-balanced diet, coupled with plenty of exercise, is important for the stud dog. You want him in top-notch condition. Be sure to check for both internal and external parasites. Worms and fleas will sap his energy, and a male in run down condition may well have a below normal sperm count.

The mental attitude of a stud dog is important. You want a lively, confident dog, who is sure of himself and enthusiastic about breeding. Therefore, he must be handled differently than a pet male. At an early age, your male dog will begin to mount and ride other dogs. Do not be upset if you find him trying to mount other males. He may even latch on to your leg and thrust enthusiastically. While it would be acceptable to chastise a pet male, you'll have to be more inventive with the future stud dog. Repeatedly telling him "No," at an early age, may discourage him. You don't want to convey the impression that breeding is wrong. If he's riding your leg, you might try distracting his attention with a favorite toy, or take him out for a walk.

If at all possible, you'll want to breed your dog, for the first time, while he's still young. Many breeders find eighteen months an ideal age to begin. By this time, the male will be physically and mentally mature, and you will be able to accurately assess his quality. Once a male has sired his first litter, he is referred to as a "proven" stud.

That first breeding is very important. You want everything to go well, as this experience will set the tone for future breedings. Take the time to observe your dog's actions closely. You will see how he responds to females in season and how he approaches the mating process. You will also be training your dog to be the type of stud you want. He will learn to respond to your encouragement. You'll aid him by holding the bitch so that he can breed her successfully and efficiently, and you will both learn to function together as a team. While it will take time and patience to accomplish this, you will find that the time is well spent, as you will end up

A photo from the past. This is Nat. Gr. Ch. Gr. Ch. 'PR' Shelton's Alexander, owned by Jennifer Walker. He received his title in the days before the Grand Champion title was officially recorded on pedigrees.

with the type of reliable and eager stud you can always count on.

It's best if your dog's first breeding is to a proven, easily bred bitch. Working with two inexperienced dogs can try the patience of the most experienced breeder. The maiden bitch is likely to flirt and to sit down when the male tries to mount her. Even worse, she may snap at him as he mounts. While some dogs will ignore this, it could confuse and discourage your inexperienced male, and spoil his enthusiasm for breeding. If you have little experience yourself and you must breed two unproven dogs, it might be wise to obtain the help of an experienced breeder.

The inexperienced male is more apt to flirt and play with the female. Some of this should be permitted for it will increase his excitement. However, you don't want him to get into the habit of playing excessively. You want him to attend to the business at hand. Verbally encourage him. You don't want to talk so much that you distract him, but you do want to let him know that you approve of what he's doing. No matter how frustrated you become, don't lose your patience. This could ruin the dog for future breedings. Take your time and don't hurry him. He'll soon have the idea.

Some breeders simply put the male and female in a run and leave them alone for several days hoping that they will breed. This is an inefficient and dangerous way of handling a breeding. They have no idea if or precisely when the female was bred. This makes it difficult to plan for the whelping. If you are controlling the breeding and for some reason the stud will not service the bitch, all is not lost. You may still have time to try another stud with the bitch. Also, accidents do occasionally happen and either the bitch or, more likely, the stud could be injured. By controlling the breeding you will be able to avoid a calamity.

It's best to teach your stud dog that you will hold the bitch for him. Some males, particularly those who've bred on their own for the first time, will have nothing to do with a female if you insist on holding her. This can lead to problems when you try him with a difficult bitch. If you are breeding a small stud to a larger female, you may have to reposition the dogs so they can breed successfully. A male who will not allow you to assist will be annoying. Encourage the stud to mount the bitch while you hold her. Beware of talking too much when he's attempting to actually penetrate her. After he's tied, you may indeed pet him and tell him how pleased you are with the job he's done. This way he will learn to be comfortable with having you touch him during the breeding process.

A good stud can continue to sire puppies into his old age. After the age of eight to ten years, however, you may note that some of the bitches he has bred do not conceive. His fertility may diminish during hot weather, for instance. If you're not ready to permanently retire your still valuable stud, you may wish to arrange for periodic sperm counts to be taken.

A dog who is destined to go down in history as one of the breed's most successful show dogs is Lynn Martin Wyza's UKC Gr. Ch., AKC Ch., FCI Int'l Ch., Mex. Ch., RBKC Ch., SKC Ch., IBKCA Ch. and Nat'l. Ch. 'PR' Winterset's Casper. He is also a respected stud dog.

Some males will undergo a personality change after they are used for breeding. They may begin to mark their territory, lifting their leg on furniture or house plants. Watch your male carefully, following breeding, and reprimand him if he exhibits such behavior. Aggression can also be a perplexing problem with males used for breeding. This is seldom a problem for males housed in kennels, where they are routinely separated. In a household situation, where another male resides in the home, this can be devastating. It takes stud dogs of superlative character to coexist peacefully in a home environment. You will need to monitor the dog's behavior, following breeding, to ensure that there are no squabbles or fights. Because of this, it's best to think very seriously before allowing your household companion to be used at stud.

HANDLING THE MATING

You may want to allow the dogs to become familiar before the breeding. Some owners place the dogs in adjacent runs so that they can become acquainted with each other. If this is your first breeding, it's advisable to have two people on hand to handle the breeding. Once you gain experience, you may be able to deal with the situation by yourself. It's important to be able to control both the dog and the bitch. If you are uncertain, placing a leash on the bitch will give you added control.

Take a few moments to plan for the breeding, before you bring out both dogs. You'll want to do the breeding in an area where the dogs will be free from distraction. It's best if the stud is familiar with the area, so that he will feel comfortable. I prefer to breed dogs in the early morning or the evening. I find this less taxing than during the heat of the day. Examine your male. If he is heavily coated, you may wish to trim any hair that's near the penis. Similarly, if the bitch is heavily coated, you may want to clip the hair around her vulva. You want a surface where your male will have good footing. This is seldom a problem if you are breeding outdoors. If you'll be breeding the dogs in the house, you may want to spread out a piece of old carpeting. Be aware that there may be a few dribbles and be sure to protect your regular carpet. If your stud is smaller than the bitch, you might try placing the dogs on a sloping surface or have a small rug on hand. This can be folded so that the male can stand on it and elevate his height.

The early Nat. Gr. Ch. 'PR' Smith's Arctic Snow, owned by Betty and Clarence Smith, is the sire of champions.

Be sure to prepare for your own comfort, too. Once the male penetrates the female, his penis will swell and the dogs will become "tied" together. A tie may last only a few minutes or it could continue for an hour. Most ties last between 15-25 minutes. Try to make yourself as comfortable as you can. If you find a position where you're able to rest your back against a wall, you may be more comfortable. You don't want to be distracted, either. If you're breeding your dogs in the house, take the telephone off the hook. If you're expecting an important phone call, try to move the telephone within reach.

If you wish you may allow the dogs to play and flirt for a few minutes. Kneel down on the ground or floor near the dogs and keep one or both hands on the bitch. Hold her firmly with one hand on her shoulders or neck and the other on her belly. After some initial nuzzling and licking, your male will probably start licking the bitch's vulva. If she's ready to be bred, she'll raise her tail and elevate her vulva. The male will then usually mount her. You'll have to be prepared to control the bitch if she starts to snap or tries to lie down. You'll want to try to line up the bitch and the stud. If he is out of position, very gently push him away and encourage him to try again. You will most likely be able to tell when the male has penetrated by the reaction of the bitch. Just make sure she stands solidly on all four feet until he stops thrusting. Your stud dog will probably slide his front feet off the bitch's back. You may notice that he is anxious to turn. Gently help him bring his hind leg over the bitch's back. Both dogs will then be standing tail to tail. If, while he's turning, your male should cry out in pain, quickly bring him back to the original position. You don't want to take the chance of injuring him.

Just when you think your back will break and your legs have gone permanently to sleep, the dogs will separate. It may take you a few seconds to realize that they are no longer linked. Some breeders like to hold

The Miniature Ch. 'PR' Maxwell's Amiego, owned by Tom and Ruth Maxwell, can be found in many pedigrees.

The extraordinary Standard male Gr. Ch. 'PR' Tinker's Toybear, owned by Carolyn Kane, is an influential stud. He is the sire of two National Grand Champions and many champions and grand champions. *Eddie Rubin photo*

One of the breed's most famous show dogs is Gr. Ch. U-CD 'PR' Winterset's Silver Fox, owned by Sheila and Frank Ruzanski. This Miniature male retired from the ring after winning 52 Grand Champion classes. He is the sire of many champions and grand champions.

the bitch's hindquarters up in the air for a few seconds to avoid losing any sperm. Others consider this a waste of time.

It's best to separate the dogs. Some terrifically enthusiastic stud dogs will mount the bitch and attempt to breed again. Give the dogs some fresh water and allow them to rest. Most breeders skip a day and then breed once more on the following day.

The Outside Tie

An outside tie occurs when the bulb, located at the rear of a dog's penis, swells outside the bitch's vagina. An outside tie is more difficult for the inexperienced breeder to handle. Nevertheless, while less desirable than an inside tie, a properly handled outside tie is often successful. Some males seem more prone to outside ties and, while they are more trouble to breed, they can and do sire puppies.

It's best to hold the penis behind the swollen bulb. Place your other hand on the bitch's belly and press her backwards. You can allow the stud to turn, but it's usually easier to keep the pair linked if he remains mounted. You'll want to hold the bitch and stud together as long as possible. Though the dogs may be restless, try to keep them together for at least five minutes.

THE PUBLIC STUD

As the owner of a public stud, you must realize that you are undertaking a great responsibility. You must insure the safety and well-being of any bitch in your care. A nervous female, in strange surroundings, may be more apt to dart out a door or escape under a fence. You could be legally liable if she's lost. You will also have to prepare yourself for some inconvenience. It's quite possible that you will have to endure a bitch who barks and whines all through the night.

Some of these problems can be abated by having the bitch's owner accompany her during the actual breeding. Some bitches are comforted when they're held by their owners. Others, however, never calm down sufficiently when their owners are present. They are more likely to be subdued without their owner around. You may be more comfortable without the presence of the owner, too. While you certainly don't want to be abusive to the bitch, it is sometimes necessary to be quite firm, particularly with maiden bitches. Stud owners sometimes find this difficult to do under the watchful eye of the female's owner.

Before you offer your male at stud, give some thought to what policies you wish to adopt. You should breed only to United Kennel Club and/or American Kennel Club registered bitches. Standard stud fees are usually equivalent to the price of a show quality puppy. It stands to reason, of course, that the stud fee for a Grand Champion or Champion will be higher than for an untitled male. Unless specific arrangements have been made, stud fees are paid at the time of breeding.

You will have to decide if you're willing to accept the pick of litter pup in lieu of a stud fee. If you do decide to accept a puppy, be sure to specify when you will make your choice. Most breeders opt to pick their puppy between eight and twelve weeks. Do try to be considerate. It's unfair to prohibit the litter owner

AKC Ch. 'PR' Northern Lights Warp Factor Ten was bred, owned and handled to his title by Donna Blews. "Zippy" has points toward his UKC title and is in obedience training.

from selling any puppies because you delay in making your pick.

Bitch owners should be told that they are paying for a service only. The fee is for the male's services, and your time and effort. Simply paying a stud fee does not guarantee a pregnancy or live litter. Most breeders will provide a repeat breeding if the bitch fails to conceive.

You should decide if you wish to offer a "return" service. Many breeders promise one free return breeding if the bitch does not conceive. Most breeders specify that the return service is good only on the bitch's next season. Some stud owners require proof, such as a letter from a veterinarian, that the bitch did not whelp a litter. You may also want to specify that you be notified in a given amount of time if the bitch fails to conceive.

Whatever policies you decide upon, it's best to put them in writing. This will help to eliminate misunderstandings. If you frequently provide stud service, you will want to prepare a standard contract which includes all your policies. If you only rarely provide stud service, it's still best to formalize the agreement. A simple list of any terms and conditions, including a receipt of any monies paid, should be signed by both parties. This precaution will take a little time and thought, but it will help to avoid hard feelings and disputes. Such foresight may well prevent a lawsuit.

Chapter 19

The Brood Bitch

Much of what we've said about stud dog selection, applies equally to the brood bitch. The beginning breeder will make no more important selection than the purchase of a good brood bitch. The strength of your breeding program will be based on your continuing production of good bitches. While many breeders make a grand splash with a sensational winning dog, the true breeder knows that a line of top-producing bitches is his ticket to success. Excellent brood bitches form the cornerstone of the carefully planned breeding program. If you are using outside studs and a breeding proves unsuccessful, it's relatively easy to change course. If, however, your female is unsuitable as a brood bitch, you must either begin again or be plagued with years of trying to breed up from a mediocre start. The brood bitch is the rock upon which the foundation of your kennel will rest. Selection of the appropriate brood bitch, therefore, is essential.

The brood bitch does not necessarily have to be a champion herself. It is imperative, however, that she be carefully bred and from a line that has a reputation for producing consistent quality. After reviewing the breed standard carefully, decide which qualities are most important to you. Select a bitch from a line which excels in those virtues. Look for a bitch who is structurally sound and one that excels in temperament. You'll be on your way to producing American Eskimos of which you can be proud.

BREEDING AGE

American Eskimo females generally come in season for the first time between six and nine months of age. All Eskies are individuals, however, and occasionally you will find bitches who come into season earlier or later than this average. I've heard of Eskies who came into season as early as four months of age and one of my own females had her first estrus at five months. As a rule, most bitches come into season every six months, thereafter.

Your female will need time to grow and mature before being bred. She must be ready, not only physically, but also emotionally and mentally, for the task of having puppies. I suggest waiting until the second season to breed your bitch. This should allow her to mature without the stress of whelping a litter. Under no circumstances should any bitch, no matter how mature she may appear to be, be bred on her first season.

Most breeders prefer to breed their bitches, for the first time, before they reach the age of four. Certainly, bitches can and do whelp successfully, for the first time, after four. Very often, however, it's more difficult for these older bitches to conceive. Like the very young bitch, the older maiden bitch may encounter difficulties in whelping.

Novices often ask when a bitch is too old for breeding. This is difficult to answer. Breeders frequently continue to breed their bitches into their sixth year. Much depends on the health and condition of the bitch. Frequently, older bitches are less regular in their seasons than younger bitches. You should be aware that older bitches are also more prone to complications during whelping, and a Caesarean may be necessary. Still, if you want one last litter from your fabulous brood bitch and she's still in good condition, you can try.

Most breeders breed their brood bitches one season, then skip the next season. This allows the bitch to recover fully and replenish her resources, in preparation for her next litter. There's nothing that grieves the dog lover quite so much as seeing a bitch bred successively, season after season, until she wears out. If you have a bitch, however, that comes into season every ten months or only once a year, it is permissible to breed her every season. If you feel compelled to breed your bitch on successive seasons, then do allow her to rest on her third heat cycle. Above all, let common sense be your guide. If your brood bitch has a litter of one or two puppies and raises them without difficulty, it might not be too much of a strain to breed on her next season.

One of Lynn Martin Wyza's brood bitches, the lovely 'PR' Winterset's Butterfly.

This Miniature bitch, Ch. 'PR' Maxwell's Sonseearay, was owned by Tom and Ruth Maxwell.

If, however, she's just finished raising a litter of eight, you're asking a great deal to expect her to raise another litter on her next season.

CONDITIONING THE FUTURE MOM

The best time to begin conditioning the brood bitch is before she's bred. Your best bet for ensuring vigorous, strong puppies and few whelping problems, is to start with a bitch in tip-top condition. Now's the perfect time for a routine veterinary visit. A fecal examination should be done to detect the presence of worms. It's best to have your bitch treated now, before she's bred. You'll also want to be sure she's up-to-date on her yearly vaccinations. Have the vet attend promptly to any vaginal infections. Immediate treatment is in order for any skin conditions that the bitch might transmit to the puppies.

Now is also the time to stop for a moment and take a long look at the future mom's physique. You want to have her in good, hard condition. A flabby, overweight bitch may have difficulty becoming pregnant. She could also encounter whelping difficulties. Place her on a diet before you breed her. Similarly, the thin, underweight bitch is apt to be dragged down by the burden of a litter. Now, not after breeding, is the best time to increase her ration until she achieves ideal weight.

Optimum muscle tone is also important. A bitch whose muscles are in tight, hard condition is likely to have fewer complications. It's usually not difficult to get American Eskimos to exercise. Thankfully, ours is a lively, energetic breed. Still, make sure your bitch gets sufficient exercise. You want her in the peak of condition. Exercise can be especially useful in helping to trim the figure of an overweight bitch. If your American Eskimo bitch would rather relax on the sofa, you'll have to encourage her to exercise. Toss a ball or a frisbee, or take her for a daily walk. While she may be reluctant to exercise on her own, chances are she'll be delighted at the prospect of spending some time with you. She'll feel better and you'll feel more confident in breeding her.

Your bitch should have a simple blood test to determine if she has the serious and highly infectious canine brucellosis. This bacteria, which affects both males and females, is found in semen and urine of dogs who have this unfortunate condition. Generally, you will not see any outward signs which is why blood testing is so essential. Brucellosis is transmitted sexually and,

The late Gr. Ch. 'PR' Denali's Country U-Kay-C was an extremely reliable brood bitch. She produced champions and grand champions in each of her litters, although bred to different studs. Owned by Nancy and Michelle Hofman, she was the constant companion of the author.

Good health and condition are important in a potential brood bitch. This is Gr. Ch. U-CD 'PR' Thunderpas Snooty Tooty Dotty, owned by Talitha Bell.

since there is no cure, bitches having this bacteria should not be bred. It's important that you insist that the stud you are using has been brucellosis tested, too.

COORDINATING WITH THE STUD DOG OWNER

Contact the owner of the stud you have selected as soon as your bitch begins her season. There's nothing as frustrating, to a stud owner, as receiving a frantic telephone call announcing that a bitch must be bred immediately. Stud dog owners have busy lives, too. Courtesy and thoughtfulness will go a long way toward friendly relations. If you aren't certain of the exact day your bitch's season began, let the stud dog's owner know. He can arrange for you to deliver the bitch a few days early.

Ch. 'PR' Snobird's Winter Break, a Standard bitch, is owned by Judy Jones.

By understanding your bitch's season, you will be better able to pinpoint the correct time for breeding. Lila and Leroy Bean carefully track Gr. Ch. 'PR' Sassi's Crystal Misty's seasons.

UNDERSTANDING YOUR BITCH'S SEASON

It's an aid to breeders to have a basic understanding of their female's heat, or estrus, cycle. If we have a general grasp of how the bitch's body functions during the breeding season, it will make it easier to determine the optimum days for breeding.

Your bitch will be in season for approximately eighteen to twenty-one days. Young bitches may, the first time, have an immature, or incomplete, season of shorter duration. It's easy to miss the first few days of a bitch's season, so close attention is essential. Your first indication that your bitch is in season will likely be the sight of a few drops of blood. You'll also note that her vulva swells, although at this early stage it will feel firm when touched. Some bitches are quite adept at keeping themselves clean. If you suspect that your bitch is in season, you may want to line her kennel, crate or dog bed with a white cloth (an old sheet or white towel is ideal) so that you will be able to confirm your suspicions. Some bitches have a pinkish discharge, but most show bright red blood.

During this first phase, you may notice behavioral changes in your Eskie female. Some bitches become anxious and nervous, while others seem overly affectionate. A bitch may be a bit testy with other females. Don't be surprised if she needs to go out to relieve herself more often than usual. These changes are due to the sudden production of hormones and are quite normal. This first phase of your bitch's season will last approximately one week. You should be aware, however, that all American Eskimo bitches are individuals and many vary from this general guideline.

Before breeding, carefully assess your bitch's conformation and temperament. This lovely bitch has both brains and beauty. AKC Ch., SKC Ch. & Gr. Ch. U-CD 'PR' Thunderpas Athena, CD was bred by Patrea Pabst and is owned and shown by her husband Robert Kalkreuter. *Teresa Yancey photo*

Gr. Ch. 'PR' Stevens' Country Princess, owned by Sandy Tocco, was the nation's top female Eskie in 1984.

The second phase of the season is the one that most concerns breeders. It is during this time that the bitch is ready to be bred. By this time, your bitch's vaginal secretion will have changed. Most likely it will become clear or take on a yellowish tinge (breeders often refer to this as "straw-colored"). A light touch of your bitch's vulva, with a piece of toilet paper, will help you to observe this change. If your bitch happens to be one of those who are fastidiously clean, the best time to check is while she's sleeping or the minute she awakens. You'll notice changes in the vulva, too. It will generally show greater swelling and will be softer and almost flabby in nature. The vaginal opening will be more prominent.

The bitch's demeanor will definitely change during the second phase. She'll flirt eagerly with other dogs. If you have her in an enclosure with other bitches, you may find that they are mounting her. Some females become quite brazen in their flirtations. Owners must exercise caution during this phase of the bitch's cycle. Not only is the bitch intensely interested in being bred, but she's extremely enticing to males. The odor of her urine will proclaim to every male that she's available. Indeed, you may find a pack of males camped out on your front lawn.

Watch closely for your bitch to exhibit the classic, telltale sign of breeding readiness...flagging her tail. She will raise her tail and flip it slightly to the side. She'll also elevate her vulva in anticipation. It's best to breed a couple of days after the bitch begins flagging her tail. This is usually on the tenth to the fourteenth day. Treat this on an individual basis. Let the bitch's behavior be your guide. Most breeders breed one day, skip a day, and then repeat the breeding. This increases their chances of selecting a day when the bitch will have ovulated.

Don't assume that your bitch's interest in males will diminish after she's been bred. Continue to exercise caution in protecting her. Your bred bitch could still slip out under a fence. Males have been known to go to extraordinary lengths in their efforts to reach a female in season. You must remain vigilant.

During the final phase of your bitch's season, she will no longer be willing to stand for breeding. She may growl or snap at any male who attempts to mount her. Her swelling will diminish and her decreasing discharge will have changed to a dull brown color. Her body is now returning to normal.

As we've said, all Eskie bitches are individuals. Some simply don't follow the commonly accepted rules. There are bitches who routinely have irregular seasons. They may be ready for breeding on the second day of their season. Conversely, one occasionally finds a bitch who should be bred on the sixteenth day. It's very difficult to ascertain the optimum breeding day for such females. You may breed this type of bitch, season after season, without getting her to conceive. You may want to coordinate with your veterinarian. He can perform vaginal smears that will help to pinpoint the ideal day for breeding.

DETERMINING PREGNANCY

The breeding has taken place and now the waiting game begins. If this will be your first litter, you will undoubtedly be anxious. You'll be watching eagerly for any sign that your bitch is pregnant. I'm afraid there is nothing to do but relax. The normal gestation period for dogs in 63 days. However, many females, particularly first time mothers, whelp their litters early.

During the first month of pregnancy, there's virtually no way to tell for certain if your female has conceived. You may be able to detect signs of pregnancy as early as the fourth week. At this stage, you might note a thickening in the width of the loin.

During the fifth week, other changes may become evident. Your bitch may become ravenous, eating her food with great relish. Bitches, particularly those carrying large litters, may look fuller in the belly. It's during the fifth week of pregnancy that you can palpate the bitch in an attempt to feel the developing fetuses. Some breeders are very skilled at palpation, while others just don't have the touch. The same applies to veterinarians. Palpation is effective only in the fifth week for at this stage the fetuses are small, hard and firm. Later, they will be too soft to detect. You should also know that if the bitch is carrying her puppies high up under the ribs, you won't be able to detect them. If you are going to palpate, above all, be gentle. You want to know if there are puppies. The last thing you want to do is harm them. With your thumb and index finger, gently feel along the bitch's abdomen. You are searching for one or more bumps approximately the size of a hickory nut. Once again, palpation is not foolproof. Don't become discouraged if you can't feel anything.

During the sixth week, you should be able to see definite signs of pregnancy. Your bitch may well have a big belly by this time. Because of the added weight, her topline may begin to sag. Even bitches with strong, sound rears may appear spraddle-legged and cowhocked. You may see that the bitch's nipples are slightly swollen and appear more prominent. The breasts may begin to fill with milk. Remember, however, that your bitch could be carrying a single puppy. Do watch her closely even if you fear that she may not have conceived.

The impressive Gr. Ch. 'PR' Tsa La Gi's Satin Doll, owned by Lynne Vickers.

CARING FOR THE MOTHER-TO-BE

Your bitch is now eating for herself and her puppies, and you will have to feed her accordingly. Most breeders have, over the years, developed different diets for use on pregnant bitches. Ask ten different breeders what they feed and you're bound to get ten different answers. This only illustrates that there is no one specific way of feeding that will insure success. There are, however, certain general guidelines that you should follow.

You will, of course, be increasing the amount of food your bitch will receive. Most importantly, you want to increase the quality of her food. Foods high in protein, with a good calcium content, are recommended. The important thing to remember is to make certain that you are using a complete, well-balanced dog ration. Some breeders give a vitamin and mineral supplement, and you may want to ask your veterinarian about this. Be aware that loading her up with additional vitamins is risky, however. Oversupplementation can cause many problems.

During the early stages of her pregnancy, your bitch can continue with her routine exercise. If she has

A beautiful Miniature bitch, Ch. 'PR' Flo Dai's Snobird Ginger Snap, owned by Judy Jones.

AKC & Gr. Ch. 'PR' Thunderpas Apollo's Gaea, owned by Rosemary Stevens, is the dam of champions, including the first AKC American Eskimo champion. *Eddie Rubin photo*

good muscle tone, the whelping will be easier. By the fourth or fifth week, however, it's best to cut down on any really strenuous exercise. Jumping should definitely be curtailed.

Unless absolutely necessary, the bitch should receive no medications or shots during her pregnancy. Some medications can cause birth defects. There have been instances where treatment has been toxic and fatal to the developing fetuses. Unless the condition threatens to endanger the bitch's life, try to delay any medications until after she's whelped her litter.

American Eskimos are, generally, healthy and hardy dogs. They usually experience few problems during their pregnancies. Your best bet for avoiding problems during pregnancy is to begin with a healthy bitch. By conditioning her carefully, insuring correct exercise and feeding her sensibly, you will have prepared her for her job as a mother. As the date she's due to whelp approaches, watch her closely. By being vigilant, you'll be able to see both the physical and behavioral changes, and avoid any problems.

Chapter 20

Having Puppies

Delivering a litter of puppies is a natural process for your bitch. We've all heard the stories of bitches that whelped their litters, without assistance, under the porch of an old farm house. There's even the old timer's story of the Foxhound bitch. It seems that the pregnant bitch was part of a pack in hot pursuit of their quarry. During the chase, the bitch stopped, whelped a puppy and cleaned it off. Taking it in her mouth, she rejoined the other pack members, continued the chase and then came home to deliver the rest of her litter.

Natural though it may be, some dogs do need assistance in bringing their puppies into the world. It's advisable for you to be there, just in case there's a problem. American Eskimos are, in general, excellent mothers. Some do, however, need a little help in getting started.

If this is the first time you've attended a mother-to-be, it's natural that you'll be nervous. Just don't let your anxiety consume you. Some bitch owners have panicked at the last moment and rushed the bitch to the veterinarian, so he could do the whelping. The place for the bitch who's beginning labor is at home, unless complications force a trip to the vet. She'll be more relaxed in familiar surroundings.

Your best bet for staying calm is to educate yourself. If you know what to anticipate, the whole experience will seem less frightening to you. By learning as much as possible about what will happen, you'll be able to tell when things are going awry. It's impossible to predict how your bitch will act, particularly if this is her first litter. She may take command of the situation and not need any assistance at all. If she has the situation well in hand, don't interfere.

As the big day approaches, you're likely to become more and more anxious. Take heart for most whelpings go smoothly, just as nature intended. To allay your fears, refer to this chapter and gather all the equipment that you might need. If you have a friend who's a long time breeder, keep the telephone close by. Many an experienced breeder has talked a novice through the process. If you truly fear that there might be a problem, check with your veterinarian. Tell him the date your bitch is due and make sure that he will be there or on call, should you need him during the night.

WHERE TO HAVE THE PUPPIES

Left to her own devices, the bitch will surely choose an inappropriate place to whelp. Stories of bitches who delivered their litters in closets, under the living room sofa, or in the middle of a bed, abound. Give some thought to where you want to house the mom and her litter. You want a place that's free from drafts and reasonably warm. Most importantly, you want a place where mom can feel secure and where she will stay calm. Look for a spot that's away from the hustle and bustle of everyday life. You will also want a location where you can easily glance in and check on her. If you have a guest bedroom, or there's a convenient corner of your bedroom, this may be ideal. It's possible that you'll have several nights when you'll be half-awake, watching the bitch. Having access to a bed, for naps, is handy. If at all possible, you'll want a telephone within easy reach, just in case you do have an emergency.

Your bitch needs to feel protected and secure. This isn't the time to plan a dinner party or issue an invitation to the family to come for a visit. Keep strangers and friends alike away from the bitch. Don't bring people in to see the expectant mother. If there are children in your home, declare the mother-to-be's room strictly off limits. Expectant mothers have been known to act unpredictably.

It's best to provide the bitch with a whelping box. There are many types of boxes, some fancy and some simple. Some breeders elect to use cardboard cartons (those with Standard sized Eskies will find boxes for televisions the appropriate size) for their whelping bitches. These are readily available from grocery or appliance stores. If you decide to go this route, be absolutely sure you know what came in the cartons. You must never use cartons which formerly contained a potentially toxic substance, such as detergents or abrasives. Cardboard cartons don't hold up as well as permanent whelping pens, so you'll need two boxes. One will be used during the actual whelping. You will then transfer mom and her puppies to the other box after the whelping. You'll have to cut an opening in one side of the box, leaving a strip along the bottom about two to three inches high. This will allow mom to get away from the puppies and yet keep them from tumbling out.

Most American Eskimos are devoted mothers. This is Ch. 'PR' Stevens' Good Golly Miss Molly, owned by Kathy Cella, with her three-day-old puppies.

Chances are, those with several bitches will opt for permanent whelping boxes. Each breeder seems to come up with a design that suits him. There are, however, several guidelines you should follow. You must be capable of easily sanitizing the whelping box. If you opt for cardboard cartons, these, of course, should be discarded after each use. You'll want to make sure that the mother has an opportunity to get away from the puppies. She must have easy access to them, but be able to escape their constant demands. Some breeders have used a child sized wading pool. You must decide on the bedding to line the whelping box. Some breeders opt for indoor-outdoor carpeting, while others prefer newspaper. If you decide on carpeting, be sure it is secured to the bottom of the box.

It's best to place the mother in the whelping box about a week before she's due. This way she can become accustomed to her new surroundings. Mothers, suddenly placed in a new and strange whelping box, have been known to try relocating their litters to a place of their own choosing. It will hasten her adjustment if you feed her in the box. Encourage her and tell her how good she is for remaining in this strange, new place. By the time she's ready to deliver the litter, she will have settled down and will be comfortable in her new home.

Most Eskies will be fine in your normal household temperature. Freedom from drafts, however, is essential. You don't want to take a chance on the puppies or the mother being chilled. If you fear that drafts may be a problem, it's a good idea to partially enclose the whelping box, with cardboard or blankets, to keep out the breeze. You may want to provide extra warmth during the whelping and for the first few days. This can be provided with a light bulb or a heating pad on the "low" setting. One caution if you opt for a heating pad. Make certain that the mother cannot get at the electric cord. It's also a good idea to insure that the heating pad does not cover the entire surface of the whelping pen. Tiny puppies can become overheated and they must have room to move off the heating pad or they will become dehydrated. If your bitch is whelping in winter and there's a heavy wind outside, you may want to place a small heater in the room where she's whelping. This will protect mom and babies until the weather warms again.

WHAT ELSE WILL I NEED?

It's best to collect a few supplies that may come in handy during the whelping. Have a good supply of *newspapers* on hand and a large *garbage bag* for bundling up the soiled papers. It's a good idea to have a *cardboard box* with a heat source. Some mothers become restless while they're whelping. You may want to remove one or more puppies and place them in this box, while she delivers the next addition. You'll want to have several *towels,* for cleaning and rubbing down the puppies. A pair of blunt nose *scissors* is excellent for use in cutting the umbilical cords. You might also prefer to have a *hemostat* on hand, for clamping the cord before you make the cut. Some breeders prefer to use *dental floss* to tie off the cords. It's best, just in case, to have some *Esbilac* or other milk replacer. You'll also want a *baby scale*, for weighing the newborns and a *pen* and some *paper* for jotting down notes.

YOU AND YOUR VETERINARIAN

We hope that you've already established a close working relationship with your veterinarian. It's reassuring to know that you have someone you can trust, if need be. Don't pester your vet with calls over trivial, insignificant matters as the day of birth approaches. You don't want to gain a reputation as "the boy who cried wolf." Make sure you keep records, such as the days your bitch was bred and the hour she went into labor. These will be helpful to your veterinarian, should treatment be necessary.

Let common sense be your guide in contacting your veterinarian for help. Some vets will tell you not to worry if the bitch hasn't gone into hard labor (had at least one contraction). However, if you honestly believe there's a problem, do make a call. You are within your rights in insisting that the veterinarian meet you at his office. Trust your instincts. While your veterinarian is a well-trained professional, you live with the bitch daily and know her better than anyone else. If you're sure there's a problem, don't hesitate to pick up the phone.

WATCHING FOR THE SIGNS

American Eskimo bitches vary in the warning they will give you as the time of birth approaches. Some exhibit virtually no symptoms. Conversely, other bitches will drive you to distraction several days before the big event. Many bitches become excited, nervous and restless as the big day approaches. There are a few, however, who will remain calm until they actually go into labor.

One of the early signs to look for is your bitch's attempt to "nest." She'll tear papers frantically, then lie down. In a few minutes she'll be up again, ripping at the papers with her paws and mouth. She continually rearranges the papers to suit herself. Many bitches refuse food, as the time approaches. Some wolf down their food voraciously, only to regurgitate it, afterward. You may notice that your bitch is shivering violently, even though the temperature in the room is very warm. Sometimes you can detect a physical change in your bitch's appearance. She may be carrying her puppies lower and have a "hollow" look in the loin area.

Some bitches, particularly household pets, want you near them at this time. Give your Eskie a few pats of encouragement, try to calm her down and tell her how well she's doing. Stay calm yourself. This period, known as prelabor, may last only an hour or the bitch may carry on like this for a day or more.

TEMPERATURE CAN BE AN INDICATOR

Most breeders will rely on their experience in determining when a bitch is due to whelp. For the beginner, however, charting your bitch's temperature can be helpful. The bitch's temperature will drop shortly before the birth of the puppies. By taking her temperature repeatedly, you will have advance warning.

The dog's normal temperature is around 101.6 degrees. Individual dogs, however, can vary slightly from the accepted norm. For this reason, it's best to take your bitch's temperature twice a day during the week before she's due to whelp. Take your readings at twelve hour intervals, such as seven a.m. and seven p.m. Avoid taking the reading immediately after your bitch has exercised, as activity may elevate her temperature. Don't be alarmed if her temperature fluctuates slightly during the day. This is normal. By taking her temperature in this manner, you'll be establishing a "baseline" that will tell you what is normal for your dog.

When you notice a steep drop in the bitch's temperature, you will want to watch her closely. The temperature will probably drop into the nineties. This is a clear sign that your bitch will whelp some time within the next twenty four hours. If you see no symptoms of labor within a day after the temperature drops, phone your veterinarian. Similarly, if your bitch has not whelped by the 63rd day after breeding, it's best to take her in for a check-up.

Ch. 'PR' Shamrc's Sunday Silence nurses her litter of one-week-old puppies at the home of Doug and Esperanza Kaz. *Doug Kaz photo*

LABOR BEGINS

During the first stage of labor, your bitch will become increasingly nervous and uncomfortable. She'll scratch frantically at her papers, lie down and pant for a few seconds and then get up to paw the papers again. She may have a pained look on her face. Don't be alarmed if she whines and trembles. Watch for your bitch to begin licking her vulva. You don't want to interfere with her at this stage. It's best to keep an eye on her from a discreet distance. Don't add to her nervousness.

The beginning stage of labor may last one hour or more. You might try speeding up the process, by letting the bitch outside to relieve herself. Offer her a drink of water. Do, however, exercise caution and keep a close eye on her while she's outside. More than one breeder has discovered that the bitch whelped a puppy outside.

If your bitch remains in this first stage of labor for more than twenty four hours, call your veterinarian. Problems don't usually occur until the bitch has gone into hard labor, but it's best to be on the safe side. Do keep an eye out for an abnormal discharge. If you see a greenish or black discharge, phone the vet immediately. Excessive bleeding should also be reported promptly to your veterinarian.

HARD LABOR

Hard labor begins when your bitch has her first contraction. The first contractions could be mild and easily missed, so watch closely. You don't want to interfere, but it's best, at this stage, to move closer and keep a steady eye on her. Jot down the time you noticed the first contraction. Don't trust your memory. The contractions will probably increase as your bitch bears down. The contractions may follow one right after the other or there may be an interval of time between them. Much of this depends on where the puppies are, in relation to the birth canal. If this is the first time you've witnessed a bitch in labor, it may look as though she's straining to have a bowel movement. Your bitch will choose a position that's comfortable for her. Some bitches have their puppies lying down and others prefer to stand.

If your bitch is having very hard contractions and she hasn't whelped a puppy in an hour, it's time to call the veterinarian. There may be an overly large puppy that she's unable to expel. It's also possible that a puppy is in an awkward position and jammed at the entrance to the birth canal. In either of these situations, you vet may elect to perform a Caesarian section. If your bitch's hard contractions stop suddenly and don't resume within an hour, call the veterinarian.

THEY'RE HERE!

After one or several hard contractions, a large, black, bubble-like sac will emerge from the vulva. This will probably be the water bag. The appearance of the water bag is an important sign, for it signals the entrance of the first puppy into the birth canal. Be alert, for the puppy usually follows quickly. Occasionally, the water bag will burst in the birth canal, but this is not a cause for alarm.

Most puppies are born head first. The puppy will be encased in a watertight, fluid filled sac. During the months of pregnancy, he has been suspended in this fluid and received oxygen through his umbilical cord. The sac must be torn away from the puppy's head immediately, so that he can breathe air, not fluid, now that the umbilical cord is no longer providing him with oxygen. Make sure the bitch attends to this immediately. If she doesn't, tear the sac away with your fingers. Move quickly. Try to be unobtrusive, so as to avoid upsetting the bitch unnecessarily.

Generally, the bitch will take over. She will pull away and eat the sac. She'll lick the puppy all over, cleaning it and stimulating it. You will be surprised at how roughly the bitch handles the newborn. She may even roll the puppy over, causing it to cry out and thrash around. Don't be alarmed. This is natural and beneficial. As the pup cries out, he's filling his newborn lungs with oxygen.

When the bitch has finished cleaning the puppy, she should attend to the umbilical cord. She will sever it with her teeth. If your bitch fails to cut the cord, you will have to step in and take over this duty. Take a firm hold on the cord, but do not pull it as this will result in an umbilical hernia. Approximately one to two inches

A beautiful picture. Ch. 'PR' Stevens' Snow Queen poses with her 20-day-old litter of five pups.

from the puppy's belly is where you want to cut the cord. Some breeders prefer to clamp the cord first with a hemostat. If you opt for this method, leave the clamp in place for a few minutes or until the bleeding subsides. Some breeders also feel it's best to tie the cord. If you want to tie the cord, encircle it with dental floss and make one or two knots. Be sure to cut off all the excess floss. If you don't trim the floss, it will worry the mother and she may tug on it and injure the puppy. You may also wish to apply a drop of iodine to the remaining cord.

Be sure to look for the placenta, or afterbirth. This is usually attached to the umbilical cord. The afterbirth is about half the size of the puppy and will resemble a dark piece of liver. Occasionally, the placenta will separate from the puppy and be expelled just after he's born or be pushed out by the emergence of the next puppy.

You'll want to be alert for the appearance of each afterbirth. There will be one for every puppy born. You may want to make a note each time you see one. After the whelping is completed, check your notes. If an afterbirth was not expelled, contact your veterinarian. Retained placentas cause very serious infection and may be fatal to your bitch.

Breeders differ in their opinions as to whether the mother should be allowed to eat the afterbirths. The afterbirth is a rich source of vitamins and nutrients. In the wild, it supplies the mother with nourishment, so that she doesn't have to leave the litter in search of food. Experts also believe that the placenta may stimulate milk production. Unfortunately, consuming the afterbirth has a laxative effect on the bitch and she's apt to have loose stools for a few days. Some breeders remove and discard all afterbirths. Many breeders allow the bitch to eat one afterbirth and remove all subsequent ones. Some breeders believe it's best to allow the bitch to consume as many as she wants. Talk with your veterinarian, or friends who are experienced breeders, to help you decide what to do.

CLEARING THE PUPPY OF FLUID

Once the mother has cleaned up the puppy, you'll want to pick him up and examine him. Some mothers object to this, while others seem to welcome the help. If the mother objects and you feel she's done a good job, you can delay. Rub the puppy vigorously, with a towel, until he's completely dried. Remember, you needn't be gentle. If he hasn't made a sound or if he seems a little sluggish, give a sharp little tug on his tail. This is akin to spanking a newborn human infant on the bottom. He'll cry out and his lungs will fill with oxygen.

A 14-day-old puppy owned by Doug and Esperanza Kaz. *Doug Kaz photo*

Hold the puppy to your ear. If you hear any rasping, rattling or bubbling, the puppy has retained fluid in its lungs. You don't want him to get pneumonia, so it's best to deal with this immediately. You'll want to "swing down" or "shake down" the puppy, as breeders call this technique. While it may sound complicated, once you try it, you'll see how simple it is in reality. Hold the puppy very securely, with his belly resting in your palm. Place the other hand over its back, with the index finger and middle finger behind the puppy's neck and head for support. Stand up straight with your legs approximately shoulder's width apart. Carefully raise the puppy, at arm's length, over your head. Make sure your grip is secure, you don't want to drop him. Swing your arms forcefully in an arc, from over your head to down between your legs. The centrifugal force generated in this maneuver will expel fluid from the puppy's lungs. You'll notice a few bubbles of moisture at the puppy's nose and/or mouth. Wipe these off and repeat the procedure. Place the puppy to your ear once again. If you still hear rasping, repeat the procedure. Continue with this until the puppy's lungs sound clear.

THE FAMILY GROWS

Bitches may deliver their puppies in rapid succession, or there could be a lengthy break before the next puppy arrives. It will calm the bitch if you leave the puppy with her, until the next contractions begin. Many bitches become restless when the contractions start again. They stand, walk around and tear at the papers. It's best to remove the first puppy, so that mom can concentrate on the task at hand. You wouldn't want her to lie on the pup or inadvertently injure him. Be sure to place him on a heating pad or under a heat lamp.

It's entirely possible that the second puppy may come "breech" or feet first. Such births are fairly common in dogs. Breech puppies may come easily. There is the possibility, however, that the puppy may hang up since the widest part of his body (the shoulders) exits last. Some bitches must give an extra push or two to expel the pup. If the hind legs emerge, but the rest of the pup does not immediately follow, you should help. Grasp the hind legs and hold them securely. If at all possible, leave the sac intact. Pull gently, steadily and very slowly. It's best to pull in time with the mother's contractions. If she isn't bearing down, massage her stomach to stimulate the contractions. Make certain you pull out and down, just as the puppy would come into the world naturally. Once the puppy is out, quickly break the sac, clean and massage the puppy, and swing him down. This is very important, as breech puppies almost always have fluid in their lungs.

Experienced breeders can often successfully turn a puppy which is in an abnormal position inside the mother. They've learned this skill from watching veterinarians, talking with breeders and, most of all, through experience. It's difficult for novices to deal with this type of problem, however. A call to your veterinarian is in order.

HELPING THE PUPPIES TO NURSE

Now that the puppies are here, it's time for them to nurse. Some puppies instinctively hunt for a nipple, almost immediately, while others may not nurse for an hour or more. First time mothers may be uncomfortable having the puppies nurse. Don't worry, with time and patience, the bitch will catch on.

The first feeding is very important. Following birth, the mother produces colostrum. This milky substance contains antibodies that transfer the mother's immunity to the puppies. If a puppy seems reluctant to nurse, you'll have to lend a helping hand. Open the puppy's mouth and place it on a nipple. Squeeze a few drops of milk onto the puppy's tongue. If necessary, support his body while he nurses. Getting a newborn to nurse is sometimes frustrating, but just keep at it. Soon you'll be rewarded by a row of contented little puppies with full tummies.

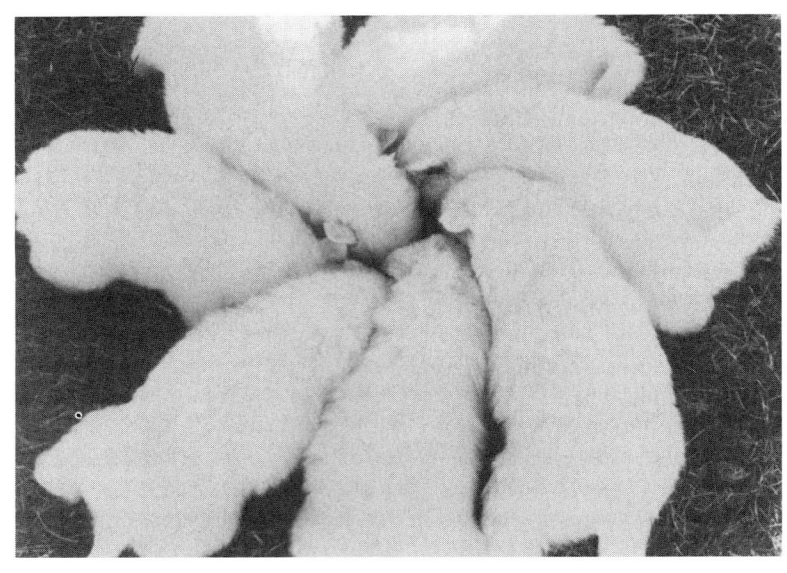

Most American Eskimo puppies are good eaters. Here is a litter of puppies learning to eat solid food at Brenda O'Sullivan's Shamroc Kennels.

THE NEW FAMILY

Now that the excitement of whelping is past, you'll be able to settle down and observe mom and her brood. Newborn puppies will nurse and sleep around the clock, during these first few days. You'll be amazed at how quickly they grow. Don't be surprised if the little whelps double in size before your eyes. If the bitch has the situation well in hand, don't interfere. This is not the time for visitors, so don't invite people over to see the babies. Do watch the puppies. You'll be able to determine when something is amiss. Healthy, vital puppies will wriggle and squirm when you pick them up. The weak, listless, limp puppy, who cries incessantly, is a problem. He may not be getting enough milk. It's also best to keep an extra close eye on any very tiny pups in the litter. Make sure that they aren't being pushed off the nipple by their stronger littermates. If necessary, place them on the nipple and make sure they get their fair share.

Make certain the dam is cleaning the puppies. Newborn pups are unable to urinate and defecate on their own for the first few days, and mom must attend to this. She should lick and stimulate them to eliminate. If you fear that the bitch is neglecting this, you'll have to fill in for her. Dip a piece of cotton in warm water and gently rub the pups' private parts.

In the days following the whelping, keep an eye on the mother. It's natural for her to have some discharge, usually reddish brown in color. She may also continue to bleed. If you notice excessive bleeding, particularly if it's bright red blood, contact your veterinarian. Be alert for any sign of a greenish discharge. This type of discharge usually means that a placenta has been retained and could spell serious trouble, if not treated promptly. If the mother seems weak or listless, has an elevated temperature, or goes into convulsions, take her immediately to the veterinarian.

Your bitch will probably have a voracious appetite. Continue feeding her as you did when she was pregnant. Allow her to consume as much food as she wishes. Also, be certain that the bitch is supplied with plenty of clean water. You'll be surprised at how much she drinks. This is normal, don't be alarmed.

The puppies' eyes will open at about two weeks of age. It's fascinating to watch them discover their new world. By two or three weeks, they'll be staggering onto their feet and trying to take their first faltering steps. In another short week, they'll be walking without difficulty. However, if you've had a litter with only one puppy, it may take him a little longer to begin walking. You'll want to clip back the puppies' toenails at this stage. The tips can be taken off with a pair of scissors or a human nail clipper. Be careful to remove only the white tip and avoid cutting into the pink vein, known as the "quick."

WEANING TIME

Weaning should begin at three to four weeks of age. Some mothers grow fussy during the third week and spend more time away from the puppies. Conversely, other mothers will stay with their pups well into the sixth week, even allowing them to nurse once the sharp milk teeth have emerged. Generally, mothers with small litters will continue to nurse for a longer period.

Most American Eskimo puppies are avid eaters and your litter will probably take less than a week to wean. I start by giving the pups two feedings a day. I begin with a pablum type human baby cereal mixed with warm water. Mixed in equal parts with the water, this has a very sloppy, gruel-like appearance. Pour the food into a shallow dish or onto a plate. A pie pan is ideal. Stick the puppies' noses in the pan, or place some food on your fingers and allow them to lick it off. Don't be surprised if your puppies are messy. They'll take a few bites of the food, walk in it, fall in it and, generally have a wonderful time making absolute messes of themselves. When they lose interest in the food, return mom to them. She'll finish up the remainder of the meal, including what's on the pups.

During their first few meals, your puppies are likely to get more food on themselves than in their tummies.

Once the puppies are eating the cereal well, you can begin introducing them to solid food. Buy some puppy kibble and soak it in warm water until it swells up and becomes soft. Mix this with a small amount of the cereal. As the puppies become familiar with this, decrease the cereal until they are eating kibble alone. A small amount of cottage cheese or canned meat can be added to the kibble. Some breeders begin their puppies on milk, but very often this causes loose stools. Be sure to provide clean water for the pups. After you have the pups eating successfully, you can gradually begin decreasing the amount of food the mother is receiving.

Puppies have small stomachs, so it is important to feed small amounts frequently. Generally, I give my puppies four meals a day until they reach three months of age. At this stage, they are usually cut back to three feedings per day. I continue this thrice daily feeding schedule, until the puppy has reached eight months of age. From eight months to two years, I feed the dog twice daily. Some breeders, however, pare the dog back to one meal a day at one year of age.

SOCIALIZATION

As the pups grow, you'll want to give them attention. After the first week or so, you'll probably pick them up, cuddle them and love them, while mom is out exercising. Puppies need love to grow into stable adults with charming personalities. You may want to expose them to household sounds. The television, radio and vacuum cleaner, as well as the clatter of pots and pans, and the ringing of the telephone, may startle and frighten them at first, but they'll quickly adjust.

If the weather is warm, pups can be taken out at about five weeks of age. Be sure, however, that they

These puppies, whelped at Rosemary Stevens' house, are eager to get out of the whelping box and explore.

have access to the shade. You may want to provide them with toys. An old work glove or discarded sock makes an excellent and inexpensive play toy. While they love squeaky toys, it's best not to allow them to play with these. They could tear apart the toy and accidentally swallow the squeaker.

VACCINATIONS

Your puppy will gradually lose the immunity he obtained from his mother. There's no precise date when this will occur. It's best to check with your vet to see when he wishes to start the immunization program. It will probably be at six to eight weeks of age.

Rosemary Reseigh's pups enjoy their stint in the exercise pen where they can see new sights.

Generally, puppy vaccinations are given as a series of two or three shots. Since there's no way to tell exactly when the mother's immunity will end, the multiple shots will ensure that the puppy is adequately protected. Don't stint or think you can save money by skipping the shots. The cost of vaccination is very small, compared to the cost of treating a dog who has contracted distemper, hepatitis, leptospirosis or parvovirus.

Your puppies are now well on their way to becoming well adjusted adult American Eskimos. More than likely, you'll decide to keep at least one of the litter. With a little luck, it could become your first homebred champion. The other puppies will go to loving homes. Be sure to check back, periodically, with their new owners. Go to see the puppy or request a photo. By keeping in touch with the people who purchase your pups, you'll be better able to evaluate the litter. This will be of great help to you in planning your next breeding.

Chapter 21

From Birth to Maturity

It's sometimes difficult for new owners to envision the growth stages that their puppy will go through. There will be many changes as your cuddly puppy matures to adulthood. We thought it might be helpful for you to follow this process, through pictures. Our model is Gr. Ch. "PR" Hofman's Country Coolpas Luke (AKC major pointed), a Standard-sized male, owned by Nancy J. Hofman and Julie D. Young. He appears in all but the birth to three-four day shots, which were contributed by Kathy Cella. It should be remembered that Miniature and Toy American Eskimos mature much more quickly than Standards.

THE PARENTS

(On the left)
The Sire: Gr. Ch. 'PR' Stevens' Max-A-Million, owned by Kathy Cella

(On the right)
The Dam: Gr. Ch. 'PR' Hofman-Thunderpas Country Solo, owned by Nancy J. and Michele Hofman

AT BIRTH

American Eskimo puppies are born white. The coat is short and satiny and the pink skin shows through. The nose and pads are probably pink, though occasionally you will see some puppies born with black pigmentation. The eyes are closed and the ears are flattened against the head. The puppies go by smell at this stage, as they cannot hear or see. They do not yet have teeth. The muzzle often has a rather blunt appearance. Check to see if your puppies have any dewclaws. Rear dewclaws should definitely be removed and you may wish to remove the front dewclaws, too. This is usually done at two days.

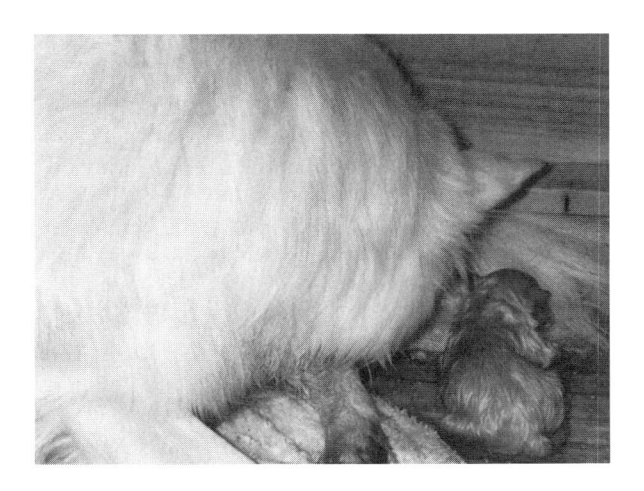

3-4 DAYS
(On the right)

Weight has increased. You will begin to see involuntary twitches, or flickers, of the muscles. On some puppies, you will begin to see the first black smudges on the nose and/or mouth. You may detect a slight grayish cast on the eyerims. This a good indication that the pigment will be black.

I begin to touch the puppies at this stage. I pet them lightly, but I don't pick them up. I do my best to get them used to human touch without disturbing them.

(On the left)
10-14 Days

The eyes are open now and are slate blue in color, although they are still unfocused. The coats are beginning to grow and become fluffy. The pups are growing and will now be about twice their birth weight. The wedge-shape of the head is now apparent. While nursing, you will notice the tails come straight up and start wagging. The pups are beginning to hear so make sure that you don't startle them.

Now that the puppies' eyes are open, I increase the amount of touching they receive. I pick them up very carefully, at this stage, pet them and talk softly to them. This should be done very gently, so as not to frighten them.

3-4 WEEKS
(On the right)

The ears are beginning to come up, though this will vary from puppy to puppy. The tails start to come up over the back and the puppies begin to use them for balance. The puppies are now trying to get on their feet, but they are rocking back and forth. They begin to move, though they totter about like drunken sailors. When they aren't eating or sleeping, they begin to play with each other. They discover they have voices and take delight in barking and growling...then they promptly fall right over! In their mind, they are "big guys" now. You start to see the appearance of sharp little teeth, much to the consternation of the nursing mother. Their little nails are starting to grow and Mom doesn't like that either. You can use a human nail clipper to very carefully take off the points. You may want to start the pups on mush now.

Now the fun really starts! This is discovery time. The pups will hang onto their mother's teats very tightly and, when she jumps out of the box, the pups will take a ride out, too. This provides them with a wonderful opportunity to explore. The adventurous will love the chance to see larger vistas, but the fearful ones will scream the first time or two. They will learn to grab hold and pull themselves up and over the box so they can get out on their own. In fact, they will attempt to get out of the box and explore at every opportunity.

5-6 WEEKS

It's full activity in the puppy pen now. They romp, play, bark, growl and have a grand old time. The coat continues to grow and the puppies are becoming very photogenic. Ears continue to come up, although they may go up and down or there may be one ear up and one ear tipped or partially down. The ears on Miniature puppies will probably be up by now. The pigmentation has, hopefully, filled in completely now. Their fat little bodies are still waddling along, but it's time to look for some features which will separate the show and pet puppies. You can begin checking the bites now. Cowhocks and weak pasterns will be clearly seen.

You will be able to tell if the puppies have correct tail sets. Ear set will also be discernible, even if the ears aren't completely up. You can now evaluate the amount of bone. In males, make sure that the testicles are properly placed in the scrotum.

The puppies are now interested in making friends with you. By all means have fun playing with them. These lessons in socialization and being handled are very important. Check with your vet to see if he's ready to give the puppies their first shots and have him check the stools to see if they need worming.

8 WEEKS

(On the right)

The pups are now fully steady on their feet and they love to run and play. Here's the time when you can really begin to select the show dogs. Some people say that this is the time when the puppies look like adults in miniature. In the subsequent months they will go through many changes, so this may be your best chance to evaluate them. In reality, choosing a show dog at this stage is 90% luck and 10% knowledge. There are so very many things that can go wrong between here and maturity. You can get a fairly good idea of what the head will look like at this point. You'll be able to see ear size and check that they are in proportion to the size of the head. Neck length and topline will be discernible. Feel under the coat to see that the shoulders are properly placed. You can clearly tell if the puppy has good feet. It's easy to tell if the puppy has cowhocks and you should look for good rear muscling. Check the males again for testicles. Pay close attention to fronts and make certain that they are straight now, since they are apt to go through changes in the upcoming months. It's a little difficult, but you may wish to try judging the puppies' movement at this time. This can be done without a leash.

Most importantly, now's the time to look for that puppy with the extra special "look at me" quality. Choose the one you can't take your eyes off.

Socialization should continue. Now that the puppies have had their first shots, feel free to invite people over to see them and play with them.

3 MONTHS *(On the right)*

The puppy coat is at it's most appealing—in full, glorious bloom. Everyone is breaking out the cameras now. The puppy is really beginning to grow, but is probably still in basic proportion. The legs, however, have begun to lengthen and you may notice that the front is not as straight as it was several weeks earlier. The ears are strengthening, but may still tip over. This is more common in Standards as the ears on Miniatures and Toys usually come up at an earlier age. Socialization continues.

(On the left)

4 MONTHS

The gorgeous puppy coat is gone! Your American Eskimo is entering the "ugly duckling" stage. While our model Luke still looks in basic proportion, many Eskies will be anything but that, now. The back lengthens, the legs seem two sizes too long, the front may be east-west and the shoulders can seem loose. The dog's topline may have altered, making him appear high in the rear. This is frequently seen in Standard sized Eskies. The rear should still be good, but the muscle may not be as pronounced. The movement may cause you to shield your eyes in disgust. The pup's ears, which were firmly up, may now tip over, as he enters the teething stage. And, when the ears are up, the pup may appear to be all ears! Don't become discouraged. Eventually, your Eskie will emerge from this stage. Remember, it's important to continue your socialization.

(On the right)

6 MONTHS

It's amazing the growth that has taken place. The head has broadened greatly, though the ears may still be a little large. If your dog is a Miniature, he is probably at his full height by now. Standards usually reach their full height at around nine months. His rear should be good. His front is probably coming back together, but may not be perfectly straight. The dog is adding coat now, but it is still far from a mature adult coat. The ruff will begin to fill out, particularly in males.

(On the left)

11 MONTHS

Your dog is finally beginning to look like the Eskie you envisioned. He's emerging from that awful adolescent growth stage. That glorious coat is back, requiring you to spend more time on grooming. The texture of the coat has also changed. The ruff is clearly visible and has become pronounced on males. The final shape of the head and ears are now in place, although the skull may continue to broaden. The rear is probably stronger and more muscled. The front should be straight now, although it may still be a little narrow. Larger standard males may still lag behind so don't despair.

(On the right)

15 MONTHS

Compare the photos of the 11 month old Luke with the one taken at 15 months. The changes are not great at this point, but they are important. The chest has definitely begun to broaden and has more depth. The body has filled out and is more substantial. It's also easy to see that the ruff around the neck is more marked. While retaining the sweet expression, so typical of the breed, Luke has begun to take on a masculine air.

(On the left)

ALMOST TWO YEARS

Luke probably won't reach full maturity until he is two-and-a-half to three years of age, but already the changes have been extraordinary. As he has matured, it has become apparent that Luke bears a remarkable resemblance to his sire. Indeed, people have even confused the two dogs. The difference in maturity from the previous photo is readily apparent. The body is more substantial, the head is broader, the neck is wider and the coat is more profuse. Luke now has a decidedly masculine look. It should be noted that Eskies reach full maturity at widely varying times. Those who mature at a young age, don't usually last. The slower maturing dog usually takes more patience, but retains his good looks into old age. Females often improve once they have had a litter. Their chests broaden, their bodies become wider and their coats improve.

TRI-CITY
AMERICAN PIT BU
TERRIER CLUB
CHAMPION OF CHAMPIONS

Chapter 22

Showing Your American Eskimo

Exhibiting purebred dogs is one of the most popular family sports in America. It is an ideal group activity, in which everyone can participate. The whole family can be involved with raising, conditioning, training, grooming, feeding and showing just one dog.

While showing dogs is a fascinating sport, knowing what to do, ahead of time, can relieve a lot of anxiety. Showing a dog is not complicated, but it is a "learning" experience and should be enjoyable to both young and old. New dog owners, unfamiliar with basic ring procedure, may easily become discouraged and confused. If their dogs are inadequately groomed or trained, they may become frustrated and disillusioned. Sometimes the other exhibitors, at the show, are too busy to offer the guidance and advice the novice needs. In this chapter, we will attempt to cover the basic information you will need to participate in UKC and AKC shows. Don't expect to learn everything at once. Go to the shows and enjoy yourself. You will learn as you go along. Not everyone has the necessary skill to become a successful exhibitor. Some people display a greater degree of natural ability than others. Don't let this intimidate you. You will never know unless you try. Many average handlers, with good dogs, win at shows and, with proper preparation, you stand an excellent chance.

Everyone loves their American Eskimo and thinks their dog is smarter and more beautiful than any other. At shows, however, you must remember that there can only be one Best in Show winner on a given day. Each and every exhibitor paid his entry fee and wants to win. Therefore, we must create an atmosphere of fun and togetherness at a dog show. This way, we will enjoy ourselves, whether we win or lose. After all these years, I do not consider myself an exceptional handler, but I like attending shows and handling dogs. I love all the fun and camaraderie that develops among show people. On the other hand, my husband is an excellent handler, but he does not enjoy showing as much as I do. He much prefers the creative challenge of breeding dogs, in an effort to improve the breed. It's his form of artistic self expression.

Professional handlers are not permitted at UKC shows. A friend may take a dog into the ring for you, but he cannot charge you a fee. Professional handlers are, however, allowed in AKC shows. Many of these people are highly skilled individuals, masters at presenting a dog at his best. Even if you intend to show your dog yourself, it will often pay to watch professional handlers. You can learn a great deal from them and may pick up some tips you can use on your own dog. You may elect to hire a handler, particularly for shows you cannot attend. Be sure to discuss the arrangements in advance and make sure that you understand them. Ask questions. What will the fee be? Will you be charged any boarding or travel expenses? What will happen if the handler has a conflict and two dogs he is handling are scheduled to be judged at the same time? If your dog wins in the Group or takes a Best in Show, does the handler receive a bonus? Remember, professional handlers generally keep any prize money that is awarded. Make sure you understand the arrangements and, if a contract is used, read it over carefully.

UNDERSTANDING UKC SHOWS

People attending their first dog show are often confused and bewildered by the entire proceeding. United Kennel Club shows, however, are well organized and follow a logical pattern. American Eskimos are entered in classes based on their size and their age on the day of the show. Miniatures are judged before Standards and males are always judged before females. By keeping these simple rules in mind, you will be able to follow the judging sequence.

American Eskimos are shown in two divisions, according to their height. To qualify for the *Miniature*

The beautiful Gr. Ch. 'PR' Apollo's Lucky Star, owned by Sandy Tocco.

class, males must stand at least 12 inches at the withers (the highest point of the shoulder) and may not exceed 15 inches. Females must be at least 11 inches tall and may extend up to and including 14 inches. Miniature male puppies are allowed to enter as long as they measure at least 11 inches and female pups must stand at least 10 inches high. *Standard* sized American Eskimo males must be over 15 inches, at the withers, and up to 19 inches. Standard females must stand over 14 inches but may not exceed 18 inches.

The first licensed class that will be judged is the Miniature *Puppy Class* for males that are six months to one year of age. Next comes the Miniature *Junior Class* for males. Entered in this class will be males that are one to two years of age. The Miniature *Senior Class* for males consists of dogs that are at least two years of age, but less than three years. The last males to be judged are those entered in the Miniature *Veteran's Class*. These are males over three years of age. After the Veteran's Class has been judged, the winners of the Puppy, Junior, Senior and Veteran's Classes will be brought into the ring, to compete against one another. The judge will select one male as *Best Miniature Male of Variety*. The same classes, in the same order and with the same age requirements, are then judged for Miniature American Eskimo females. After the class judging, the female winners of all the classes will be brought into the ring, and the judge will select the *Best Miniature Female of Variety*.

At the completion of the Miniature judging, the Standard sized American Eskimos will enter the ring. Once again, males will be judged before females and the classes have the same age breakdowns listed above. A *Best Standard Male of Variety* and a *Best Standard Female of Variety* will be selected. The judge will then call the Best Miniature Male and the Best Standard Male into the ring, to compete against each other. The winner is declared the *Best Male*. The Best Miniature Female and the Best Standard Female next enter the ring, and the *Best Female* is selected. The Best Male and the Best Female are required to enter the ring for a final time. The judge will select one of these Eskies as the *Best of Winners*.

Most American Eskimo shows include a *Champion of Champions Class*, which is judged after the Best of Winners has been selected. Both Miniature and Standard males and females compete against each other in this class, which consists of dogs who have already earned their UKC championship titles. Some American Eskimo shows also feature a *Grand Champions Class*. To qualify for this class, males and females must have already earned the UKC Grand Championship title. The Best of Winners, winner of the Champions class and winner of the Grand Champions class all compete for *Best of Breed*.

American Eskimo shows usually offer some non-licensed classes, too. A *3-6 Month Puppy Class* is frequently offered. This class enables breeders to gain valuable ring exposure and experience for their pups. *Stud Dog* and *Brood Bitch* classes are also offered. Here a dog or bitch appears with two to four of their progeny. UKC also permits *Brace* classes, in which two dogs of similar type are shown together. *State Bred* classes reward breeders and owners who reside in the state where the competition is being held. The *Seasoned* class is for those old-timers over the age of seven. *Parade of*

UKC shows include a Pee Wee Junior Showmanship class. Two-year-old Edward Kalkreuter poses with his buddy, AKC Ch. & Gr. Ch. 'PR' Thunderpas Icebreaker CDX, bred by his Mom, Patrea Pabst.

Five-year-old Brieanna O'Sullivan shows 'PR' Daybreak's Bit of Mischief, owned by her Mom, Brenda O'Sullivan.

Titleholders is a popular event at specialties and may be held at other shows, too.

Junior Showmanship classes are also commonly offered by show giving clubs. These classes allows youngsters to participate and gain ring experience. Classes offered may be *Pee Wee,* for children two and three years old; *Sub-Junior* for 4-7 year olds; *Junior* for those 8-12 years of age; and *Senior* for 13 to 17 year olds. The *Best Junior Handler* is selected from the winners of the *Junior* and *Senior* classes. The Junior handler is judged on his ability, not on the dog's conformation. Judges take time to offer tips to the youngsters and may quiz them on dog care or points in the standard. For children, emphasis should be placed on having fun.

How UKC Championships Are Earned

The United Kennel Club awards *Champion* (abbreviated Ch.) and *Grand Champion* (Gr. Ch.) titles. Points toward a championship are earned by winning first place in the Puppy, Junior, Senior or Veteran's classes. In both Miniatures and Standards, the winners of each of these classes receive five points toward their UKC championships. The Best Miniature and Best Standard Males of Variety and the Best Miniature and Best Standard Females of Variety receive an additional eight points toward their titles. The Best Male and Best Female are awarded an extra ten points for their achievements. Finally, the dog selected as the Best of Show receives an additional twelve points. Thus, a miniature male that won first place in the Junior Class, for example, and then went on to be judged Best Miniature Male, Best Male of Variety and then Best of Winners would earn a total of 35 points toward his championship. This is the maximum number of points that can be awarded at any one show. There must be at least three dogs entered in order for championship points to be awarded. In order to earn a championship, an American Eskimo must accumulate a total of 100 points. Furthermore, these points must have been earned under at least three different licensed judges. For an American Eskimo to complete the championship requirements, the dog must also have been awarded at least two Best Male or Best Female awards enroute to the title. Dogs who began their show careers as Miniatures and then matured into Standards, keep any points garnered in the Miniature classes.

The Grand Championship title can be earned by American Eskimos who have already completed and been confirmed as UKC Champions. In order to earn a Grand Championship, dogs must compete in the Champion of Champions class. They must win the Champion of Champions class in at least five shows under three different licensed judges.

A special and highly esteemed title is offered only once a year. At the national specialty, the winner of the Grand Champion Class is christened the Natonal Grand Champion (Nat. Gr. Ch.). The dog who is fortunate enough to win this title receives a special certificate and this title becomes an official part of the dog's name and is shown as such on pedigrees.

The UKC Grand Championship title is highly regarded by American Eskimo breeders. This is Gr. Ch. 'PR' Hofman's Lil' Bit Country, owned by Nancy and Darrel Hofman. He is the sire of grand champions and champions.

UNDERSTANDING AKC SHOWS

To those familiar with UKC shows, an AKC event may be confusing and overwhelming. There are likely to be a thousand dogs or more (some shows have upwards of 3,000 entries) with over 130 breeds in attendance. Rings swirl with activity as dogs are judged all around you. Despite the seeming chaos, though, AKC shows are well organized and follow a logical pattern. Once you become accustomed to AKC procedures, you'll find their shows easy to follow.

AKC shows are a process of elimination. They start off with a large group of dogs and eventually whittle that down to the one dog who is declared Best in Show. When you first arrive at an AKC show, you should purchase a catalog. These are on sale at the table where you pay to enter. In the front of the catalog, you will find a judging schedule. This will tell you when American Eskimos will be judged and in what ring they can be found. All AKC shows are pre-entered, several weeks before the show. When you receive a confirmation of your entry, it will include information on the time when Eskies will be judged. Judging can never start before this time.

While only *Standards* and *Miniatures* are shown at UKC shows, the AKC also allows *Toys* to compete. Toys must stand 9-12 inches at the shoulder. Dogs over 19 inches and under 9 inches are disqualified

A growing number of American Eskimos are competing in AKC shows. This is the impressive AKC Ch. & Gr. Ch. Winterset's E-Z Goer, owned by Esperanza and Doug Kaz.

from competition. At most AKC shows, Standards, Miniatures and Toys all compete together at the same time, rather than having a separate series of classes for each size. At some larger shows, the show giving club may decide to offer separate Open classes for each size.

At UKC shows, Eskies are referred to as "Males" and "Females." At AKC shows, they are called "Dogs" and "Bitches." It is important to remember that all the male classes are judged first and, when they are completed, all the female classes are then judged. There are six classes for each sex. The first class will be *Puppy Dogs, 6-9 Months,* followed by *Puppy Dogs, 9-12 Months* and the *12-18 Month* class. Next comes the *Novice* class. In order to be eligible for this class, a dog cannot have any points toward his championship. He cannot have won a first placing in the Bred-by-Exhibitor, American-bred or Open class. Puppies may compete in the Novice class, but once a dog has scored three first places in Novice, he will have to enter another class. The *Bred-by-Exhibitor* class comes next. Many breeders take great pride in finishing a dog's championship with wins from this class. A dog in this class must be handled by one of his breeders or a member of the immediately family (husband, wife, father, mother, son, daughter, sister or brother). Again, all dogs who are not champions, even puppies, can compete in this class. The *American-bred* class is open to all dogs mated and whelped in the United States. The *Open* class is often the largest class in the show and is open to all dogs, including puppies. It is here that you will generally find the most mature dogs.

Those unfamiliar with the American Eskimo once thought that the breed was inferior to AKC recognized breeds. As the Eskie has become better known, that myth has been exploded. Our breed has proven it can compete with the best of them. If there are still any doubters out there, they should meet UKC Gr. Ch., AKC Ch., FCI Int'l. Ch., Mex. Ch., RBKC Ch., SKC Ch., IBKCA Ch. & Nat'l Ch. Winterset's Casper. The most titled conformation dog in history, "Casper" is owned by Lynn Martin Wyza. *Eddie Rubin photo*

It is apparent from this description that you have a wide range of choices for which class you wish to enter. Once all the male classes have been judged, the winners of those classes are brought into the ring to compete against one another. *Winners Dog* will be chosen from these class winners. This is the only dog who will receive points toward his championship. A *Reserve Winners Dog* will be selected from the remaining dogs in the ring. Should anything happen to disqualify the Winners Dog, the points will go to the Reserve Winners Dog.

Dog showing can be a fun hobby. Ch. 'PR' Eskipade's Hello Dolly, owned by Lisa Castelan, poses with some of her trophies.

Once all the male classes have been judged, the same classes, in the same order, will be offered for bitches. A *Winners Bitch* and a *Reserve Winners Bitch* will be selected.

When the dog and bitch class judging is concluded, the champions join the Winners Dog and Winners Bitch in the ring. Both sexes compete together, however, in very large classes, the judge may ask all the males and females to line up separately. From this group, the judge will select his *Best of Breed*. He will also choose a *Best of Opposite Sex*. Thus, if a male was chosen Best of Breed, a female will be selected Best of Opposite Sex. From the Winners Dog and Winners Bitch, the judge will also choose a *Best of Winners*. This dog or bitch will receive the highest available number of points in the breed on that day. So, if there are three championship points allotted to males and only one to females, but the female goes Best of Winners, she will receive the three points because she has defeated the male.

If all this sounds complicated and hard to follow, don't worry. Let the catalog guide you through the judging order. The classes will be listed, in the order they are judged. You will find the armband number, name, registration number, sire and dam and breeder and owner, along with his address, of every dog entered in the show. There will be spaces for you to fill in the armband number of the Eskies who were chosen Winners Dog, Winners Bitch, Best of Breed, Best of Opposite Sex and Best of Winners. Be sure to mark which dogs were absent. Either before the breed listing or in the back of the catalog, you will find a chart which tells you how many championship points are available for Eskies at this show. Just be sure to deduct the absentees when determining the number.

When the breed judging is concluded, *Group* and *Best in Show* judging will begin. There are seven groups at AKC shows: Sporting, Hound, Working, Terrier, Toy, Non-Sporting and Herding. The American Eskimo is in the Non-Sporting Group. The dogs who represent each breed, all the Best of Breed winners, assemble in the same ring to compete for Best in Group. First through fourth places will be given. Those dogs who earn Group First wins are, once again, brought into the ring. It is from these dogs that the prestigious Best in Show will be chosen.

You'll also find other activities at the show. There will usually be obedience judging and *Junior Showmanship*. As at UKC shows, this class judges the youngster's ability, not the dog's conformation. Any youngster from 10-17 years of age is eligible to compete in Junior Showmanship. Such classes are divided into *Novice* and *Open*. Once a competitor has won three first places in the Novice class, he moves on to Open. At larger shows, classes are sometimes further divided into *Junior* and *Senior* divisions. Juniors are for children aged 10 to 12 and Seniors are for those 13 to 17. At some shows the classes are also divided into boys and girls.

At the largest shows, there may be other classes, too. Sometimes shows offer *Brace* classes, in which an owner shows two dogs, closely matched in appearance, together. There may also be *Team* classes, in which four dogs, closely matched, are shown together. Brace and team classes are judged at the conclusion of the Best of Breed judging. Dogs in these classes compete for Best Brace or Team of Breed, Best Brace or Team in Group and Best Brace or Team in Show. Though they occur infrequently at shows, Brace and Team competitions are always fun to watch.

Some AKC shows are known as *Specialty shows*. Specialties usually feature only one breed or, sometimes, one Group. They are usually hosted by a local or national breed club. At these shows, special classes may be offered. There can be a *Veteran's Class*, in which dogs over a certain age compete. They may offer a *Stud Dog* and *Brood Bitch* class, in which a dog or bitch appears with their progeny. There may be a *Membership* class open only to members of the club. There may be a further breakdown dividing the classes into different sizes and colors. For instance, if there was an Eskie Specialty, there would likely be separate classes for Standards, Miniatures and Toys. Some clubs also hold *Sweepstakes*. Some National Clubs sponsor annual *Futurities*. If you believe that you have just done a mating which will produce superior puppies, you send in a nomination form when the bitch is bred. Once the puppies are actually born, you have a period of time in which to select the most outstanding and nominate them. You are betting on the future quality of your pups. All of these puppies will compete with each other at the specialty and will share in the pot of money which came from the nominations.

Many AKC clubs also host *Fun Matches*. No points are offered at these shows and the atmosphere is more relaxed and easygoing. Fun matches typically offer classes for young puppies. There is usually a 3-6 month class, but some shows have 2-4 month and 4-6 month classes. By all means take advantage of fun matches. They are excellent training grounds for both you and your dog. They will help to socialize your dog and accustom him to what he will face at a real show.

How AKC Championships Are Earned

In order to earn an AKC championship, an American Eskimo must accumulate a total of 15 points under three different judges. This must include two *major* wins. A major is a win at a show where three, four or five points are awarded. The maximum number of points available at any show is five.

Each year, the AKC examines its records and sees how many dogs, of each breed, are shown. The country is divided into several "zones," or regions. From these studies, it is determined how many dogs are necessary for each point. For instance, it may take an entry of 30 Great Danes to earn three points, while you may need only 5 American Eskimos to get the same three point major. The purpose of this method is to help insure that only worthy dogs become champions.

As we've pointed out, the dog that goes Best of Winners automatically qualifies for the highest points available in that breed for the day. If your dog should win Best in Group from the classes, he will receive the highest number of points available for classes within the Group. For example, let's say you have the sole American Eskimo entry and are fortunate enough to win the Group. There were no other Eskies present so no points were offered in the breed. However, there were many Chow Chows (another member of the Non-Sporting Group) present and there was a five-point major in that breed. By virtue of winning the group, your dog would be entitled to those five points. In the unlikely event that a class dog wins Best in Show, he takes the largest number of points offered in any breed on that day.

Once a dog has earned his championship, he may retire or continue to compete, with other champions, for Best of Breed wins. The AKC does not offer a Grand Championship or its equivalent.

SHOW TRAINING

At dog shows, the rank novice with his first dog can compete side by side with the person who has finished many champions. If his dog is best, chances are the beginner will win. In order to compete successfully, however, your dog must have some show training. Without this basic schooling, he is apt to lose despite his superior quality. While this may seem unfair, it is actually quite reasonable. A judge has only a limited amount of time, in the ring, to assess the quality of the dogs exhibited. If a dog refuses to stand still so that he can be adequately examined or balks at moving around the ring, the judge has a difficult time seeing his virtues. This is particularly true in large classes, where there are many top quality dogs from which the judge can make his selection. Show training is not difficult and, with a little practice, your dog will be ready for the big time.

Working With Puppies

You can begin training your young pup as soon as he's mastered walking on a lead. Working with young pups can be great fun. It can also, at times, be extremely frustrating. Puppies have short attention spans and you must keep this in mind. Make the training fun. If your

A well posed dog. This is the Standard male Gr. Ch. 'PR' Country's Lucky Diamond, owned by Sandy Tocco.

Future Ch. 'PR' Shamroc's Kaz Sunday Silence, owned by Doug and Esperanza Kaz, was Best Puppy at the National Specialty.

puppy is more interested in playing, it's best not to fight him. Let him play and return to the training later. Limit your training sessions to five minutes. In training pups, you must have patience. Refrain from working with the puppy if you are tired or irritable. Screaming, yelling or hitting can only damage the relationship you are trying to build.

As a rule, American Eskimos do not approach strangers readily. Therefore, as soon as your puppy has had his shots, you will want to get him out in public. Take him to shopping centers and public parks where he will come in contact with many people. He'll soon learn to cope with the strange surroundings, noises, distractions and crowds. Eskie puppies are tremendously cute and you and your pup are sure to be approached by strangers. Encourage them to talk to and pet the puppy. Such training will do nothing to alter your dog's guardian instincts. Instead, it will build self confidence and your dog will feel comfortable in any situation.

Puppies learn at their own pace. Some learn very rapidly, while others take a little longer. I've had one puppy that learned to pose beautifully after only three five minute sessions. Most, however, take longer. Don't try to push your puppy too quickly. Overtraining can break his spirit and thwart his enthusiasm for showing. Remember to praise your puppy often.

Posing Your Dog

You will need to purchase a "show lead" for your dog. Most owners use one-piece, lightweight show leads. These can be obtained at pet stores, from supply catalogs and at some shows. It's best to use the show lead only when training or actually showing your dog. When you want to take him for a walk, switch to a regular leash. This way, the dog will quickly learn that, when you put the show lead on, he is expected to settle down and work.

Dogs are "stacked" or "posed" in the show ring. This is also sometimes referred to as "setting up" your dog. You need to train your dog to stack perfectly and remain motionless while the judge examines him and evaluates his conformation. Teaching your dog to stand four-square in the show ring is really a simple task, which can be accomplished with a minimum of training. Most American Eskimos are self-stacking and will strike a naturally attractive pose. Often, however, they may have a foot or two out of position. It will help if you learn to adjust the dog's stance. You don't want your Eskie to look as though he has faults which aren't really there.

In working with your Eskie, remember to keep the dog on your left. Tell your dog to "heel," and move him around in an imaginary circle. Come to a stop and tell your dog to "stand" and then to "stay." He will soon learn to stop immediately. If your dog starts to sit, take him forward a couple of steps and repeat the stand/stay command. If he once again tries to sit, slide your left foot, very gently, under him. This will keep all but the most determined dogs from sitting.

Take a moment to look at your dog. Is his stance square? His front legs should be placed beneath his shoulders and facing straight forward. His hindlegs should be slightly farther apart than the front and his hocks should be vertical. His topline should appear strong and level. At rest, your American Eskimo may carry his tail down. Many breeders, however, prefer to see the tail carried over the back.

If your dog is not standing correctly, you will want to reposition him. If his front is out of line, there are two ways to correct the stance. Place your hand under his chest and lift him an inch or so in the air. Slowly lower him. If your dog has a naturally straight front, he will be standing correctly. If only one foot is out of position, you may wish to correct only that leg. If it's the dog's left foot, reach over his shoulder and grasp the leg at or just below the elbow. Shift the dog's weight onto the other foot and place the errant foot correctly.

Before repositioning the hind feet, you need to hold your dog's head up. This is done either by using the show lead or placing your hand under the dog's muzzle. If the dog's left leg is out of position, reach beneath the stomach and gently grasp the stifle. Shift the dog's weight off the foot and place it in the proper position. The right rear leg is positioned in an identical

Doug and Esperanza Kaz taught this puppy to stack naturally on a loose lead. *Linda Cummings photo*

manner but, of course, there's no need to reach under the belly.

Males should become accustomed to having their testicles touched. In the ring, the judge must check to make certain that both testicles are present. Run your hand down the dog's back and then gently reach underneath and touch the testicles. After a few sessions, your dog will not object to this.

Take a final look at the topline. If it is sagging, gently prod or tickle your dog's stomach. Run your hand gently down the dog's back and, if he's dropped his tail, place it in proper position. Most Eskies hold their tails properly, but if your dog tends to drop his, hold it in position. A tickle on the underside of the tail's base will usually help to keep the tail up. Once again, tell your dog to stand and stay. Try to get the dog to hold this pose for a few seconds at first. You'll want to gradually extend the length of time he can stand posed.

In the show ring, you will be required to show your dog's bite to the judge. Most dogs object to this initially, but your dog will soon learn to accept this. To show the bite, place your right hand under the dog's jaw and your left hand on top of his muzzle. Pull down the lower lip at the same time you bring up the upper lip. What the judge wants to see is the dog's incisors (his front teeth).

You want to learn to pose your dog quickly and efficiently. As you gain experience, you will learn to stack the dog with a minimum of fussing. It can sometimes be difficult for the novice to tell if he has his dog properly positioned. You might want to try stacking your dog in front of a mirror. This way you will immediately be able to see when you've struck the ideal pose. You'll also be able to experiment in posing the dog in various ways to determine what's best for your dog.

Gaiting Your Dog

Your Eskie will be gaited, or moved, in the show ring. This helps the judge to discover faults that may not be apparent when the dog is standing still. There is nothing quite so beautiful as seeing an alert American Eskimo gait effortlessly around a ring. At shows, dogs are moved in a counter-clockwise circle about the ring. They will also be gaited individually. Proper movement is very important in our breed, so it will pay to practice gaiting your dog at home.

Always hold the show lead in your left hand. Fold or ball up any excess lead in the palm of your hand. Held properly, you will be able to fully control your dog on a show lead. When moving your dog, you can adjust the tension on the leash simply by raising or lowering your arm, or by feeding out or gathering up the lead. Move your dog in an imaginary circle. If he begins to lag behind you, give a quick jerk or two on the lead and he will speed up. If the dog moves away from you, a little jerk will bring him back in line. Likewise, if he veers toward you and begins to crowd in too close, an outward jerk will straighten him out.

It will take a little practice to determine the ideal speed at which to move your dog. Eskies should be moved at a brisk animated trot. You don't want to run full out as though you and your dog were in a race.

At UKC shows, professional handlers are forbidden. Thus, most Eskie breeders feel quite comfortable in the show ring. Lynda Gagnon successfully handles her Ch. 'PR' Stevens' Diamond Mystique to a win.

Neither do you want to walk along, taking small mincing steps. You want to move at a speed which allows your dog to hit an easy, free moving stride. To determine the correct speed for your dog, it is best to enlist the help of a family member or friend. Have them watch from the side as you move the dog. Tell them to let you know when the dog moves the best. You might also want to watch, yourself, as someone else moves the dog. With a little experience, you'll be able to tell when your dog is moving at his best speed.

Gaiting should be included in your practice sessions. Drill your dog in gaiting both in a circle and in a straight line. It's best to prepare the dog for any eventuality that may occur at a show. You will want to practice both indoors and out. Accustom him to a variety of surfaces. He should learn to move willingly, whether he is on a floor, cement, grass or bare ground.

Polishing The Act

In the show ring, you want your American Eskimo to perform with zest and animation. There's nothing more irresistible than a lovely Eskie, with eyes sparkling, ears up and head held high. While the judge will be comparing the dogs' conformation, in a close decision, that extra spark might give the decision to your dog.

In UKC show rings, baiting, or attracting the dog's attention by the use of food, is not permitted. Squeaky toys and other devices may sometimes be used, but this is solely at the discretion of the judge. A handler is allowed to speak to his dog or to snap his fingers to attract the dog's attention. UKC judges, however, often use attention getting devices, to help them see the dog's animation and expression. They may use keys, a squeaky toy or a piece of cellophane, such as a candy wrapper. Many judges also drop a pair of keys on the floor. This aids them in determining that the dog has good hearing and is not deaf.

At AKC shows, you will be allowed to use devices to keep your dog's attention. Bait is commonly used at AKC shows. Boiled liver, which can then be broken off and parceled out, is popular for baiting. While humans may not like it, dogs are crazy about the taste and will often respond with great enthusiasm. Commercially available dog treats are also routinely used. With a little experimentation, you will soon learn what your dog prefers.

You may wish to practice, at home, with food, squeaky toys or other devices. Beware, however, of overdoing it. If the dog becomes too accustomed to hearing keys jangling or a squeaking noise, he may not respond in the show ring.

Many Eskies, including Gr. Ch. 'PR' Stevens' Toybear's Snoball, owned by Carolyn Kane, enjoy going to shows.

The Value of Praise

Be sure to give your American Eskimo plenty of praise while working with him. Eskies are very intelligent and they respond well to training. It is never necessary to handle your dog roughly or to hit him. Always remember that this breed will work for the sheer joy and fulfillment of pleasing you. The Eskie wants your approval. Patience, persistence and training will pay off, and you will have a beautifully behaved show dog, who performs like a champ.

LOCATING A SHOW

Now that your dog is trained for the ring, you'll be anxious to show him. How do you locate a UKC sponsored show for American Eskimos? Subscribe to *Bloodlines*. All UKC shows are advertised in this magazine. One of the best ways to learn about local events is to join a breed club (the names of such organizations are available from the UKC). By joining a club, you will be able to meet people you have something in common with...you all love American Eskimos. In addition to learning about shows, you will make friends and learn more about the breed.

Information on shows is listed in the "UKC Upcoming Events Listings" in *Bloodlines*. The listings give the name and location of the club and what classes (conformation, obedience, agility) will be held. The judges for any classes offered will be listed. Directions to the show may appear. Many ads will tell you whether the show must be pre-entered only or whether the club will accept entries on the day of the show. If the club permits entries on the day of the show, the hours for making entries will be specified. Entry fees are less for pre-entered dogs. You will be given the name of two people, along with their phone numbers and, possibly, address to contact for additional information. These folks will often send you a premium list in response to your inquiry. This will often include helpful information such as directions to the show grounds and the names of motels or hotels close to the show site which will accept dogs. They will also tell you whether food will be available or whether you should plan on bringing lunch from home. Blank entry forms appear in *Bloodlines*.

Detailed lists of the thousands of AKC conformation shows, obedience and agility trials, tracking tests and a whole host of other activities are included in a supplement to *Pure Bred Dogs, The American Kennel Gazette,* known as the *Events Calendar*. The names and address of show superintendents are also listed. You may want to contact superintendents in your area and ask them to put you on their mailing list. They will send you regular premium lists which give detailed information about every show which is offered. These lists include the name of the show giving club, the location and directions to the show grounds, the names of the judges who will be presiding, all awards that will be offered and, usually, information on area hotels and motels which will accept dogs. An entry form will also be included. Pay strict attention to the closing date for the show. Typically, this is about three weeks before the actual show date. If your dog is not pre-entered, he will not be able to compete. Some shows limit the number of dogs which can be entered so get your entry in early so that you won't be disappointed. There are fax and on-line services which will facilitate entry of your dog.

Once your entry has been received, the superintendent will mail you an entry ticket and a judging program. The ticket will list your dog's identification number, which will also be the armband number you will use in the ring. The judging ticket will break down the American Eskimo entry, showing you exactly how many dogs and bitches have been entered in the show. The program will also show you what time judging will begin.

PACKING YOUR BAGS

A day or two before the show, you will want to gather all the supplies and equipment you intend to take with you. Until you become a seasoned show hand, you may want to make a list, so you don't forget anything. Take along all the material about the show. If you will be entering your dog on the day of a UKC show, take along a filled out entry blank. If you are going to an AKC show, take along your entry ticket and the judging program. Be sure to take along the directions to the show and the address of the motel or campground where you will be staying. Pack an extra show lead, in case you misplace yours or it breaks. I always bring along a can of disinfectant spray. Gather together all your grooming equipment. Be sure to bring a gallon of water from home, and your dog's food and water dishes. If the show is being held in the summer, freeze water in milk cartons. These can be placed in the dog's kennel, to keep him cool and, once melted, will supplement the water supply. To cope with an unforeseen emergency, you may want to bring along a first-aid kit for both you and your dog. Paper towels, plastic garbage bags, moistened towellettes and a pooper scooper will also come in handy.

You may wish to bring along lawn chairs, a blanket or a rug. If food is not available at the show site, pack an ice chest. Include sodas, food and munchies for your dog. Be sure to pack a raincoat, in case there's a downpour. You might also want to include a change of clothing, in the event you should get drenched. A large fluffy towel or two will come in handy, if you have to dry your Eskie.

PROPER SHOW RING ATTIRE

You want to wear comfortable clothing that's appropriate for the season. Your clothing need not be dressy, but it should be in good taste. Avoid tight fitting

Many owners like to compete in both UKC and AKC shows. Though the rules vary somewhat, it's easy to adjust to both venues. This is a Champion of Champions class at a UKC show. It's equivalent to the "specials" class at AKC shows, in which only champions compete. *Photo courtesy of Ann DeTavernier.*

clothes that may restrict your movement. Women should refrain from wearing low cut blouses. Very full skirts are also inappropriate, since the material can catch under your shoe as you bend down to pose the dog. Such skirts also make a swooshing noise, which is distracting to the dogs. Shoes are very important. They should be comfortable and practical. High heels or sandals are never appropriate for a ring appearance. I've seen more than one person twist an ankle, or fall, because of improper footware. Heavy charm bracelets that clank will distract your dog and the judge. Likewise, long heavy necklaces, that brush against your dog when you pose him, should be left at home. It's also best to prepare for emergencies. Be sure to take a raincoat and, if the weather is cool, take along a warm jacket.

It is best to wear dark clothes when showing your American Eskimo. The Eskie's white coat will contrast best against a dark background. Black, blue and red outfits show the Eskie's coat to advantage. Your choice of color will be particularly important if your dog wins. Photos will be taken of the winning dogs. I have a beautiful picture of one of my champion bitches. Unfortunately, I wore a white jacket and the dog's head does not stand out against this background. The photo was taken the day she completed her championship. It was a very special day and I would have liked a wonderful photo to capture the moment.

Doug and Esperanza Kaz's Eskies love to travel to shows. *Doug Kaz photo*

Many exhibitors allow their dogs to rest in exercise pens. Here Standard-sized Eskie Gr. Ch. 'PR' Shamroc's Miss Tuff Stuff and Miniature Gr. Ch. 'PR' Sassi's Shamroc All Wound Up, owned by Brenda O'Sullivan, relax before going into the ring.

WHEN YOU ARRIVE AT THE SHOW

The large AKC shows, with thousands of dogs entered, often look chaotic to those not familiar with them. They may be held in arenas, convention or civic centers or may sprawl through parks or outside acreage. If this is your first show, you will doubtless wonder where in the heck you should go! Sometimes your judging program will include a diagram of the show grounds. If not, you'll have to look for yourself. For indoor shows, search for the main entrance. At outdoor shows, keep an eye out for the largest tent. This will be the place for you to purchase a catalog and ask directions to your ring.

Go to ringside and approach the steward's table. Tell him the number for your dog (the one on your entry ticket) and he will give you the armband. There will be a bag of rubber bands nearby. Secure your armband to your left arm. If you are showing a number of dogs, it's easier to place all your armbands on at once, in the order the dogs will be going in the ring.

At present, UKC shows are generally smaller and less formal than their AKC counterparts. However, interest in these shows is growing rapidly so we can expect significant future growth. If you have pre-entered your dog, be sure to go to the Stewards table to confirm your entry. You will usually receive your armband here. If you haven't entered, now is the time to present your completed entry form and pay your fee. Be sure to get there in plenty of time.

BEFORE YOU GO IN THE RING

Let your dog relax before you go into the show ring. It's a good idea to walk him so that he can eliminate, if need be. Permit him a small drink of water, but don't let him drink too much, or he's apt to have a "pot bellied" look.

If you aren't in the first class, be sure to observe the judging. It can be very valuable to see how

Eskies are natural show dogs. AKC Ch. & Gr. Ch. Kaz Cntry Western Harmony, owned by Doug and Esperanza Kaz, has learned to pose naturally in an attractive stance.

the judge organizes his ring. You will see if he prefers to gait the dogs around the ring immediately or if he examines the dogs before moving them. Perhaps the judge examines all the dogs before gaiting any of them individually. Or he may examine each dog, gait him and then proceed to the next dog. By paying close attention, you will know what to expect when it's your turn to go into the ring.

IN THE RING

The big day has finally arrived, and you and your dog are ready for your show ring debut. Chances are you will have butterflies in your stomach and your knees may knock. It's quite likely that your dog can sense your nervousness and will be tense, too. Take a deep breath and try to relax. Remember, everyone else in the ring was a beginner at one time.

Each judge has his own procedure for conducting the judging in his ring. While there may be variations, I will describe the most commonly followed pattern, here. When your class is called into the ring, enter promptly. Don't make the other exhibitors wait for you. Most judges signal everyone to go counterclockwise around the ring. This allows the dogs to settle down and gives the judge an overall impression of the class. Move your dog out at a brisk trot, but remember this isn't a race. If your dog starts to run, give a quick jerk on the lead to get him under control. You want the judge to see your dog moving at the pace that's best for him. Don't run into or crowd the dog in front of you. Neither should you move so slowly that the dogs behind you jam up. After one or two circuits of the ring, the judge will indicate (usually by holding his hand up) that he wants the dogs to stop.

The first handler in line should stop his dog. If your dog stops in an awkward position, you will need to adjust his stance. Either take a step or two forward until the dog is standing squarely or reach down and place him in the proper position. Unless instructed otherwise, remain in the same order you entered the ring.

The judge will now begin his individual examinations of the dogs. Toys and Miniatures may be judged on tables. Most judges wisely approach from the dog's front and often extend a hand so the dog can sniff it. He will either ask you to show him the dog's bite or examine it himself. The judge will begin by examining your American Eskimo's head. He will be looking at the shape, length and width of the head and the placement of the ears.

The judge will then look over your Eskie's front and shoulders. You don't want to get in his way and obstruct him. Stand inconspicuously to the side while the judge is examining the dog. Each judge has his own procedure for evaluating the front and shoulders. The judge will feel to determine the dog's shoulder layback. Some will lift the legs and release them, seeing how they drop naturally into place.

Next, the judge will look at the dog from the side. He may span his hands over the dog's ribs to judge their spring. He will probably run his hand down the dog's back and may apply slight pressure, to insure that the topline is strong and straight. He will then move to the dog's rear. As the judge moves to the rear, you should move to the dog's head to steady him. The judge will examine the hind legs and may reset the rear himself. If your American Eskimo is a male, the judge will feel to make sure that both testicles are present. If your dog has dropped his tail, the judge may lift it to the proper position.

When he's completed the examination, the judge may step back to take a final look at your dog. If your Eskie has moved out of position, quickly place him in the proper stance. When individual examinations are completed, the judge will want to see you move your dog. He will ask you to gait in one of several patterns. If you have been paying attention, you will know what to expect. If yours is the first dog to be judged, and you are not sure of the judge's instructions, by all means ask for clarification. Check your show lead, to make sure it's in the proper position, and then gait your dog as the judge requested. This is an important exercise, so gait your dog at his best speed. If your dog breaks into a gallop or acts up, stop. Give your dog a jerk to get his attention and then begin again. Remember to keep your dog between you and the judge. As you are returning, keep an eye on the judge. The judge may hold up his hand, indicating that he wants you to stop a few feet in front of him. Slow down and bring your dog to a stop. Try to maneuver him into correct position, but do not manually position him.

Return to the line of dogs as the judge continues his individual examinations. Make sure you keep an eye on the judge. If you are competing in a very large class, you may allow your dog to relax. When the judge begins examining the last dog, it's time to pose your dog. The judge may walk up and down the line, giving the dogs a final look. In a large class, he may pull out one or two dogs and ask them to move again.

At this point, the judge will likely have decided on the winners. He will ask all the dogs to circle the ring again. Even if you think you have lost, don't let up. Judges have been known to change their minds on the final go-around. As you circle the ring, the judge will usually call out and point to the winners, "One, two, three, four." If you are one of the lucky winners, go to the appropriate placement marker. You will then receive your ribbons and any trophies for your class. If you placed first in your class, don't leave the show grounds. You will be called back into the ring for further competition.

What an exciting day for any breeder! Ch. 'PR' Hofman's Sabrina Royale and Gr. Ch. 'PR' Maxwell's Illamar Hofman complete their championships on the same day.

BE A GOOD SPORT

You should always act in a courteous, considerate fashion at a dog show. It's very bad form to interfere with other dogs, while you are in the ring. Don't allow your dog to lunge or growl at other dogs. Your dog may be excused from the ring if he becomes a nuisance. Pay attention while you are in the ring. Don't indulge in conversations with those standing at ringside. There will be plenty of time for that later. While you may talk to other handlers in the ring, keep your voice low and don't break the judge's concentration. Remember, the judge is in the ring to do a job. Don't engage him in con-versation. Some judges will barely speak with exhibitors during judging. If the judge realizes that you are a novice, he may say a few words, in an attempt to calm and relax you. This does not mean that he's inviting you to have a lengthy conversation. It is inappropriate to tell the judge about your dog's show record or any of his previous wins. The judge will not be persuaded if you tell him, "My dog needs only one more win to finish his championship."

Not everyone can win and you must learn to take both the wins and losses with equal grace. Learn to control your emotions. Don't jump wildly about, screaming and yelling, if you win. This will only distract the dogs. Likewise, don't storm out of the ring, stamping your feet, if you should lose. There will be another show on another day and your dog will have another chance to win. Thank the judge graciously for the ribbon he gives you. Be sure to sincerely congratulate the winner. Extend your hand or give the person a hug. By acting courteously, you will help keep dog showing a fun sport.

Ch. U-CD 'PR' Lucky's Fuzzbuster CD, owned by Sandy Tocco, wins the novice class while earning an AKC Companion Dog title.
Mitchell photo

Chapter 23

Training Your American Eskimo

American Eskimos have long been star performers in obedience trials. It's no wonder. This breed combines inherent intelligence with a strong desire to please. Furthermore, Eskies are a relatively easy breed to train. Even novices, who've never before trained a dog, find their Eskies easy to work with. Many owners find great satisfaction in presenting their American Eskimos in the obedience ring. In general, Eskies are happy, enthusiastic workers. Their eyes sparkle and their tails wag as they perform the exercises. While you may not be interested in gaining an obedience title or winning trophies, your Eskie will still benefit from basic obedience training.

Let's look at some of the day-to-day, practical applications of training. Have you ever watched someone taking an unruly dog for a walk? The dog drags the poor owner along, tugging and lunging, until it appears that the person's arm will be yanked from the socket. Sometimes the dog wraps the leash around his owner's legs, tripping him. Walking such a dog quickly becomes a chore, rather than an enjoyable outing. A properly trained dog walks quietly at his owner's side, even on a busy street. How many times have you opened a door or gate, only to have your Eskie run out? If your dog knows the "stay" command, he'll remain in place, when the door or gate is opened. It's also very convenient to have your dog trained to "come" on command. Surely, you've watched someone attempt to chase and corner an Eskie. The dog runs wildly about, darting here and there, just out of reach. With growing frustration and rising blood pressure, the owner chases the dog. By the time the dog is finally captured, the Eskie is exhausted and the owner is fuming. How much nicer to tell the dog to "come" and have him respond immediately. Should your dog escape from your yard, obedience training might well save his life. If your dog hightails it for the street, a "down" command will cause him to drop immediately. This response might prevent him from ending up under the wheels of a car.

In addition to the practical advantages of owning a trained dog, there are other benefits. Obedience training is an ideal way to form a close bond with your dog. No other activity develops such an intimate rapport between owner and dog. You and your Eskie will learn to function as a team. Most American Eskimos are eager to please and they genuinely enjoy learning. Training will constructively channel your dog's abundant energy. Furthermore, trained dogs are generally happy dogs. They are a pleasure to take out in public and they help to give people a positive impression of the breed.

A BRIEF INTRODUCTION TO TRAINING

Obedience training your dog is not difficult. Dog clubs, in many cities, hold weekly training classes, during which the owner is taught to train his dog. There are also numerous books which give step-by-step instructions for training. By devoting a few minutes each day to working with your dog, you can have a well-trained companion in short order. Even if you have no desire to participate in obedience competition, your dog will benefit from learning the basic commands. While we cannot include in-depth training instructions here, we will give you an idea of how to teach your dog the basics.

For basic training, your dog will need a suitable collar. A slip (often called a "choke" collar) is best. For American Eskimos a medium link chain which slides easily, is preferred. It's important that the collar fit properly. When the collar is pulled tight against the dog's neck, there should be about three inches of spare collar. Contrary to its name, the choke collar is not meant to choke a dog. Used properly, it applies quick pressure to the dog's neck and is immediately released. Such collars are not cruel or harmful. You'll also need a leash. A five or six-foot leather or nylon web leash is best. Chain leads are hard on the hands and will telegraph any corrections to the dog.

The proper way to put on a choke chain. The model is Ch. 'PR' Country's Kaz E-Z Money, owned by Doug Kaz.

Every dog should learn the five rudimentary exercises that are the basis for all obedience training. The dog should be able to "sit" on command. He should walk at your side, or "heel," on and off the leash. He should be taught to drop, or "down," when ordered. He should also learn to "stay" when so instructed. Finally, he should "come" when called. We'll describe for you, briefly, the basic methods of teaching each of these five essentials. Regrettably, space allows us to give only the briefest of instructions.

Heeling

There are a few basics to remember when teaching your dog to "heel." The dog is always on the handler's left side. This is referred to as the "heel" position. In heeling, the dog should walk quietly at your left side. His shoulder should be in line with your leg. He should not forge out in front of you, nor should he lag behind. Your dog should be attentive and learn to keep up with any changes in your pace. If you speed up or slow down, the dog should, too. If you make a turn or a turn around, the dog should turn with you.

Place the dog in a sitting position, at your left side. Take a step forward with your left foot. Simultaneously, give a little jerk on the collar and command, "Sam, heel." Remember, this is an active command, in which the dog will be moving. Therefore, use his name first. Start by walking in a straight line or a circle. If the dog starts to forge ahead or move off to the side, give a quick jerk and repeat the command, "Sam, heel." A small jerk, which brings the dog back in position, is all that is necessary. If needed, several successive jerks may be used, but you do not want to drag the dog. You may want to talk to your dog enthusiastically while he's heeling. This will keep the dog's focus on you. Remember, you want the training to be fun, not drudgery. Now, halt. Tell your dog to "sit." Be ready to reach down and help guide the dog into an automatic sit. Anytime you stop, your dog should routinely sit. Keep heeling with your dog, giving small jerks whenever he veers from heel position.

Next, you'll want to teach your dog to do an about turn. When executing an about turn, you want to either pivot or take small mincing steps. You should always reverse your direction by turning to the right. Your Eskie may well continue on in the direction he was going when you made your turn. As you begin your turn, give your dog a quick jerk and reiterate the command, "Sam, heel."

Your dog should also be taught to make right and left turns. Your turns should be abrupt and sharp in angle. Right turns are seldom a problem. Simply, give the dog the heel command and a short jerk when beginning your turn. Left hand turns are a little trickier. Early in the training, use the lead to let the dog know what is coming up. Nudge or brush the dog with your leg, when making the turn. If the dog starts to move away, a small jerk will bring him back to position.

Rosemary Stvens and her Int'l. Ch., RBKC Ch., SKC Ch., Gr. Ch. U-CD 'PR' Lucky's Tynee Tygrr CD, ARBA CD, ASCA CD, CGC scores High in Trial en route to her ASCA title, with a score of 199.

Your dog has now learned the basics of heeling. Eventually, you'll want to try heeling off leash with him. Don't be too quick to try your dog off leash, however. Starting him too soon may set back the training. Make sure your dog is working perfectly on lead and paying close attention to you, before you try working off leash.

The Sit

To teach the sit, place your dog on a leash. With the dog at your left side, give him the command to "sit." Hold the leash in your right hand. Pull straight up on the leash, while applying downward pressure to the dog's haunches with your left hand. Repeat the command so that the dog associates it with the action. Take your hand away. The dog should remain in a sitting position. Beginning dogs will likely stand up. Don't be annoyed. Place your dog back in a sitting position and tell him, once again, to "sit." When he has remained in place for a few seconds, praise him. Be sure to tell your dog how wonderful he is for obeying you.

The Down

There are two ways to teach the "down" and both are effective. With your dog in a sitting position, give him the hand signal and the command, "down." You can give a small downward jerk with the leash and pull the dog down. Or, with one hand, pull your dog's front legs so they are extended out in front of him. With the other hand, press down on the dog's shoulders. As soon as your dog is down, tell him "down, good." Now, remove your hands from the dog. If he stays where he is, all is well. It's likely, however, that he will sit up again. Repeat the procedure. You may want to pet the dog while repeating, "down, good." If the dog starts to rise while you're stroking him, tell him "no," place your hand on his withers and press down, repeating "down, good." This will keep him in place. When your dog stays for a few seconds, praise him. American Eskimos often feel vulnerable in the "down" position, so it may take several sessions to teach your dog this command. Be persistent and your dog will soon learn what you want.

The Stay

This is one of the most important of the obedience commands and one that will come in handy in everyday life. Have your dog on the leash and place him in a sitting position. Stand in front of your dog. Hold the leash, partially folded, in your left hand. Hold the leash tautly, slightly behind your Eskie's head. Give

Ch. U-CDX 'PR' Tocco's Mister Ruffy, owned by Sandy Tocco, takes the high jump.

the dog the "stay" signal and the voice command. With the taut leash, you'll be able to keep your dog in place should he try to move. If he doesn't try to get up, take a couple of steps backward and let the leash go slack. The dog may get up and try to follow you. Tell him "no," put him back in position and tell him, again, to "stay." Gradually, you will increase your distance from the dog until you are at the end of the leash. You will also want to lengthen the amount of time you spend away from your dog. The "stay" should be used with both the "sit" and "down" commands. Be sure to praise your dog when he stays successfully.

The Recall

Place your dog in the "sit" position. Tell him to "stay." Walk to the end of the leash and call your dog. You'll note that in the other exercises, you have given the dog a single word command. However, since you want the dog to move in this exercise, you'll use his name first. In an excited voice, say, "Sam, come." Keep the tone of your voice light and enthusiastic. Praise the dog as he moves toward you. Most dogs will immediately come to you. Use both hands to reel in the leash, as he comes to you, so that he won't get tangled in it. Tell your dog to "sit" when he is in front of you. If your dog does not respond to the "come" command, give a jerk and reel him to you with the leash. If your dog seems lackadaisical about coming, give the leash a quick jerk and, with small steps, run backwards. This usually prompts the dog to run to you. As before, have the dog sit. Your dog has now learned to "come" on command and much praise is due him.

Training With Treats

While the vast majority of American Eskimos respond well to the above training methods, some owners prefer to make use of treats when training their dogs. Mike Neil, trainer of the highly successful U-UD Ch. "PR" Zal's Prince Nikolas TT, TDI, CGC, UD, CDX, CD, CD, OFA, believes that training with treats makes for a happier, more animated worker. If your dog doesn't seem to take to the methods we have described or is particularly responsive to food, you may want to incorporate the rewarding of treats into your training program.

Use special treats to reward your dog for coming to you. Teach him to sit by holding a treat directly above his head until, to keep his eye on it, he is forced to sit. Hold the treat at ground level until your dog is forced to go into a down in order to get it.

At first you will want to reward even minimal success. Don't be a tease...if you promise a treat, be sure to give one. Later, as your dog learns the commands, give him the treats only if he performs the exercise properly. And remember, although your are using food to motivate your dog, make sure that you accompany this with lavish praise.

Children can excell at obedience, too. Seven-year-old Sherri Blews, daughter of Donna Blews, handles Ch. U-CDX 'PR' Northern Lights Calah CDX, S-CD, TT, CGC to a High in Trial win with a score of 194.

Unfortunately, the above discussion gives only the briefest possible treatment of the basics. We strongly encourage you to sign up your Eskie for obedience classes. If none are available in your area, purchase a book on obedience and start at home. Both you and your American Eskimo will benefit from the experience.

One final note regarding obedience training. Praise and correction are the basis for all training. Most American Eskimos are eager to please. You will build on this by giving your dog profuse praise, whenever he does anything right. Always try to be consistent in everything you do. Variations in the way you give commands, or corrections, will confuse your dog and delay the training process. Keep the training light and make it fun. Your voice should radiate enthusiasm and delight. Never, under any circumstances, lose your temper. This can be very difficult to carry out. There will be times when you will become frustrated and angry. You'll be tempted to scream and yell, and may want to hit your dog. Don't! Hang up the leash and begin again when you've calmed down. Just don't give up. Patience and consistency are important in all types of training.

Chapter 24

Obedience Competition

American Eskimos have established a consistent record as top obedience performers. The breed's intelligence, desire to please and natural agility make them ideally suited for the sport of obedience. Most Eskies are happy workers who seem to take delight in displaying their talents. Training your dog, honing his skills and readying him for competition can provide a creative outlet for a dog who may be bored around the house and tend to get into trouble. Obedience competition is also the natural choice for a show dog who has retired from the ring. Such dogs often hate being left home, while their younger counterparts accompany you to conformation shows. They may become despondent and jealous. Why not take the dog along and show him in obedience? As an added bonus, dogs who have been spayed or neutered can compete in obedience.

There's a camaraderie that exists among obedience enthusiasts that is quite different from what exists in the breed rings. This attitude is one that makes for devout obedience fans. In the breed ring, only a few dogs are winners. Many people will go home disappointed. Not so in the obedience ring. While dogs are given ribbons for first through fourth placings, many dogs will receive qualifying scores toward the titles for which they are competing. Theoretically, every dog in the ring could qualify and thus be a winner. Thus, you will often find obedience exhibitors applauding, supporting, encouraging and offering advice to each other.

Never before have there been so many arenas in which the American Eskimo can demonstrate his proficiency in obedience. Many Eskies have long competed in UKC shows. Now, with recognition by the AKC, Eskies are successfully competing in their obedience events, too. Furthermore, the breed is eligible to compete in obedience events sponsored by other organizations.

Before you decide to compete, it's a good idea to request the rules and regulations from each organization and read them thoroughly. There are some times when the handler is penalized, although the dog may have done the exercise perfectly. You will be able to avoid such instances by understanding the rules. You'll also save a lot of money spent on entry fees if you study the rules and avoid errors.

In this chapter, we'll try to give you a brief overview of the titles offered by each of these organizations. We would also like to share with you the accomplishments of some outstanding obedience Eskies. Perhaps their accomplishments will inspire you to train and compete with your Eskie!

AKC OBEDIENCE

The American Kennel Club offers five obedience titles to dogs who demonstrate their proficiency in trials. These are the Companion Dog (CD), the Companion Dog Excellent (CDX), Utility Dog (UD) and Utility Dog Excellent (UDX) titles. Dogs who have earned the Utility Dog title are eligible to compete for an Obedience Trial Championship (OT CH).

A specified series of exercises is required for each level of competition. A perfect score is 200 points, and a dog must score at least 170 points to earn a "leg" toward his degree. It is called a "leg" each time your dog earns a qualifying score. Furthermore, the dog must score at least half the points allotted to each exercise to earn a qualifying score. An American Eskimo must demonstrate his proficiency by earning three legs, under different judges, in order to earn his degree.

Dogs who complete their titles, receive certificates from the AKC. They use the initials, CD, CDX, UD or UDX *after* the dog's name. Dogs who earn an Obedience Trial Championship may use this

SKC Ch., Gr. Ch. U-UD 'PR' Northern Lights Nokomis CD, SKC UD, TT, CGC, owned by Donna Blews, demonstrates the broad jump.

title *before* the dog's name. The AKC has done this to show that they consider an obedience championship to be just as important as a show championship.

In order to earn a CD, dogs compete in "Novice" classes. AKC offers two classes: Novice A and Novice B. "A" is for the handler who is new to the sport and has never before earned an obedience title. "B" is for the experienced handler who has already earned a CD on another dog or is a professional trainer. Both Novice classes consist of the following exercises: Heel on Leash, Figure Eight, Stand for Examination, Heel Free (off leash), Recall, Long Sit for one minute and Long Down for three minutes.

In order to earn a CDX, dogs compete in "Open" classes. Once again, AKC offers both Open A and Open B classes. Retrieving and jumping exercises are introduced in Open classes. Your dog will have to perform the following exercises in order to earn his CDX: Heel Free, Figure Eight, Drop on Recall, Retrieve on Flat, Retrieve over High Jump, Broad Jump, Long Sit and Long Down.

Dogs wishing to earn a UD title compete in either Utility A or B. This is the most advanced level of obedience work. The dog is expected to respond to hand signals and to determine a handler's article by means of scent discrimination. Utility B is for the handler who has previously earned an Obedience Trial Championship on another dog or who is a professional trainer or judge. The Utility class consists of the following exercises: Signal Exercise, two Scent Discrimination exercises, Directed Retrieve, Moving Stand and Examination and Directed Jumping.

Earning a Utility Dog Excellent title is a challenging and demanding task. A dog must not only be proficient in executing the exercises, he must also be a consistent performer. In order to earn a leg toward a UDX title, you must show your dog in both Open B and Utility B on the same day and earn a qualifying score in each class. Making the title even more difficult to obtain, he must earn 10 legs! There must be at least six dogs competing in the Open B class and at least three in Utility B.

Dogs who have earned their UD titles, may earn points toward their Obedience Trial Championships. The dog earns these points by competing in Open B and Utility B. Dogs who place either first or second in the class receive points which are determined by the number of dogs in competition. The dog must earn a total of 100 points. Regardless of how many points he has earned, a dog must have at least one first place in *both* Open B and Utility B and another first in either one of those classes.

UKC OBEDIENCE

Many fanciers consider the UKC obedience program second to none. In many respects, the program is more challenging than some of the other programs offered. The UKC offers four titles: Companion Dog (U-CD), Companion Dog Excellent (U-CDX), Utility Dog (U-UD) and the newly added Obedience Champion Dog (U-OCH). UKC titles are shown *before* the dog's name.

. As in the AKC program, a perfect score is 200 points and a dog must earn at least 170 points to qualify for a leg. He must earn at least 50% of the points allotted to each exercise. Three legs are required to earn each title and these must be given by at least two different judges.

Many of the UKC exercises are quite similar to those of the AKC. A dog should be able to compete in both organization's trials with only minimal retraining. Jumping is required in each level of UKC obedience. There is one exercise that is unique to UKC events. This is the "Honoring" component, used in each level of activity. In the Novice class, one dog is brought into the ring and placed in a down position and given a stay command. The handler walks to the opposite end of the ring and stands facing his dog. The dog should stay in place while another competitor performs the Heel on Leash and Figure Eight exercises. In the Open class, the Honoring dog stays in place, with his handler out of sight, while another dog/handler team does the Heel Free and Figure Eight. In Utility, the handler places the honoring dog in the down position, walks to the opposite side of the ring and turns so that his back is to the dog. This is done during the Signal exercise.

To earn a U-CD title, your dog must compete in "Novice" classes. Novice A is for owners or handlers who have never earned a CD title with the UKC, AKC or any equivalent organization. The dog must be shown by the owner or a member of the immediate family. Novice B is for owners who have already put an obedience title on a dog with the UKC or AKC. The UKC also has a "Novice C" class. This is for dogs who already have a U-CD, but have not yet earned a qualifying score in Open. While dogs in Novice C cannot earn a title, they are eligible to compete for High in Trial awards. U-CD exercises include: Honoring, Heel on Leash, Figure Eight, Stand for Examination, Heel Off Leash, Recall over a Jump and Long Sit for one minute.

Dogs vying for the U-CDX title, compete in "Open" classes. Open A is for dogs who have not previously earned a CDX title from either the UKC or AKC. Again, the dog must be shown by the owner or a member of the immediate family. Open B is for dogs who have already completed their AKC or UKC CDX titles. CDX exercises include: Honoring, Heel Off Leash, Figure Eight, Drop on Recall, Retrieve on the Flat, Retrieve over the High Jump, Broad Jump and the Long Sit.

Dogs seeking for their Utility titles, compete in "Utility" A or B. These follow the same general rules as the previously referred to categories. Utility exercises include: Honoring, Signal Exercise, Scent Discrimination, both Marked and Signal Retrieves, a Consecutive Recall and Directed Jumping.

In order to earn an Obedience Champion Dog title, a dog must qualify in Open B and Utility B at the same trial, with a combined score of at least 370 points. He must repeat this feat in at least five trials. The UKC has established a point system, from one (for scores of 170 to 174.5) to eight (199 to 200), and the dog must accumulate at least 100 points. At least 30 of these points must be earned in Open B and 20 must come from competing in Utility B.

U-CDX 'PR' Kaz Northern Bandit retrieves the dumbbell over the high jump. Bandit is owned by Doug and Esperanza Kaz.

OTHER ORGANIZATIONS

Once your dog has earned the AKC and UKC titles, you may wish to compete in trials held by other organizations. This gives you an opportunity to earn additional titles.

The **States Kennel Club** awards titles using the same rules as the AKC. The Eskie is also eligible to compete at shows hosted by the **American Rare Breed Association,** which uses AKC rules. The **Australian Shepherd Club of America** welcomes American Eskimos at its obedience events. Like the other groups, the ASCA uses AKC rules, although they do differ with regard to the group exercises. These are often performed at the beginning of the trial. Despite the name, the **American Mixed Breed Obedience Registry** does permit Eskies to compete. Once again, AKC rules reign. Dogs may also earn legs toward their AMBOR titles at UKC and ASCA shows.

COMPETING FOR TOP AWARDS

If your Eskie turns out to be a star performer, the cream of the obedience crop, you may wish to compete in tournaments or see if he qualifies for a special award. Even if you don't compete, you may wish to attend some of these events. You'll see the top scoring obedience dogs in the nation and, we can assure you, they are a joy to watch!

Dog World Award

If your dog earns his legs in three consecutive shows with scores of 195 or above, he qualifies for an award given by *Dog World* magazine. You must send your dog's name along with a list of his scores, and the shows at which he competed, to *Dog World,* along with a check for $5. Your dog's name will be printed in the magazine and you'll receive a nice certificate.

Cycle Competitions

Cycle Dog Food Company sponsors the Cycle Dog Obedience Competitions. Regional competitions are held annually in an Eastern, Western and Central location. They use AKC rules.

In order to qualify to compete at a Regional competition, you dog must have earned a title before the closing date for the show, with three scores which average 193 or better. The dog's title must have been awarded by the AKC, UKC, American Mixed Breed Obedience Registry or Canadian Kennel Club. Only Australian Shepherds may compete on the basis of titles earned at Australian Shepherd Club of America events.

If your dog has earned titles from more than one organization, he must compete in the Regional class of his highest earned title.

Dogs who perform well at the Regionals can go on to the US Cycle Dog Obedience Classic. Dogs who win first through tenth place in each class in the Regional competitions are automatically eligible to compete in the Classic. Dogs who competed at the Regionals, but did not place in the top ten, may also be eligible. In order to win admittance, they must show three scores, within the calendar year, which average 195 or better.

UKC's Top Gun

Once a year, the UKC sponsors an event which draws the most avid obedience exhibitors. This is the Top Gun competition. Unlike the Cycle competition, there are no minimum requirements for entering Top Gun. Your dog simply needs to be UKC registered. This event draws both novices and experienced exhibitors alike.

World Series of Dogs

The World Series of Dogs is held annually and is open to all dogs who have earned a degree with the AKC, UKC or Canadian Kennel Club. This competition allows great flexibility. You may use the rules of the organization from which you earned your title. The World Series uses a three judge panel. All three judges score the dog simultaneously as he competes in the ring.

RATING SYSTEMS

If your dog proves to be a top performer, you may want to keep track of his awards as he racks up those scores. There are several different rating systems which track top obedience winners. They not only compute the top obedience dogs in the nation, but also tabulate the top dogs in each breed. All of them score dogs who participate in AKC events only. Who knows? Maybe your dog will be the top obedience Eskie!

The Delaney System

Under the Delaney rating system, you earn a point for each dog you defeat if your dog earns one of the top four placements. Dogs may win points no matter what class they are in. If there are 20 dogs competing, for example, the first place finisher will receive 19 points; the second place dog will get 18 points; the third place dog will receive 17 points; the fourth place winner will score 16 points. If your dog is fortunate enough to score HIGH IN TRIAL, which means that he has the highest score of the day, he will receive one point for every dog who competed in the entire show. With the popularity of obedience, it's easy to see how you can rack up the points if you win that coveted High in Trial.

First and Foremost System

This rating system is based solely on the dog's score, not any placements he wins. It is open exclusively to dogs competing in Open A and B and Utility A and B. The First and Foremost System

Mike Neil and his tremendous obedience dog Ch. U-UD 'PR' Zal's Prince Nikolas TT, TDI, CGC, UD, CDX, CD, CD. Nikki is the first American Eskimo to earn the AKC's CDX and UD titles.

assigns points to each qualifying score from one (170-174.5) to eight (for a perfect 200).

The Whitehead System

This is a system for the elite. The Whitehead ratings tabulates scores of dogs when they earn a HIGH COMBINED IN TRIAL award. This award is given to the dog who has the highest combined score for his performance in both Open and Utility.

AMERICA'S TOP OBEDIENCE STAR ESKIE

One of the brightest lights in the obedience ring these days is U-UD Ch. "PR" Zal's Prince Nikolas TT, TDI, CGC, UD, CDX, CD, CD, OFA. "Nikki," as he is known has earned a U-CD, U-CDX and U-UD from the United Kennel Club and a CD, CDX and UD from the American Kennel Club. He is the *first* American Eskimo to earn the both the Companion Dog Excellent and Utility Dog titles. You will note that another CDX and two CDs follow the UD in Nikki's title. These are not an error. The talented Eskie has earned a CDX degree from the Australian Shepherd Club of America and CDs from both the States Kennel Club and the American Rare Breed Association. In addition, Nikki has earned a show championship from the UKC. The "PR" before his name is the "Purple Ribbon" designation given by the UKC. The "TT" shows that Nikki has been certified by the Temperament Testing Society. He has also been certified by the Therapy Dogs International (TDI) and has earned his Canine Good Citizen (CGC) title (see the next chapter). Nikki has also received certification from the Orthopedic Foundation for Animals (OFA) declaring him to be free of hip dysplasia.

In the quest for his many titles, Nikki has scored some impressive wins. He has earned an impressive five *Dog World* awards, for his scores of 195 (out of a possible 200) and above. Nikki is the first Eskie eligible to qualify for the 1995 Cycle Regional competition. He has the right to compete in either the Utility or Super Dog class. To qualify for this honor, Nikki earned scores, in AKC shows of 198.5, 198 and another 198 in the Open B class. His scores in Utility A were 195.5, 195 and 195. Nikki's high scores automatically make him eligible to compete in the Cycle Classic. At last year's Western Regional, in Denver, Colorado, Nikki finished in 11th place. His scores earned him a place in the Cycle Classic, held in Memphis, Tennessee, where he finished in 16th place.

Much credit must go to Nikki's owner and trainer. He is owned by Pamela J. Neil and handled, in the obedience ring, by Michael Neil. All has not gone smoothly for Mike and Nikki and they are a lesson in persistence. When the duo first began training, they attended classes which used forceful methods. "Nikki worked for a while," Mike says, but the dog eventually turned on him. "He would growl and attempt to bite. It was his way of letting me know that if you want to teach me something, you had better be fair and make it fun to learn." The instructors weren't very encouraging. They told him that Spitz dogs were just too stubborn and would refuse to learn.

Mike did his homework. He researched other training methods, reading books and trying to find out what methods the top obedience instructors both in this country and abroad used. He concluded that "with food and fun most dogs can be taught anything, and will learn it quickly and readily."

Mike Neil is now the Director of Training for the American Eskimo Dog Club of San Diego. As such, he's had the opportunity to work with many Eskies. Mike stresses food, fun and praise in his classes. Dogs trained with force methods will not be as animated in the obedience ring, he believes.

If you would like to compete in obedience, Mike recommends that you buy a dog from a reputable breeder. As soon as you get the dog home and his shots are in order, start to socialize your new puppy. Above all, be sure to keep the training fun. It should be pleasurable for both you and the dog. Your dog doesn't really care if he earns a title. He merely wants to please you and have fun. If you're not having fun, try another method of training and make sure your quest for a title is not making the task into drudgery for your dog.

SKC Ch., Gr. Ch. U-UD 'PR' Northern Lights Nokomis CD, SKC UD, TT, CGC, owned by Donna Blews, earned his AKC CD with scores of 193, 193 and 195 at the grand old age of 14 years! *The Standard Image photo*

Donna Blews, and her daughter Sherri, have proven that age is no barrier to obedience competition—for either humans or canines. Ch. U-CDX 'PR' Northern Lights Calah UD, S-CD, CGC, TT became the second Eskie to win an AKC UD title at eight years of age. Calah is currently competing for her UDX title. *Ashbey photo*

Mike and Nikki have won many friends for the breed and convinced many people that the American Eskimo is a worthy obedience competitor. One of Mike's biggest thrills is the response he gets when he walks out of the obedience ring. Nikki often earns an ovation from those who see him work. Complete strangers, as well as his fellow competitors, often come up to offer their congratulations. They tell Mike how much they enjoy Nikki's enthusiastic upbeat attitude in the ring.

SENIOR STARS

Not only do most American Eskimos make terrific obedience dogs, but they retain their enthusiasm into old age. Indeed, they can remain competitive, earning top honors even at an advanced age.

Donna Blews, of Northern Lights American Eskimos, in Feeding Hills, Massachusetts, is one of the breed's most avid long-time obedience exhibitors. A UKC licensed conformation and obedience judge, Donna and her Eskies have set a number of records in the breed. Her Gr. Ch. and SKC (States Kennel Club) Ch. U-UD "PR" Northern Lights Nokomis CD, S-UD, CGC, TT, OFA was the very first American Eskimo to earn a UKC Utility Dog title. Along the way, he earned eight High in Trial awards and became the first Eskie to win all five titles available from the United Kennel Club. In 1987, he became the first Eskie to compete in the Gaines Regionals in the Super Dog division. When the American Eskimo became eligible to compete in AKC shows, Nokomis returned to the obedience ring. He earned his CD with scores in the 190s, at the grand old age of 14! He also earned his Canine Good Citizen award and a Temperament Testing certification. In addition, he has received his hip certification from the Orthopedic Foundation for Animals. "Nikki," as he is known, has been retired as Donna doesn't wish to jump him at his advanced age.

Donna has had other senior stars, too. Ch. U-CDX "PR" Northern Lights Calah CDX, CGC, TT is owned by her daughter. Calah is now approaching ten years of age, but completed her AKC Companion Dog and Companion Dog Excellent degrees with several placements and High Scoring Junior Handler awards. All of the scores earned were in the mid-190s. Utility Dog competition proved too daunting for Donna's daughter, so she took over. So far, she and Calah have earned two legs toward the UD title and taken a second and fourth place.

Donna's very first American Eskimo was Justus J. Barabbas CDX, S-CD. He's the dog who first introduced Donna to the sport of obedience. In 1989, Justus earned his States Kennel Club CD title at the age of 14!

Mrs. Blews has owned a number of other obedience titled Eskies, including Gr. Ch. U-UD "PR" King Arthur Pendragon TT, the first Grand Champion to earn his U-CDX and only the second Eskie to earn a Utility Dog title. He was the second Eskie to earn all five UKC titles in both conformation and obedience.

Mrs. Blews is adamant in her insistence on both beauty and brains. She's a firm believer that the American Eskimo can and does excel in obedience. This breed, she insists, makes an eager, active and enthusiastic worker. She's proven something else, though. It's never too late to teach an American Eskimo new tricks!

Chapter 25

The Good Neighbor

We all hope that our canine companions will become "good neighbors." A well-behaved dog is a joy to own. He can also be an ambassador for the breed, making a good impression wherever he goes.

This is particularly important in these days when some cities and counties have passed laws restricting dog ownership. It was in response to such legislation that, in 1989, the AKC instituted the "Canine Good Citizen" program. For those who want a well-behaved pet, but don't want to go through the rigors of formal obedience, this program provides a welcome alternative. Anyone can train their dog for these exercises, at home, without formal education. In fact, most well-behaved and well-socialized Eskies will have little trouble passing this evaluation.

The test is judged on a pass or fail basis and includes ten exercises which are designed to demonstrate a dog's confidence and control. Dogs who pass the test receive a Canine Good Citizen certificate and may use the initials "CGC" after their name. Mixed breeds may even compete at tests which are not held in conjunction with AKC shows.

Before taking the test, you will be required to present a rabies' certificate as well as any other locally required licenses or certificates. The exercises covered in the test are as follows:

1. Appearance and Grooming: This exercise demonstrates that your dog will accept being touched by someone, such as a groomer, or examined by someone, like a veterinarian or his assistant. The evaluator will gently brush the dog, check his ears and pick up each foot. The dog should gracefully accept this.

2. Accepting a Stranger: The evaluator will approach you in a friendly manner, just as though you met on the street. He will ignore your dog, but shake your hand. The dog should not shy away or act resentful, and should remain in position and not go to the evaluator.

3. Walking on a Loose Lead or Out for a Walk: This exercise shows that you, not the dog, are in control when you take a walk. The dog should walk calmly at your left side on a loose lead. He should stay with you as you turn, make an about turn and stop. He is not required to maintain the strict heel position seen in obedience competition.

4. Walk Through a Crowd: This exercise demonstrates that your dog is under control when you take him out in a public place, such as a park. You and your Eskie will walk around and pass close to at least three pedestrians. The dog must not strain on the leash. He can show interest in the strangers, but should never be shy, aggressive or show resentment.

5. Sit for Exam: While your dog sits at your left side, a stranger will approach. He acts friendly and pets the dog's head and body. Your dog should accept this approach without showing shyness or resentment.

6. Sit and Down on Command: This shows that the dog has had some training and will respond to your commands. When you tell your dog to sit and down he should do so. You may give more than one command, but you cannot reach down and force him into position.

7. Stay in Position (Sit or Down): You have your choice of giving your dog either the sit or down command. You will then tell your dog to stay. The evaluator will tell you to leave your dog and you should drop the leash and walk about 20 feet away. You will then turn and go back to your dog. The dog should remain in the stay position until the evaluator tells you to release him.

8. Reaction to Another Dog. This exercise shows that your dog can remain well-behaved when he is in the presence of another dog. You and your dog will walk along and encounter another handler who is walking

Rosemary Stevens and her Int'l. Ch., RBKC Ch., SKC Ch., Gr. Ch. U-CD 'PR' Lucky's Tynee Tygrr CD, ARBA CD, ASCA CD, CGC pass their AKC Canine Good Citizen test.

his dog. You and the other handler will stop and shake hands. The dogs should demonstrate only casual interest in each other.

9. Reaction to Distractions: Your dog should be confident, even though he may face distracting conditions. Your Eskie may be curious, startled or interested, when faced with a strange distraction, however, he should not bark, become aggressive, panic or run away in fright.

10. Dog Left Alone: Your dog should still show good manners, even when he is left alone. With your dog on a 15-foot leash, you will go out of sight for five minutes. The dog may be mildly agitated or nervous, but he should not whine, bark, howl or pace.

Good luck!

Chapter 26

American Eskimo Heroes

Dogs are often called "man's best friend" and we know that American Eskimos are known for their loyalty to their owners. We all like to think that our dogs will be there to save our lives, should the situation arise. Thankfully, they aren't often put to the test. On more than one occasion, however, American Eskimos have risen to the challenge. We salute both the following dogs and all the other unsung Eskie heroes.

NORI

Nothing strikes fear in the hearts of parents more than the thought that their children may be kidnapped. And that's exactly the fate that would have befallen two Colorado Springs, Colorado tots had it not been for the intervention of an American Eskimo named Nori.

Sharon Stubbs left her two-year-old daughter, Hannah, and her playmate, two-year-old Michel Felli, alone in her fenced yard for only a moment, as she went in the house. A man in his forties approached the fence, called the children and then leaned over and grabbed them. With a child under each arm, he ran down the street. Thankfully, Nori, who was in the house, must have seen what was going on. She began growling and pawing frantically at the door to get out.

"When I went to pat her to tell her she couldn't go out, she turned and tried to bite me! That was very strange because Nori's normally very passive," Mrs. Stubbs told a reporter.

"So, I said: 'Fine, go out!' As soon as the door was open, Nori took off around the house. Mrs. Stubbs was amazed that the dog was snarling as she ran. "That's when I got a feeling something dangerous was happening. I ran after her and saw her jump the side fence."

Mrs. Stubbs ran after the dog and was amazed to see a stranger running away with the children. Without hesitation, Nori planted her teeth in the man's buttock. "He yelled in pain, shook off Nori, dropped the girls in the next-door neighbor's yard and ran down the street.

"If it hadn't been for Nori, I shudder to think what might have happened. She's amazing."

We often tell people that the American Eskimo makes an ideal playmate and guardian for children. Nori has certainly proven that these are not empty words.

SHASTA

In 1989, a 20-pound American Eskimo made headlines in California newspapers. She was dubbed "Shasta, the wonder dog." The little white dog had been given to a group which found homes for unwanted dogs and was temporarily staying with Luella Ball, 75, of Arcadia. Mrs. Ball often served as a "foster mother" for dogs looking for homes.

One January night, Mrs. Ball laid in a fire and retired to her upstairs bedroom. Shasta went to sleep in the living room. Around two a.m. an ember from the fireplace escaped through the firescreen and landed on the carpet, igniting a chair. Soon, the whole living room was ablaze. The flames licked up the drapes and spread to the sofa; the television and stereo melted into black lumps. Thick clouds of smoke enveloped the room and began rising toward the second story.

Shasta, an inveterate barker, was so overcome with smoke that she could not sound an alarm. Yet, she rushed upstairs to Ball's bedroom and threw her little body repeatedly against the door. "I was asleep and heard a thump on the door. I opened the door and saw flames and a lot of smoke," Ball told the papers. She was more specific when she wrote to the author about the incident. "When I opened the...door, the room exploded 'red' fire. I could hear the TV blowing its tube and the glass on the windows and doors shattering.

"Shasta, the Wonder Dog," saved the life and home of 75-year-old Luella Ball.

I couldn't see and only managed to locate Shasta with my feet. I picked her up and rushed through the kitchen door. I put her down, called 911 and ran from the house.

"Shasta was my smoke alarm," Mrs. Ball said. "She...saved the house from more damage....without the dog being here, there might have been very different circumstances for me." The firemen were more explicit. They credited Shasta with saving Mrs. Ball's life.

Mrs. Ball was taken to the emergency room and Shasta was rushed to a veterinarian. Thankfully, both were fine.

Shasta's heroics did not go unnoticed. The Los Angeles chapter of the SPCA chose the Eskie as their Dog Hero of the Year and her deed was immortalized on a plaque. Shasta and Mrs. Ball also received a $100 check. The California American Eskimo Association made Mrs. Ball an honorary member and presented Shasta with a special award.

MAVERICK

A seven-month-old puppy, "PR" Silver Maverick, also helped save his entire family and their property from destruction. In 1973, an electrical fire broke out in the home of Mr. and Mrs. Bill Phifer, of Avery, Oklahoma. Soon, thick clouds of ominous black smoke filled the house. Maverick ran into the bedroom, determined to wake his owners. He jumped on the bed, pawed the couple and began pulling at their blanket until he had roused them. The Phifers and their daughter, Vesta, managed to escape in time. Due to Maverick's quick reaction, the damage to the house was minimal.

NORKY, SHAWNEE AND MITZY

A trio of American Eskimos, Degeraty's Snow King Norky, Snow Queen Shawnee and Snow Princess Mitzy became heroes to their Rio Rico, Arizona neighborhood. Indeed, they are credited with saving some $130,000 in property.

Will and Diane Degeraty, and their children, Michelle, Rhonda and Micheal, had gone out for the evening. Two of the adjoining property owners had also decided to make it a night on the town. Neighbors, a few doors down, were surprised when they heard the Degeraty's American Eskimos frantically barking. The dogs "never barked unless sounding an alarm of danger," the neighbors told a reporter. Thankfully, the neighbors decided to investigate. A carelessly set fire was rapidly spreading, the flames licking up the hillside toward the Degeraty home. Neighbors raced to phone the fire department.

By the time firefighters arrived, the inferno was a scant three feet from the dogs' kennels and spreading fast. Both neighbors and firefighters worked furiously to bring the fire under control. The Degeratys arrived soon after and pitched in.

Had the American Eskimos not sounded the alarm, fire officials told reporters, three houses would have been destroyed. Norky, Shawnee and Mitzy were certainly top dogs on their block!

TEE TEE

For the elderly, living on their own can be both lonely and dangerous. There's always the danger that a fall could result in a serious injury and no one would be around to help out. That's what would have happened to 84-year-old Marie Lancaster, of San Pedro, California, had it not been for an American Eskimo named Tee Tee.

While walking outdoors, Marie fainted and collapsed in a heap. Fortunately, her faithful dog was at her side. Tee Tee didn't hesitate. She ran next door and barked insistently at the neighbor's door. She wouldn't stop. Sensing that something was wrong, the neighbor followed the excited dog and found Marie on the ground. She helped the woman to her feet and led her back to the house. Thankfully, nothing was wrong.

Ms. Lancaster never assumed that her American Eskimo would be a lifesaver. Instead, it was loneliness that led her to the breed. She confided in her good friend, Kitty Burich, that she was lonely and would love to have a little dog to keep her company. Kitty phoned author Nancy Hofman and told her of

"Tee Tee," officially known as Ch. Hofman's Country Tiara, ran to a neighbor's house to bark when her owner collapsed. When her owner died, Tee Tee went to live with Catherine Burich, who co-owns her with Doreen Rhoan. After her owner passed away, Nancy Hofman showed the bitch to her title at the age of nine years.

Lancaster's plight. The next day a beautiful white puppy, daughter of Gr. Ch. "PR" Hofman's Country Diamond, arrived at the senior's house.

"I am proud of my little dog," Marie wrote. "...She is the very best friend I could ever have. She takes good care of me...Tee Tee has filled my life with happiness, and she is the greatest treasure of all."

TASHA

We often hear stories about dogs who save the lives of people, but Jenny and Gary Shelton, of Highland, Michigan, own a dog who saved another dog's life.

The utility room seemed the ideal place for their new puppy, Stacy (bred by author Nancy Hofman) to settle in for the night. It was warm, comfy and, the Sheltons believed, safe. No sooner had they settled in for the night than they heard some mild banging and whining from downstairs. They didn't think much of it until one of their adult Eskies, Tasha, bounded into the room, clearly agitated. "...Tasha made a bee-line downstairs," Jenny Shelton recalled in *Bloodlines*. "We followed fast." There they found their puppy, Stacy, on her back with an electrical cord still in her mouth! "We've always been very careful to hide plugs and wires and the like," Jenny says, "but the unexpected can happen, especially with our dear nosey little Eskimos."

Thankfully, the Sheltons got to little Stacy in time. They observed her closely for the rest of the night, fearing that she might go into convulsions, but all seemed well. They looked closely for burns, but could find none. Jenny and Gary congratulated themselves on their good luck and were grateful that no harm had come to the puppy.

"The following morning, Tasha was pacing and carrying on something awful," Jenny writes. "We figured she was nervous from the night before. Finally, Tasha grabbed my hand and led me over to where Stacy was sitting. She stuck her nose inside Stacy's mouth and snorted." Jenny looked again and saw a burn that she'd missed the night before. "There was a dime size hole on the inside of Stacy's cheek; it was blue-green in color and had quite an odor...To the vets we went in a hurry."

Once again, Tasha had saved the day and prevented what could have been a very serious, even fatal, infection. For a time there was speculation whether the hole would go all the way through the cheek or whether it would leave a serious scar. Fortunately, Stacy recovered completely and bears no scar today.

"We were lucky," Jenny declares. "We hope it never happens to you. If it does, or comes close, we hope you have another Eskimo nearby to save the life of someone, or something, you love dearly."

Chapter 27

The Versatile American Eskimo

For those who believe that the American Eskimo is "just another pretty face," this chapter will quickly dispel that notion. Never before have there been so many opportunities for our dogs to prove themselves in so many different arenas. And Eskies are quickly rising to the challenge.

THERAPY DOGS

Studies have conclusively proven that dogs make a difference in our lives. They reduce stress, lower blood pressure and help us to live longer. Heart patients who own dogs live longer than their non-dog owning counterparts. Time and again it has been shown that dogs are capable of improving the mental and physical health of confined patients. Mentally disturbed patients, the handicapped and those confined to institutions or nursing homes often show little interest in their surroundings. Yet scientists have discovered that these people respond in a very positive manner to dogs and cats.

Eager to be of service to their community, many dog owners have volunteered their dogs in this worthy endeavor. Many years ago, Elaine Smith, a nurse in England, took her German Shepherd and Shetland Sheepdog to the hospital where she worked. One of the patients the canine duo encountered was a woman who hadn't spoken a word in years. Her desire to communicate with the dogs was so strong that she began trying to talk. Elaine was convinced of the powerful benefit of dogs. When she moved to the United States, she established Therapy Dogs International. The group trains and certifies dogs for such work.

"...to me the essence of the program (is) helping people understand the significance of the human/animal bond," says Eva Shaw, Public Relations coordinator for TDI, "showing people what it means to be a responsible dog owner, and sharing our canine friends in a way that can help others."

If you have an Eskie with a calm, stable, outgoing temperament, he may be ideally suited for therapy work. Your dog must enjoy meeting people and being kissed and hugged. He must be well-behaved and refrain from jumping on folks. You must attend carefully to his grooming and insure that he is parasite free. Proficient therapy dogs become accustomed to being around wheelchairs, walkers and other medical apparatus.

A number of American Eskimos participate in therapy work and both the dogs and owners greatly enjoy the work. In California, U-UD Ch. "PR" Zal's Prince Nikolas TT, TDI, CGC, UD, CDX, CD, CD, OFA, owned by Pamela and Michael Neil, has earned his TDI certification. He often takes time out from his busy schedule to visit area nursing homes.

Donna Blews, of Feeding Mills, Massachusetts has also been involved with therapy work. Donna got together with several of her obedience class chums to take their dogs out. "We would visit nursing homes, schools, day cares, etc.," Donna says. "We put on demonstrations and, when we had finished, allowed the children or elderly to pet the dogs. My Eskies loved to do it and the patients and children loved the dogs."

Kim Moyer, of Line Lexington, Pennsylvania is an enthusiastic therapy advocate. All her life, Kim had owned cats, but when she saw a little American Eskimo, "I just fell in love with the face.

"I had seen pamphlets about pet therapy years before," Kim says. "When I got Austin and he grew into a wonderfully friendly and sociable guy, I took my chance. We went through basic obedience and he passed his Canine Good Citizen and Therapy Dogs International tests.

"Whenever he sees someone new he's just so happy and eager to meet them. He has that great 'happy Eskimo face.' We work with the elderly at a facility in Doylestown, Pennsylvania. Often people there ask me if he is an Eskimo. They remember the breed from 30

"Austin," owned by Kim Moyer, brightens the day of 94-year-old Clara Dolderer. Austin is one of a growing number of American Eskimos who are licensed for therapy work.

years ago when it was more popular. Sometimes they had one of these dogs themselves.

"Austin is still occasionally a little afraid of wheelchairs and walkers, but I know he'll get used to them. When he realizes there is a warm hand and a friendly pat behind the walker, he relaxes quickly. Therapy work is very rewarding for me and Austin is always excited when he realizes where we are going." It's our belief that the patients at the nursing home enjoy the visits just as much.

HEARING EAR DOGS

Most people have heard of dogs that guide the blind. Since the 1970s, however, some dogs have been used to aid those who are deaf or hard of hearing. The dogs perform such services as alerting their owners to a knock on the door or the ring of the bell, telling them when a baby is crying, the alarm clock sounds, the buzzer on the oven goes off, the telephone rings or the smoke alarm sounds. Such duties could, of course, be lifesaving.

Dogs for the Deaf, Inc., headquartered in Central Point, Oregon, selects dogs from humane societies and trains them for this valuable purpose. They pick dogs which are small to medium in size and between 8 and 24 months of age. After the dogs have been given an evaluation, checked out by a veterinarian and spayed or neutered, they begin a four to six month training schedule. During these sessions the dogs are taught to respond to hand signals and verbal commands and to alert to a variety of sounds.

Dogs are trained for three types of work. *Certified Hearing Dogs* receive basic obedience and sound alert training and are extensively socialized. Just as with guide dogs for the blind, certified hearing dogs may accompany their owners to all public places and ride on public transportation. *Working Companion Dogs* are obedience trained and sound trained, but work only in the home and are not permitted to enter public places. *Social Dogs* receive basic obedience training, but have not been found suitable for advanced training. They are placed with folks who need a trained companion. Sometimes they are given to deaf youngsters, who need to learn how to care for a dog. These children will later receive certified dogs.

Currently, there are three American Eskimos which have been placed in homes with the hearing impaired. "Dodger" is a Certified Hearing Dog, living

"Tipper" is part of the Dogs for the Deaf, Inc. program which trains dogs to assist those who are deaf or hard of hearing.

in Arizona. "Dodger was laid back and independent," writes Julie Smith, Applicant-Recipient Coordinator for Dogs for the Deaf, Inc. He proved to be quite reliable in public. "He was not easily spooked when in new situations—a perfect trait for a Certified Hearing Dog," Ms. Smith says. "Dodger is a dog that requires consistency and practice, but, is a good worker and likes to please his master."

There are two other Eskies in the Dogs for the Deaf program. Sugar, who was not completely comfortable in public, is being used as a Working Companion Dog. She has had full obedience and sound training. Tipper is a Social Dog living with a woman who is slightly hard of hearing.

AGILITY

Agility is one of the most dynamic and exciting of all the sports dogs can participate in. While the course is demanding, it is also fun for both dog and owner. It's a great crowd pleaser, too. Agility is basically an obstacle course for dogs. Off-lead dogs make their way up and down an A-frame, negotiate a see-saw, weave through closely spaced poles, run through a tunnel and jump through hoops. Owners are allowed to run along with their dogs, guiding them, encouraging them and giving them commands. Scores are based on a combination of speed and accuracy.

The sport of agility was introduced at England's premier dog show, Crufts, in 1978. The demonstration so delighted the crowd that it quickly caught on. In 1979, the Kennel Club established a set of rules for the sport. Soon, Americans were taking an interest in this new activity. In 1986, the United States Dog Agility Association was formed. The USDAA offers Agility Dog (AD), Advanced Agility Dog (AAD) and Master Agility Dog (MAD) titles. In USDAA trials, the jumps are higher and the times faster than in competitions authorized by other organizations. They also include separate classes for veterans and special games events.

Both the AKC and the UKC now offer Agility titles. When competing in AKC courses, you can earn Novice Agility (NA), Open Agility (OA) Agility Excellent (AX) and the Master Agility Excellent degrees. Dogs must earn three qualifying scores under at least two different judges. The UKC offers Agility I (U-AGI) and Agility II (U-AGII) titles.

American Eskimo owners are becoming interested in agility in ever increasing numbers. Indeed, the sport seems ideal for the breed. Eskies are an alert, high energy breed...just what's needed to score big in an agility ring. Dogs who have become bored by the repetition of obedience will also find agility to their liking. Lisa Castelan and her U-CD Escapades Little Jake CD and Tracy Vittetoe, with her Jan's Spirited Timberwolf are among the Eskie pioneers in this sport. But the star among Eskies is clearly

An American Eskimo agility star. 'PR' Lambert's Princess Kimo, owned by Karen Lansing, earned High in Trial with a perfect score of 200! *Joseph Lambert photo*

Agility is becoming an increasingly popular sport with American Eskimo owners. Lisa Castelan leads her U-CD 'PR' Eskipades Little Jake CD on the A-Frame.

Tracy Vittetoe and her agility dog 'PR' Jan's Spirited Timberwolf. Tracy and Timberwolf have recently begun mountain climbing together.

Lambert's Princess Kimo, owned by Karen L. Lansing, of Island Park, Idaho. This lovely lady completed her basic agility degree with a perfect score!

FLYBALL

Flyball is another growing sport which is fun for dogs, owners and spectators. Teams of four dogs run in a fast paced relay race. Released one at a time, the dogs quickly jump over a series of four hurdles and step on a foot pedal mounted on a box. This releases a tennis ball which the dog catches. He then takes the hurdles again, returns to the starting line with his ball and the next dog is released. The win goes to the team that accurately completes the course in the fastest time.

The sport is overseen by the North American Flyball Association. There are different divisions. Teams competing in Novice take longer than 28 seconds to run the course. The Open division is for dogs who can complete the relay in 24-28 seconds. Dogs in the highly competitive Championship division must complete the course in less than 24 seconds. The NAFA awards Flyball Dog (FD), Flyball Dog Excellent (FDX) and Flyball Dog Champion (FDCh) titles.

Judith Edwards, of Guelph, Ontario, is one of the breed pioneers in this sport. Her dog Rebel competes on one of North America's most famous flyball teams. Rebel serves as lead dog on a team composed of Border Collies, a breed renowned for its prowess in flyball. The 15 1/2 inch dog easily handles the jumps and completes his segment of the relay in under six seconds, an excellent time. In fact, Rebel's team held the world record for flyball competition, with a time of 20.39 seconds.

One of the breed's most recent stars is UKC Ch. "PR" Ann D's Mandolin, owned by Ann DeTavernier. Flyball is Mandy's favorite sport and it shows. Her eagerness and enthusiasm impress all who see her and will, we hope, encourage other Eskies to try a "paw" at flyball.

FRISBEE

Many American Eskimo owners have enjoyed taking their dogs into the backyard or to the park for a game of frisbee. Eskies have the combination of characteristics that make them ideal frisbee dogs. They are agile, alert, energetic and eager to please. Jumping and running are sure to delight most Eskies. Indeed, frisbee is a wonderful outlet for house dogs, who sometimes become bored and have no way to release their abundant energy. All of my dogs are avid frisbee fans.

In order to play frisbee, you will need to teach your Eskie how to retrieve. Many dogs tend to catch the frisbee and then strut proudly, urging you to "catch me if you can." Try practicing retrieving in the house, where there's limited room for this tactic, before you attempt to play outside. If your Eskie reverts to this practice when you switch to the outside, put his leash on and, when he catches the disc, reel him in. Once your dog gets the hang of retrieving, try to teach him a few commands. Point in the direction you will be throwing the frisbee and try to get him to prepare for the throw.

Should you and your American Eskimo become really proficient at the sport, you may wish to appear in competitions. The Gaines Ashley Whippet Invitationals (P.O. Box 1683, Encino, CA 91426) hold regional competitions and a national final. The competition is named after the extraordinary Whippet, Ashley, who, together with his owner, Alex Stein, began the sport. Anyone can enter the regionals and the winners are "invited" to attend the national competition. Should you be lucky enough to make it to the finals, Gaines will pay your travel expenses and the winners receive savings bonds. In one phase of the competition, the dog and handler are judged on how many successful returns they make in one minute. There's a Freeflight competition in which the team is judged on its showmanship, teamwork, leaping and agility. Here's where you will see the fantastic acrobatic catches and tricks.

K-9 Disc Masters (Route 4, Box 455C, Bakersfield, CA 93309) was formed by frisbee enthusiasts who wanted more opportunity to compete with their dogs. The Gaines regionals and annuals just weren't enough for them. They hold informal meets, formal competitions and regional and annual finals. They often perform at events, such as the Rose Bowl, and are in great demand at charity functions.

TRACKING

Tracking is unique to dog competition. In most sports, the owner gives commands and the dog responds. With tracking, the dog is in the driver's seat, for only he can tell where the scent lies and the track leads. Despite this fact, even naturally gifted dogs do take training and you will have to practice.

The AKC has long supported tracking and offers several titles. Dogs may compete for a Tracking Dog (TD), Tracking Dog Excellent (TDX) and the newly added Variable Surface Tracking (VST) and Champion Tracker (CT) degrees.

To earn his Tracking Dog title, a dog must complete a 440-500 yard long track, laid by a stranger. The track must include at least two turns and be aged for two hours. A wallet, glove, or other object is laid at the end of the track and must be picked up by either the dog or his handler.

The Tracking Dog Excellent title is much more demanding. The test is composed of an 800-1,000 yard track, which includes five to seven turns. To challenge the dog further, the track is aged three to five hours. TDX tracks include different types of vegetation and obstacles which the dog has to overcome. Four articles are placed along the track and the dog or handler must retrieve all of them.

The Variable Surface Tracking degree requires that dogs work on a variety of surfaces besides the traditional grassy or brushland vegetation. Here the dog has to follow the scent on concrete, gravel and sand, too.

The Champion Tracker degree is available to dogs who have scored well when winning all three of their tracking titles.

Currently, the UKC does not offer tracking degrees although plans are in the works to add a tracking program in the future.

Few American Eskimos have participated in tracking to date. In a 1979 issue of *Bloodlines,* however, Patrea Latson (now Patrea Pabst) tells of her adventures with "PR" Laika's Arctic Wolf. "...Eskimos not only can track but take to it like they do to water," she writes. "Woof was able to follow a trail the on his first attempt, at less than a year of age. He's not perfect, but he's convinced both of us that tracking makes for a great outing. Try it!"

Who knows, perhaps one day you'll will be able to put your dog's nose to the ultimate test, tracking down a lost child. Well-known breeder Mrs. Don Catlin supplied several drug sniffing Eskies to a police force in Colorado!

Ch. 'PR' Ann D's Mandolin, owned by Ann DeTavernier, is an avid flyball enthusiast. "Mandy" waits eagerly as the ball is released.

CARTING AND DOG SLEDDING

When we think of carting and sledding, we typically picture Siberian Huskies, Alaskan Malamutes and other traditional sled dog breeds. In recent years, though, Eskie owners have begun to express an interest in these activities.

Many American Eskimos love to pull, as novices often learn when they try to walk their untrained Eskie down the street. To participate, you will have to get a cart and a harness for your dog. Carts can be purchased or made from plans offered in dog supply catalogs, which also sell harnesses.

Mandy's got the ball and will race back to the starting point.

Gr. Ch., Int'l. Ch., RBKC Ch., SKC Ch., U-CD 'PR' Lucky's Tynee Tygrr CD, ARBA CD, ASCA CD, CGC, owned by Rosemary Stevens, is the first American Eskimo to earn a carting title. Tygrr has also competed in herding competitions.

It's important to start slowly with your Eskie. Weight should be kept to a minimum, during the early training phase. While you can begin getting older puppies used to the apparatus, be sure not to add any weight until your dog is physically mature.

By all means, take advantage of any classes that are available in your area. Some breed clubs offer training sessions and give advice on this activity. Newfoundland clubs are often very active in carting. Rosemary Stevens and her U-CD Gr. Ch., International Ch., States KC Ch., Rare Breeds K.C. Ch. "PR" Lucky's Tynee Tygrr CD attended a clinic held by the Southern California Bouvier des Flandres Club and went on to earn a carting title. Who knows, your American Eskimo may soon be giving rides to neighborhood children.

Donna Blews has trained her American Eskimos to pull a sled. "I played around with sledding on my own," Donna says. Mrs. Blews used five dogs on her team. "I would hitch the dogs up and give my daughter rides around the neighborhood." At first Donna encountered trouble because of her dogs' obedience training. The dogs would follow her when she led them, but seemed confused when she stood behind them, on the rear runner of the sled. After awhile, they got the idea and began to pull. Donna and her dogs enjoyed their outings on the sled, but the Massachusetts woman does offer some advice. Should you wish to sled with your dogs, she says, conditioning is essential—otherwise your Eskies will not be able to sustain a rapid pace.

WEIGHT PULLING

As we've said, many American Eskimos love to pull. They are also surprisingly strong dogs for their size. Weight pulling can be a fun and rewarding activity, for both you and your Eskie, but you will have to exercise caution. Remember your dog may not know his own limits and it's up to you to prevent injury.

Start very slowly. Be sure you purchase a special weight pulling harness, which includes padding for the shoulder and chest straps. It's best to work with adult dogs. Pulling may put too much of a strain on growing bones and muscles.

Some of the sled dog breeds offer titles for weight pulling. Sometimes they allow other dogs to participate in their competitions, even though they cannot earn titles. Sometimes all-breed or obedience clubs will hold weight pulling events at their matches or shows. Contact the clubs and ask around or get in touch with a sled dog fancier. They may be able to lead you to a competition.

In competition, dogs are strapped to loaded carts which they pull over a specified distance. The owner's encouragement is often a help in motivating the dog. The classes are divided by weight, with bags of dog food often used to accurately measure the weight. If the dog succeeds in pulling the load, he progresses to the next level, where more weight is added. The dog who pulls the most wins.

During the early 1980s, a number of American Eskimos participated in weight pulls. Karla Cole was among the breeders who entered her dogs in these contests. She and others found that Eskies were very successful and the experience was enjoyed by all.

HERDING

Many Eskie owners have reported that their dogs have a natural tendency to herd. They will often circle and attempt to move children or other pets around the yard. If your dog shows these tendencies, you may wish to try your hand at herding.

For years, American Eskimos were kept on farms and sometimes assisted their owners by herding the livestock. In the May 1946 issue of *Bloodlines,* Mrs. E. E. Ash, of Missouri, tells of one such dog. It is interesting to note that Mrs. Ash acquired her foundation stock from some of the breed's most famed early kennels: Halls, Ottens and Bobands. "I have handled a number of breeds and found the American Eskimo to be the easiest of all to train. Our first Spitz, Sport and

Donna Blews' all-Eskie dog sledding team, composed of Gr. Ch. U-UD 'PR' King Arthur Pendragon TT, CGC (lead dog); Ch. U-CDX 'PR' Princess Pandora Ivanhoe; Ch. U-CDX 'PR' Northern Lights Calah UD, S-CD, TT, CGC; 'PR' Justus J. Barsabbas CDX, S-CD and Gr. Ch., SKC Ch. U-UD 'PR' Northern Lights Nokomis CD, SKC UD, TT, CGC, takes Sherri Blews for a ride.

Trixie, were not registered but they were really keen. Mr. Ash had a team that was hard to get in from the pasture. He took Sport along to help a few times then all he had to do was tell him to bring in the horses. Just in a few minutes, Sport would have them in the barn and would stay by the door and keep them there until his master came to shut the door."

You can get more information about how to train your dog for herding from those who own herding breeds. There are many seminars and classes around the country which teach the basics. Beginning dogs often start out working on ducks. Your dog must learn to remain calm despite the flapping of wings and the quacks from the alarmed animals. He must be constantly on the alert and ready to respond. Herding is a team effort and both you and your dog will have to learn to work together.

U-CD Gr. Ch. "PR" Lucky's Tynee Tygrr, owned by Rosemary Stevens, may well be the first Eskie to compete in a herding competition. Eager to see what her dog would do, Rosemary asked Australian Shepherd folks about their trials. She was encouraged to try Tygrr who had no trouble handling the ducks used in the basic event.

HUNTING

We often read that American Eskimos, like their Spitz forebears, lack hunting instinct. Indeed, it is supposed to be one of the hallmarks of the breed. Yet some Eskies have proven to be quite adept in the field. Many of our most prominent early breeders lived in the country and often took their dogs afield with them. Indeed, *Bloodlines* advertisements often proclaimed the breed's hunting ability. John L. Wilson, first president of the national club, included the following in his kennel ad: "Why have more than one dog when the multiple-purpose American Eskimo will do the following when trained correctly...?" Among the talents Mr. Wilson listed were "Good rabbit, squirrel, possum and coonhunter; Good ratters, mice, moles and snakes...."

It's certain that the Eskie will never replace the traditional gundog or hound breeds. But the next time you take to the field, you just might want to take your Eskie along and see what happens. You may be pleasantly surprised.

There are many other activities in which American Eskimos can participate. Indeed, the talents of our dogs seem to be limited only by the imaginations of their owners. By trying your hand at some of these activities, you will come to appreciate the versatile nature of the breed. You'll soon become convinced that Eskies can do it all!

The New American Eskimo

Chapter 28

Those Lovable Clowns

American Eskimos are born clowns. Take out a camera or camcorder and most Eskies instantly become real hams. This may well be why the breed excelled as a rodeo and circus dog. Most Eskies will joyfully share in their owners' desire to dress them up in comical garb or place them in unusual settings. Indeed, it is hard to imagine another breed that is so universally photogenic. The breed's high energy, desire to please and downright comical nature is appealing to all of those who adore these wonderful white dogs. Our sincere thanks to Talitha Bell, Judy Jones, Nadine Petit, Lorraine Spangenberg, Rosemary Stevens and the other owners who shared their clown photos with us.

The New American Eskimo

206

Those Lovable Clowns

The New American Eskimo

Chapter 29

A Tribute to the American Eskimo

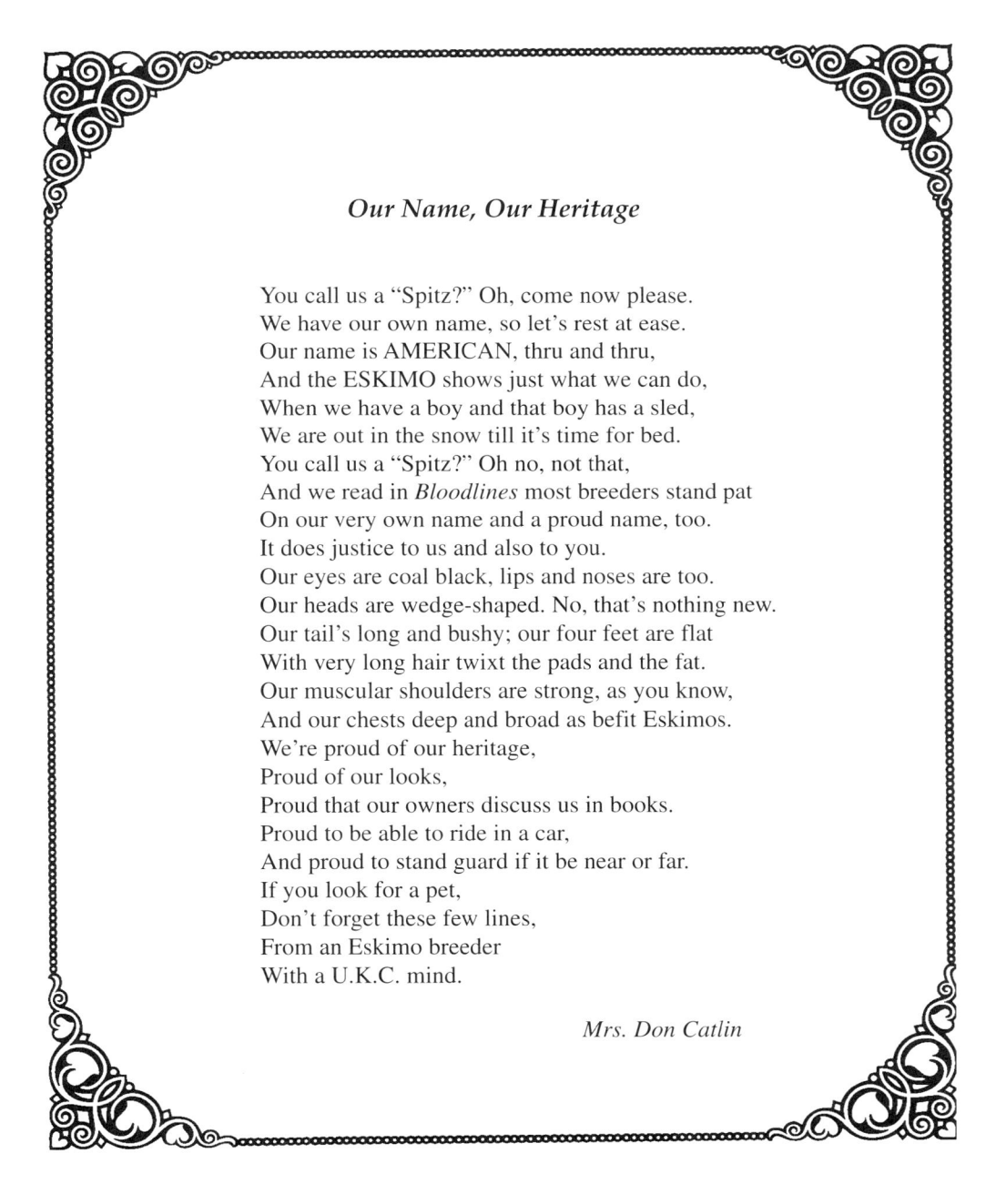

Our Name, Our Heritage

You call us a "Spitz?" Oh, come now please.
We have our own name, so let's rest at ease.
Our name is AMERICAN, thru and thru,
And the ESKIMO shows just what we can do,
When we have a boy and that boy has a sled,
We are out in the snow till it's time for bed.
You call us a "Spitz?" Oh no, not that,
And we read in *Bloodlines* most breeders stand pat
On our very own name and a proud name, too.
It does justice to us and also to you.
Our eyes are coal black, lips and noses are too.
Our heads are wedge-shaped. No, that's nothing new.
Our tail's long and bushy; our four feet are flat
With very long hair twixt the pads and the fat.
Our muscular shoulders are strong, as you know,
And our chests deep and broad as befit Eskimos.
We're proud of our heritage,
Proud of our looks,
Proud that our owners discuss us in books.
Proud to be able to ride in a car,
And proud to stand guard if it be near or far.
If you look for a pet,
Don't forget these few lines,
From an Eskimo breeder
With a U.K.C. mind.

Mrs. Don Catlin

Softness Is...

Do you know what softness is?
The downy feel of a
    puppy just whelped...
The watching of new born puppies as
    they struggle for life...
The fear that they won't respond after
    the sac's removed...
The tiny toes that wiggle back and forth
The pinkness that slowly turns to a
    startling black...
The love you feel inside to see how
    wonderfully God works.

        To touch and feel and hold a tiny
            mass of fur...
        A wiggly body, a tiny mouth...
        To watch each day a new experience...
        The growth and development of
            beautifully formed little bodies.

                A twitch here, a twitch there,
                    a flicker, a movement...
                Eight little bodies of excitement...
                The wonder of the mad rush to the
                    "dinner table"...
                The amazement of knowing they
                    cannot see
                      They cannot hear...
                But through some lovely
                    reasoning, they know...

Nancy J. Hofman

A Tribute to the American Eskimo

A Puppy's Prayer

Please God of puppies, take care of me.
When I find my new home that's readied for me.
Don't let them maul me and toss me around.
I'm just a baby.

When I go to a place tha is new and strange.
I try to be good, and I'm easily trained.
If you'll have patience and treat me fair,
You will never know how I might despair.
I'm just a baby.

I will love you all if you give me a chance.
Just let me rest when I'm tired and tense.
Feed me often and plenty of milk
And encourage me when I tend to wilt.
I'm just a baby.

In the weeks that go by, you will see such a change.
I will grow big and strong and will guard my domain.
Take care of the children and grown-ups too.
And prove, with fierce loyalty, thanks to you
I'm no longer a baby.

Mrs. Don Catlin

Growing Up

We open our eyes when we're ten days old,
We don't see too much and we're not too bold,
But there's nothing wrong with our ears and our nose
That a bowl of warm Pablum won't soon disclose.

We like our warm Pablum and wade right in,
More gets on the outside than gets on the in.
Then we each get a bath and we go to sleep,
We don't even take time to count puppies or sheep.

Another day and we learn some more,
Who moved that paper on the floor???
And who put that puddle beside the door?
And what's that thing around our necks?
They call it a collar. Ye gods, what's next?

Now, Pablum is just for the little pups.
We're big guys now, so more cups.
We have our own dish, but it won't stand still,
It's all over the floor, and it sometimes spills.

Next comes a thing that they call a lead,
That's tied on that collar, and that's not feed.
And first we walk on a little short chain,
To struggle and lunge is all in vain.

We walk with that thing just ten minutes a day,
So we won't get too tired and there's still time to play.
And soon we are walking out on the street
Close to the side of our mistress. That's neat.

We feel we know something and somebody cares,
Which means a whole lot on just how we fare.
Our aim is to please, and we do that with joy.
We're much more obedient than some girls and boys.

Mrs. Don Catlin

A Tribute to the American Eskimo

Broken Bones and All

This broken leg deal is a pretty good thing.
The "hurt" soon gets over, then this cast brings
Friends that I never knew I had.
Boy friends and girl friends, Moms and Dads.

It happened out in my own back yard,
I was on my long chair, and I was off guard.
The other dogs stood in their kennel runs,
Not to well pleased at *my* having fun.

A big black Lab from across the street
Came tearing over...(he's just a dead beat)
He was taught by his boys to grab anything small,
My front paw was there, I went down for a fall.

There was startled silence, then you should have heard
My own dogs to the rescue. An explosion occurred.
A vocal one, but the Lab ran home,
But there I was with two broken bones.

It didn't hurt then, it was numb all over,
And I limped toward my pen...my fun all over.
My mistress came out and covered me up.
We ended up at the local vets
With a cast on my leg, thanks to big black Jett.

I kind of feel sorry for big black Jett,
He has had no training, no shots, no pets
I think that he senses, and probably knows
That his 'cross the street neighbors, the White Eskimos
Have the warmth, love and security he fails to get,
And that's half what's the matter with big black Jett.

Pretty soon it is back to the runs for me,
I've been kept in the house to heal properly.
You'd never know now that I'd had a cast,
Those weeks in the house have surely gone fast.

Mrs. Don Catlin

True Love

You call me a "thing," but I'll tell you, Lee,
There's nothing else in this world that I'd rather be
Than a little white dog belonging to you,
To live in your house, to do as you do.

I know I'm a "thing," but the world is mine.
I've found me a boy, a boy who is kind,
A boy who cares what happens to me,
A boy I depend on and who depends on me.

It isn't always a beautiful coat,
"Eight inches each side" or you "miss the boat."
It's what's in a doggy heart that counts,
And that really makes these doggy points mount.

A boy and a dog. They're hard to beat.
When you see them walking down the street
You see love and devotion, loyalty all,
They're meant for each other and they both walk so tall.

Mrs. Don Catlin

A Tribute to the American Eskimo

To Give

A little blonde boy and a little white pup,
There's not too much difference in bringing them up.
They both have to learn the meaning of "No."
They both must be taught the wrong way to go.
They both have to give and they both have to take,
They both have to realize their own mistake.

In the years to come, both have to grow up,
The boy to a man, the dog, not a pup.
They find that the world is a good place to live
If they think back and remember that little word "Give."
Such a small little word, but is it so rare?
"For the gift without the giver is bare."

Mrs. Don Catlin

Linda Voight illustration

This Worming Deal

Do you know what she gave me, my "human" mummy?
A great big pill to put in my tummy.
Do you think that that was a nice thing to do?
It sure got me in an awful stew.

First, she gave me a nice little piece of meat,
All chopped up fine. A regular treat.
I gobbled it down. Boy, was it good.
It was twenty-four hours since I'd had any food.

Then she gave me some more, and I ate that too.
Then do you know what I thought I'd do?
I thought I would take a nice little nap,
But something happened. I felt a rap.
It seemed to come from my little old tummy.
You needn't start laughing, cause this isn't funny.

It rapped again, and I though, Oh Gee,
Just what on earth is this going to be?
What was in that meat that I thought was so rare,
Do you 'spose my "Mummy" didn't play fair?

It rapped again, and I sat down quick.
The lights went out, *and was I sick*.
My tummy throbbed and my head did too,
And I didn't know what in the world to do.

My "Mummy" came over and held me tight,
And said, "Poor baby, you'll be alright."
But I didn't care then if I would be or not.
My feet were cold and my tongue was hot.

But it's all over now, and the worms and me
Mutually agreed to part company.
But next time, by gosh, when I'm offered raw meat,
I'll be a little bit more discreet.

Mrs. Don Catlin

Vacation Time

We went fishing, the bosses and me,
To a mile high lake amidst tall pine trees,
It was the very first time I had seen a boat,
And at the sound of that motor, I nearly choked.

I looked in the water and what did I see,
Another Eskimo looking at me.
His ears stood up just like mine,
And his nose and his eyes were just the same kind.

I wasn't about to let things go
And let a strange dog, whether friend or foe,
Spoil a perfectly wonderful ride in a boat,
And to catch **my** fish and to get **my** goat.

I bristled right up and started to growl,
As the boss caught a fish and I swallowed that growl.
And the big boss roared a few choice words,
So I kind of figured I'd be seen, not heard.

We had a perfectly wonderful day,
In the cool mountain valley, but we had to pay
When we came down that mountain,
Boy, was it hot...110 by the "heat o'clock."

I'll dream all night how I loved my day
Curled up in the boat, and I must say
That up there, where it's quiet and peaceful and cool
You're closer to something akin to rare jewels,
You know God made man and animals, too,
And the lake and the pines and the beautiful view.

Mrs. Don Catlin

What Do You Dream?

What are you dreaming, my baby pup
When you turn and you twist and you sound so gruff,
Or is it a gain in your tummy so small,
Or is it either one at all?

What do you dream, my baby pup,
When I hold you and stroke you...my bundle of fluff,
Are you far away in the frozen North
Pulling your pack sled back and forth?

Or are you high in a penthouse tall,
Where you can look down and watch things so small,
And I'll bet you are proud to have people know
In the Northland, in a penthouse, pet or show
That you're quite at home wherever you are,
And your black eyes sparkle like northern stars.

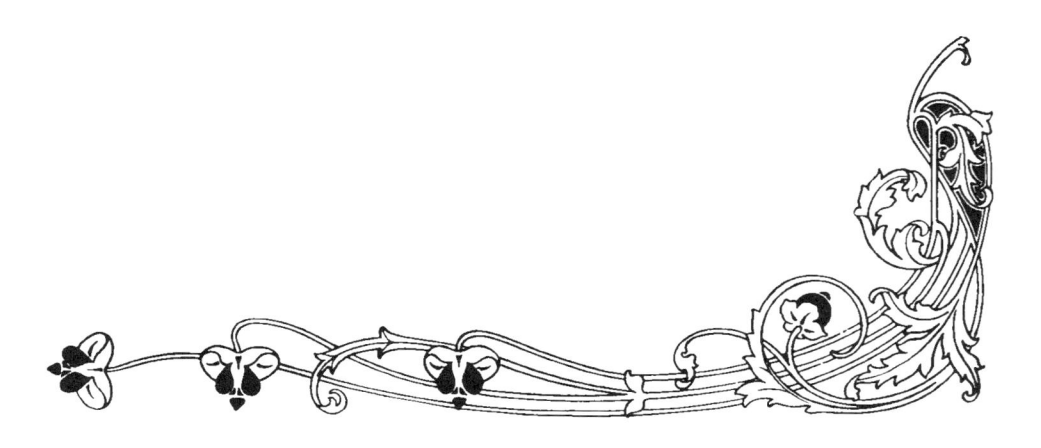

Mrs. Don Catlin

Those Nervous Owners Sez They

This obedience school is really fun,
But the whole thing **could** be overdone.
Don't they know what we do, we do to please?
We know what the trainer says, we don't freeze.

We understand English and what to do.
So why the fuss. Getting all in a stew
Isn't going to help us, and it won't help you.

So let's keep our cool and let's find the pace,
We're not going to fall down flat on our face,
No we're not going to bring you any disgrace.

We **all** do well, that's a well known fact.
We don't use diplomacy and we don't use tact,
We just act natural, so why don't you?
So we'll get our trophy and ribbons too.

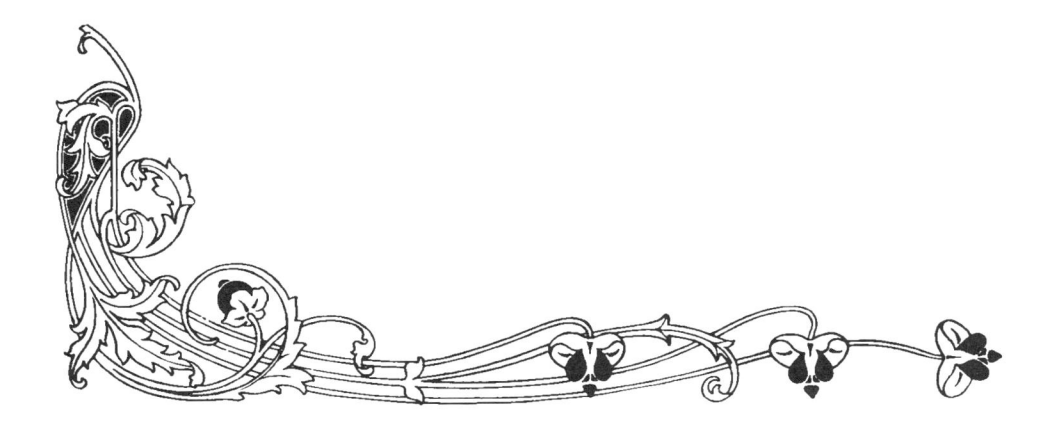

Mrs. Don Catlin

My Little Kitiza

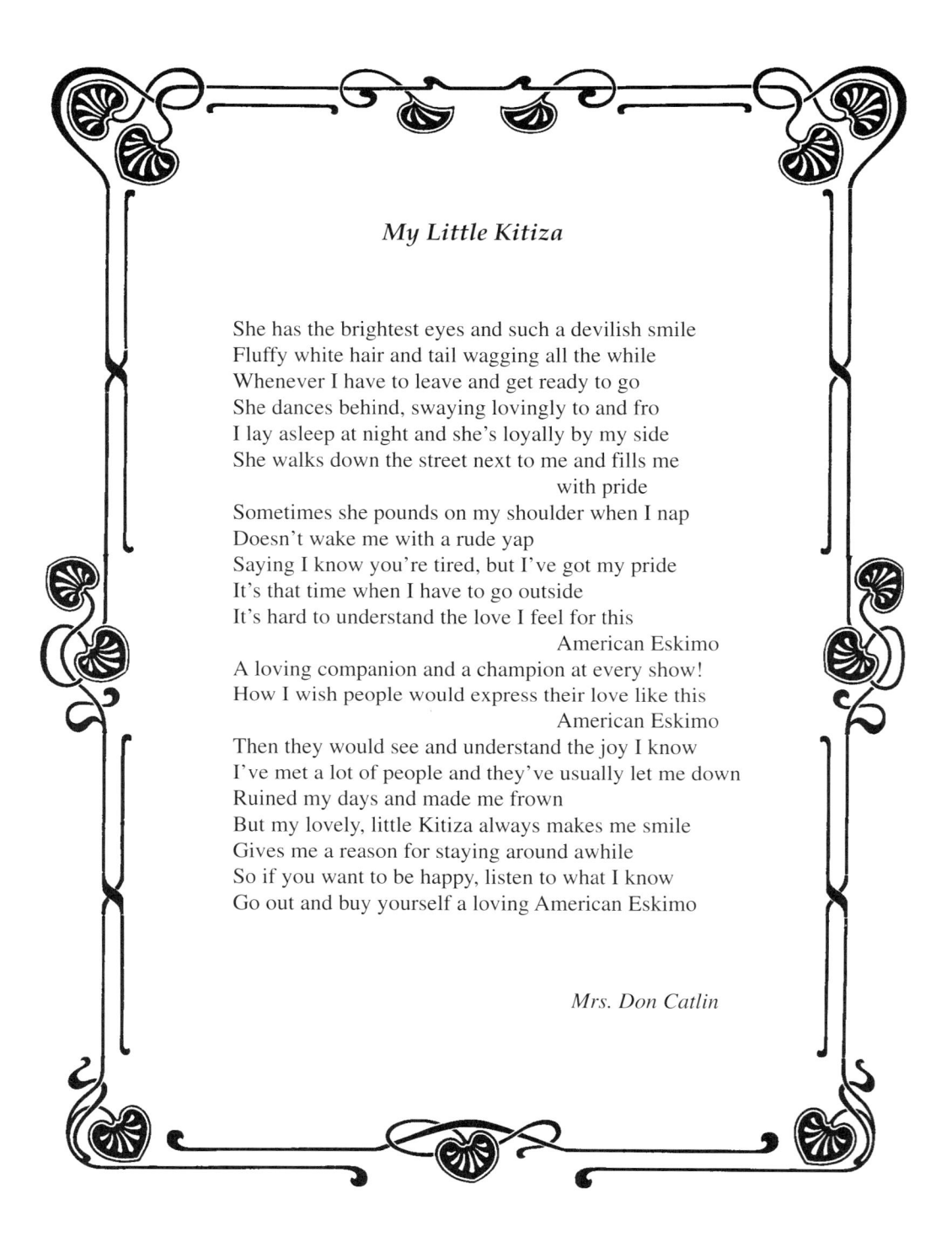

She has the brightest eyes and such a devilish smile
Fluffy white hair and tail wagging all the while
Whenever I have to leave and get ready to go
She dances behind, swaying lovingly to and fro
I lay asleep at night and she's loyally by my side
She walks down the street next to me and fills me
                              with pride
Sometimes she pounds on my shoulder when I nap
Doesn't wake me with a rude yap
Saying I know you're tired, but I've got my pride
It's that time when I have to go outside
It's hard to understand the love I feel for this
                              American Eskimo
A loving companion and a champion at every show!
How I wish people would express their love like this
                              American Eskimo
Then they would see and understand the joy I know
I've met a lot of people and they've usually let me down
Ruined my days and made me frown
But my lovely, little Kitiza always makes me smile
Gives me a reason for staying around awhile
So if you want to be happy, listen to what I know
Go out and buy yourself a loving American Eskimo

Mrs. Don Catlin

A Tribute to the American Eskimo

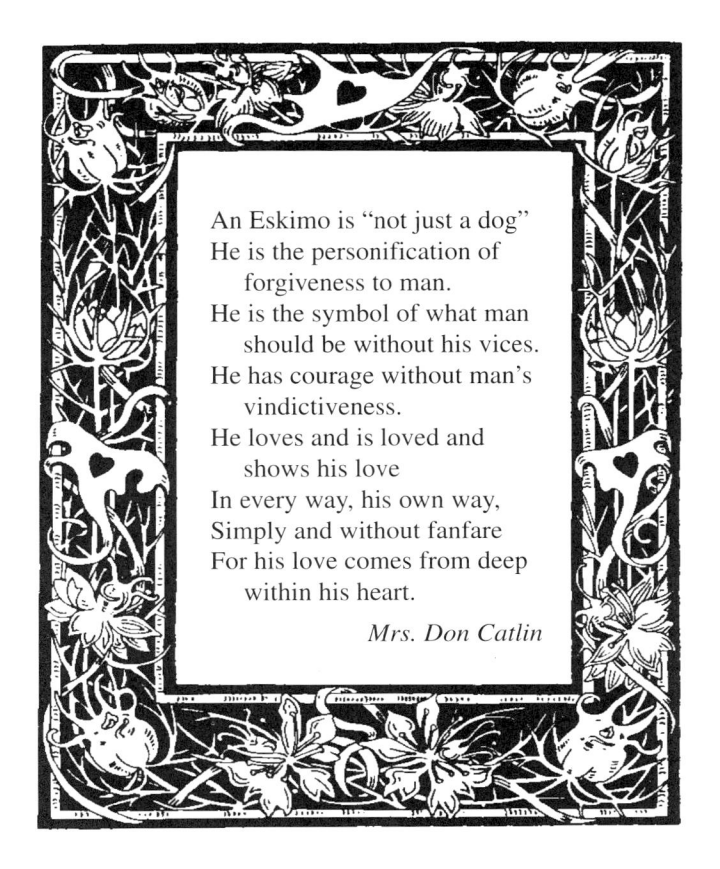

An Eskimo is "not just a dog"
He is the personification of
  forgiveness to man.
He is the symbol of what man
  should be without his vices.
He has courage without man's
  vindictiveness.
He loves and is loved and
  shows his love
In every way, his own way,
Simply and without fanfare
For his love comes from deep
  within his heart.

  Mrs. Don Catlin

Future AKC Ch. & Gr. Ch. Thunderpas Apollo's Gaea, owned by Rosemary Stevens. *Eddie Rubin photo*

OTHER FINE BOOKS FROM OTR

The Tibetan Spaniel, A Gift from the Roof of the World
by Susan Miccio

This stunning new book will appeal to all Tibbie lovers around the world, veteran and novice alike. This gloriously illustrated work fuses practical hands-on information with a plethora of entertaining and endearing anecdotes that are sure to delight lovers of this Tibetan breed. Award-winning journalist Susan Miccio tells all you need to know about selecting, breeding, caring for, training and showing your Tibbie. The extensive chapter on the breed's health will serve as a valuable reference. Mrs. Miccio's extraordinary research traces the breed from Tibet to every country in the world. You won't want to miss this outstanding book. $39.95 + $4.50 p&h. ISBN 0-940269-12-0

The Great Dane Handbook
by Mary J. McCracken

"This is one of the best breed books I have ever read. Not only is there a wealth of practical 'Dane information,' but much of the material applies to other large dogs and dogs in general....this book rates a perfect 4 star rating..." *Debbie Eldredge, DVM*. Learn everything you need to know about living with a Great Dane and loving it! This practical, witty, joyful book is the most complete guide to selecting and raising a Dane ever written. $27.95 + $2.50 p&h. ISBN 0-940269-08-2

The Goodger Guide to the Pug
by Wilhelmina Swainston-Goodger

Now, under one cover, two of the most famous books ever written on the Pug. *The Pug Dog, Its History and Origin* (1930) and *The Pug Handbook* (1959), were penned by one of Britain's most successful and knowledgeable breeders. Her landmark research has never been equalled by another writer. "I strongly urge all Pug owners...to obtain this book for your library; you will...refer to it frequently." *Pat Allen, Pug Talk*. "Ms. Goodger combines scholarly research with common sense and good humor...there is much conventional wisdom and good sense in Ms. Goodger's advice. And shining through at all times is Ms. Goodger's spirited defense and true love for her dear 'Pug Dogs.' All in all, a very enjoyable book and a definite plus for any Pug lover's library." *Debbie Eldredge, DVM*. The original books now sell for over $200 from rare book dealers. Seize this opportunity. $29.95 + $2.50 p&h. ISBN 0-940269-11-2

The Tibetan Mastiff
by Ann Rohrer & Cathy J. Flamholtz

"...this is a great read. Peruse the TM volume as a travel/adventure tale crammed with exotic information....It is reminiscent of the memoirs of...19th century explorers of mysterious lands. Rohrer is a keen observer whose eye takes in far more than the bearlike TM. Ms. Flamholtz, whose able pen and elegant style are apparent throughout, adds much to the joy of following Rohrer's and the breed's saga...This book is a treasure. Read and enjoy." *Deborah Lawson, Dog News*. $16.95 + $2.50 p&h. ISBN 0-940269-02-3

The Venerable Tibetan Mastiff
by Max Siber; revised and edited by Cathy J. Flamholtz

For the first time, American fanciers can read one of the rarest breed books of all time! Originally published in 1897, in German, *Der Tibethund* was written by esteemed Swiss writer and judge Max Siber. His extensive research and the observations from his travels are detailed in this remarkable translation. "This book is a must have for any Tibetan Mastiff fancier." *Debbie Eldredge, DVM* $24.95 + $2.50 p&h ISBN 0-940269-09-0

A Celebration of Rare Breeds, Volume I and II
by Cathy J. Flamholtz

Here they are—America's most popular books on rare breeds. Both nominated for top honors by the Dog Writers' Association of America. Volume I covers 53 breeds, including some which have since gained AKC recognition, including the **American Eskimo.** Volume II covers an additional 35 breeds, including some in the AKC line-up. See why the critics rave: "...a bold, sweeping yet homespun style holds your interest through every one of the breed stories...great new canine classic!" *Kathryn Braund, Dog Writers' Assn.* "...a true treasure...carefully done...free of baloney...a superior reference book that belongs in every library." *Maxwell Riddle, Dog World.* Volume I: $24.95 + $2.50 p&h ISBN 0-940269-00-7; Volume II: $27.95 + $2.50 p&h ISBN 0-940269-06-6.

The Working Airedale
by Bryan Cummins, PhD

In this landmark work, Dr. Cummins has penned an extensive account of the historical and contemporary uses of the King of Terriers. You'll learn of the breed's skills as a hunting dog, a livestock herder and guardian, a police dog, military dog, sled dog, as well as in obedience, tracking, canine therapy, schutzhund, search and rescue, flyball, agility, carting, backpacking...the list goes on! "The author's detail and easy style ensure that all Airedale aficionados will want to add this breed book to their libraries." *Dogs in Canada.* "...written by a careful historian who has great insight into the breed...Pick up the phone now to order the most important book ever written to focus on the working aspects of the breed!!!" *No. American Working Airedale Assn News.* $24.95 + $2.50 p&h. ISBN 0-940269-07-4

Livestock Protection Dogs
Selection, Care and Training
by David E. Sims, PhD & Orysia Dawydiak

Selected **Best General Reference Book** by the Dog Writers' Assn. of America, this highly acclaimed work has earned praise from both breeders and ranchers alike. This complete guide will tell you all you need to know about the various breeds, from the moment a puppy arrives to the care and management of the adult. This unequalled paperback includes a revolutionary chapter on temperament testing and evaluation geared specifically to these dogs. "A new and important book..." *Maxwell Riddle, Dog World.* "...an excellent book...extremely well written...If you are interested in knowing the 'How To's' of training a livestock protection dog in a step-by-step manner, this book is a must." *The Ostrich News.* $9.95 + $2.00 p&h. ISBN 0-940269-05-8

The Toy Fox Terrier
by Eliza L. Hopkins & Cathy J. Flamholtz

Praised by breeders and judges alike, this is the finest work yet on this popular toy breed. Famous breeder and judge Eliza L. Hopkins, who has produced more than 60 champions over the past 30 years, teams with award-winning writer Cathy J. Flamholtz, to present this invaluable handbook. Don't miss this superior hands-on paperback guide. "United Kennel Club, Inc., is very pleased this book is now available. (We) recommend this book." *Bloodlines, the UKC magazine.* $9.95 + $2.00 p&h. ISBN 0-940269-01-5

Order Today

VISA and MASTERCARD customers may order toll-free at 1-800-367-2174.
Or, if you prefer, mail your check or money order to :

OTR Publications, P.O. Box 481, Centreville, AL 35042-0481

UPS service, $2 extra

Foreign orders, U.S. funds only and $2 extra